THE BRIGHT PASSAGE

Books by MAURICE HINDUS

THE BRIGHT PASSAGE

THE COSSACKS: THE STORY OF A WARRIOR PEOPLE

MOTHER RUSSIA

RUSSIA AND JAPAN

HITLER CANNOT CONQUER RUSSIA

TO SING WITH THE ANGELS

SONS AND FATHERS

WE SHALL LIVE AGAIN

GREEN WORLDS

MOSCOW SKIES

THE GREAT OFFENSIVE

RED BREAD

HUMANITY UPROOTED

BROKEN EARTH

THE RUSSIAN PEASANT AND THE REVOLUTION

MAURICE HINDUS

The Bright Passage

DOUBLEDAY & COMPANY, INC.
Garden City, New York, 1947

Preface

    During the war years I met in Africa an American officer who, like myself, was of immigrant origin. He, like myself, had emigrated to America in his early teens, had grown up on an American farm, studied in an American college. We had much in common not only in our American experience but in our early background, which, though his was Polish and mine Russian, was rural and Slav.

We speculated at length and with some zest as to the type of human beings we might have been had we remained in the lands of our birth. We agreed that we never should have acquired the mutual interests and sympathies we now cherished. The very word *Russian* might have roused in him all the historic Polish choler against Russia, and the very word *Pole* might have stirred in me the proverbial Russian disdain for what Russians term "Polish levity and Polish romanticism." We were of one mind that it was our American experience and education which, by dissolving our old culture and assimilating it with the new, had changed our personalities and our attitude toward each other and the world.

Preface

We were living symbols of national and cultural reconciliation, whereas the Europe from which we had sprung was a caldron of national strife, kept boiling by economic separatisms and inequality of economic development.

"If only," said my Polish friend, "the nations of Europe could liberate themselves of their hostilities and assimilate each other's culture and integrate their economies even as you and I and millions like us have done in America. Why don't they?"

Why indeed? If only the Slav, the Teuton, the Anglo-Saxon, and the Latin could evolve a common political language and a common human and cultural solidarity which would transcend national exclusiveness and exorcise the fears and the hates, the torments and the brutalities of today!

Yet there is one nation in Europe which may yet achieve or at least set the pattern for this reconciliation. That nation is Czechoslovakia. That is why, despite the smallness of its size and all its shortcomings, which include an overanxious nationalism, Czechoslovakia is to this writer the most interesting and challenging country in Europe.

To understand what it is and whither it is going, we must see it in the context of a Europe that is experiencing the greatest change since the Reformation.

For Americans who are firm in their faith in free enterprise, the social climate of post-war Europe must seem not only unreal but painful to envisage and appraise. Yet the facts speak for themselves. Hitler, who pledged himself to cleanse the world of "the Bolshevik plague" and to entrust political and economic power in the hands of "the elite" as he understood the term, wrecked and bankrupted most of Europe. The wreckage and the bankruptcy have drained private enterprise of its lifeblood and left it, in his own and other lands, gasping for breath and staggering to an uncertain fate.

Not even Great Britain, mother of parliaments and the machine age, pioneer in modern finance and international trade, can any longer afford the free economy which America and Canada, with their vast wealth, enjoy and foster and regard as sacrosanct. The people of Great Britain have voted a Socialist government into power.

France has felt the impact of the great change even more powerfully. Despite continuous political wrangling, and with the support not only of Socialists and Communists, but also of Catholics, France has already nationalized key industries such as coal, transport, gas and electric power, the Bank of France, the big Deposit banks, the famous Renault Works, the aviation industry, insurance.

In Germany itself, Great Britain has anticipated Russia in the promotion of socialization.

Nation after nation in Europe is seeking to retrieve itself from the wreckage of war and bankruptcy by means of two-year plans, three-year plans, five-year plans, ten-year plans—the by-product of a new concept and a new practice of national economy.

With the pillars of free economy shaken or shattered, Europe is under compulsion to forge something new that would fit the changed temper and conditions of its peoples.

Czechoslovakia, more than any other nation in post-war Europe, is, in its own bold and peaceful manner, pioneering for a new principle and a new method of social and economic accommodation.

Consider these rather startling facts: Here East and West meet not only geographically but culturally; here the Communist is powerful, the Catholic politically strong; here individualism and collectivism stride side by side; here humanism and Marxism are having a continuous rendezvous; here statism and democracy dwell under the same roof; here the contentions and contradictions that beset other nations, the pressures and challenges not only of history but of the big powers are as ever-present as the sky. Yet here, instead of conflict, there is reconciliation, instead of fratricidal strife there is social adaptation.

Czechoslovakia is no paradise. The average man lives nowhere nearly as well as in America or Canada. The order of the day is arduous toil and prodigious sacrifice, made all the more imperative because of the evil heritage of Munich, the World War, the German occupation. As in other countries which have suffered protracted German occupation, there is a certain demoralization of character and degradation of work habits. Deprived of proper education and the social and mental discipline which Czech schools inculcated before the war, the youth, while not given to sex laxity or crime, is inclined to be wayward in its responsibility to everyday duties, whether in the shop or the office. Only time, proper guidance, and a fresh discipline can educate it out of this post-war waywardness.

Like weeds in a field, the new bureaucracy, often as callous as it is uninformed, here and there blights many a tender shoot of new life. This is as true of the newly created national councils as of the factory committees and sometimes of the ministries. The battle against this bureaucracy is not the least of the formidable tasks the new government is facing.

The expulsion of the Germans and the loss of eight hundred thousand workers, among them some of the most skilled in the country, has left a marked void, especially in the light industries which in the pre-war years were famed for the high quality and low cost of their products—glassware, china, textiles, toys.

Starved for merchandise, American and other buyers have flocked here as to a land of promise, only to discover that many a Czech manager or director who has replaced a German has neither the business acumen nor the business rectitude of his predecessor. These buyers wail, fume, and despair of a better day when, as in the pre-war years, transactions can be consummated with none of the uncertainties and derelictions that so often encumber business procedure now.

It would of course have been a miracle had the corruption and demoralization engendered by the enemy occupation blown away like the smoke that puffs its way out of the peasant's chimney. It is too much to expect that men entrusted with high responsibilities that are new to them should discharge their duties without some injustice in policy and some error in performance.

Yet the incident of the moment, however grave, the adversity of today, however dire, need not obscure the magnitude nor detract from the momentousness of the national effort. The new chapter in human history which Czechoslovakia is enacting is too noteworthy and too solemn an event to be dismissed with the easy disdain which it often evokes from the impatient foreign businessman or the glib-tongued foreign diplomat.

It is significant that, unlike Poland, Hungary, Yugoslavia, Rumania, Greece, Bulgaria, Iran, and Turkey, Czechoslovakia, like Norway or Finland, has given rise to no serious diplomatic clash between the big powers. Its effort to work out its own destiny in its own way, its discharge of international obligations are one of its greatest assets at home as well as abroad.

Let the reader ponder the implication of a recent statement in an editorial of the *Lidová Demokracie* (People's Democracy), organ of the Czech Catholic party: "Our national coalition is half Marxist and half non-Marxist. Yet its sole concern is that the citizens work in peace and calm for the upbuilding of the republic and the elevation of the people."[1]

This is my third book on Czechoslovakia. *We Shall Live Again,* which appeared in 1939, was an account of the country as I knew it in the pre-Munich days and observed it during the stormy Munich events. *To Sing with the Angels,* a novel pub-

[1]*Lidová Demokracie,* September 1, 1946.

Preface

lished in 1941, was the story of the struggle of a Czech village against the German invaders. In the present volume I have attempted to present a picture of the country and its people since liberation and to describe the effort to launch and realize a new type of revolution.

This book does not exhaust the subject. Perhaps I have no more than hinted at its momentousness. Many phases of Czech and Slovak life and certain aspects of the revolution, which I should have liked to include in this volume have been omitted because of considerations of space. Despite its shortcomings, I hope the book will awaken in the reader a fresh understanding of "the little-known country," as the late Neville Chamberlain once called Czechoslovakia.

Maurice Hindus

October 10, 1946
Prague

Contents

xiii

Contents

Illustrations

Part One: PLACES & PEOPLE

1. Specter and Flash

Czechoslovakia is both paradox and hope. It is paradox because history seems to have conspired to make this small country, inhabited by a calm and unspectacular people, a supreme testing ground for the massive struggle of ideas which has long been moving on all mankind. It is hope because its people may meet the test. If they do they will achieve reconciliation between the Western ideas of individual liberty and the newer ideas of collective effort and individual security which Russia has been championing. Success in the experiment would do much, more perhaps than any other circumstance, to lift the dread of inevitable war from man's minds. It would redeem and re-create the progressive pattern of western European civilization with its basic belief in the capacity of men to adapt themselves to pressing changes without fury and carnage.

This aim is central and pre-eminent in Czech thinking; recent events in the country demonstrate that, so far, it has proved stronger than the specter of Communist dictatorship and the specter of the atomic bomb, the two nightmares that haunt men's minds.

Not that Czechs are actuated by a messianic complex and are spilling over with fervor to rescue mankind from the dilemmas in which it is enmeshed. They are too prosaic and too hard-boiled a people to cherish any illusions of grandeur or to imagine themselves saviors of anybody but themselves. Someone once suggested to a Czech diplomat that his country might serve as a bridge between Russia and the Western world. With typical Czech wit the diplomat replied: "A bridge is something for people and horses to walk over." Czechs are motivated solely by the desire to wrest for themselves, from nature and from a chaotic world, a tranquil and promising life. Yet like the sun that rises over their land as over others, their efforts to attain these ambitious ends trespass and transcend the barriers of geography.

It is no accident that Czechoslovakia has become the testing ground of a historic struggle. Besides the obvious geographical reasons, its racial kinship with Russia, and its cultural affinity with the West, there are extraordinary and powerful strands in Czech history which are being woven together by President Beneš and his associates to make the fabric of a new society.

Among these associates are the best minds in the Czech Catholic and Communist movements.

The fact that Catholic and Communist, despite mutual suspicions and antagonisms, co-operate with one another with an earnestness unrivaled in other lands in which the two are eminent makes Czechoslovakia all the more fertile a testing ground for the world conflict that is upon us. Above all, history has so molded its destiny that Czechoslovakia has become the classic land of the little man. Czech folk have long hailed him as the *malý český člověk*—the little Czech fellow. Lord Charnwood, in his brilliant life of Abraham Lincoln, writes: "The South suffered to the full the political degeneration which threatens every powerful class which, with a distinct class interest of its own, is secluded from real contact with the competing classes with other

4

interests and ideas." These words apply unreservedly to any feudal society. They do not apply to the Czechs. Groups with competing and antagonistic interests did and do exist, but without what Emerson terms "the pitiless division of classes." Too many and too powerful have been the links which have bound all groups into one—a community of "the little Czech fellow."

For over three hundred years the Czechs have had no hereditary aristocracy. This alone would make them a unique people, not only among Slavs but in all Europe. In the Battle of the White Mountain, in 1620, which ended Czech independence for three centuries, the aristocracy was slaughtered by the Hapsburg conquerors. The feudal barons who survived the carnage were eventually absorbed into the Austrian aristocracy, except for quite a negligible number, who never sundered themselves from their own people, yet never grafted on them their own habits of thought or their own way of life. Thus the Czechs have been saved from "the political degeneration" of which Charnwood writes.

The great personalities whose ideas and deeds have molded the character and fathered the spirit of the Czechs of today have risen from the ranks of the little man. The Czech Reformation in the early years of the fifteenth century was, in its secular aspects, a tempestuous and far-reaching social revolution. Jan Hus, its leader, was a peasant of peasants. František Palacký, the historian, spoken of as "the father" of the modern Czech nation, was the son of a village schoolmaster. Thomas Masaryk, founder and builder of the first Republic, was the son of a coachman. President Beneš is the tenth child of a peasant family. Even Thomas Baťa, the most creative industrialist the country has known, "the shoe king of the world," was the son of a village cobbler.

The roster of distinguished names, particularly those of the intelligentsia, who fashioned the ideas and fostered the spirit of national independence, tells of similar origins. They had deep roots in the land and never forgot the social simplicities nor forswore the democratic amenities that flourished there. The folk democracy of the Slav village remained not only a sentiment and a memory but a guide and a reality.

Unencumbered with the traditions of feudal nobility, these men, when they became leaders and teachers of their people, never aspired to be anything else but common folk. They had no pretensions to swagger or superiority, and, what is equally notable, to authoritarianism. Quite the contrary, they fought the threats and spurned the blandishments of authoritarian rule.

That is why throughout the years of subjection to Austria-Hungary it was not their class-consciousness but their national consciousness that was stirred and galvanized. Class and nation fused into one. In defense against their masters, Czechs drew together to succor and strengthen one another, to prepare themselves in the university, at the workbench, in the peasant cottage, and in the gymnastic hall—under the banner and tutelage of the conveniently and innocently named *Sokol* (Falcon), a physical-culture society—for the day of independence and the achievement of their own national state.

With no aristocracy and feudal cast to combat and debase their efforts, František Palacký, and after him Masaryk and Beneš and the others, lifted Czech nationalism out of the parochial rigidities and the feverish lusts that burden so much of the nationalism of Europe. They summoned to their aid the humanistic glories of Jan Hus and his followers. They merged these with the progressive enlightenment of the American and even more of the French Revolution, with its emphasis on individual rights, on social equality, and its prodigious faith in a higher and more beneficent social order. They built their nationalism not on power but on ideas. Being a small nation, they knew they could never match physical force against more populous and aggressive-

minded neighbors. For them it was a question of a more enlightened against a more powerful nation. As Beneš once expressed himself: "To survive at all we have had to be more
progressive and more reasonable than others."

During a recent visit to Holland a highly placed Dutchman
said to me: "The Czechs have double the unpleasant qualities of
my people; they are so middle class." Whether the Czechs are
more middle class than the Dutch is open to debate. But that
they are eminently middle class in their manner of living, in
their cast of mind, in the virtues they emulate, in their own
purely Czech fashion, is beyond dispute.

In many ways the Czechs bring to mind the Scots. They are
as thrifty and labor-loving, as skilled with tools and possess as
abiding a love for craftsmanship. They are expert farmers and
superb artisans. They are as cool-minded as the Scots and as
rational. "The Czech thinks" is a universal saying. "No wonder," said a Czech woman whose home I was visiting, "that foreigners say we have no charm. We never give our brains a vaca-
tion." The "reason and conscience" which Thomas Masaryk
made the cornerstone of his philosophy and statesmanship would
be applauded by all Scotsmen. Like the Scots, the Czechs erect
monuments to their poets and preachers more often than to their
soldiers. They are as family-loving as the Scots and as proud of
their person. Pride more than any other circumstance keeps even
the poorest from soliciting alms. Rarely does one see a beggar
in Czech towns or villages.

Like the Scotsman, the Czech, stalwartly independent, is as
loath to borrow as he is to lend, and he shares with the Scotsman
an almost dour love of privacy. In this respect the Czech is unlike any other Slavs I know, least of all like the Russian. In the
land of the Soviets, when traveling on trains it is impossible not
to talk to fellow passengers. They insist on it. Russians must

talk. They do not mind telling a stranger all about themselves and are hurt if the latter fails to reciprocate. In Czechoslovakia I have traveled on trains for hours and days without my neighbors saying a word to me, precisely as in Scotland. Yet I only had to make the advance and their chill aloofness vanished and they grew communicative and comradely.

If the Czech does not share the Scotsman's preference for potent drinks—he belongs to the beer- and wine-drinking human family—he is as stubborn as the Scotsman, yet as reasonable, as shrewd a bargainer, and as ready a compromiser. He is less austere in his habits of living, for his Slav nature is always with him, but is far more critical of himself than is the Scotsman. How often have I heard Czechs say: "We are such gruff people," or "We are really a disagreeable people," which testifies to a propensity for self-analysis and self-reproach which only the pre-Soviet Russian can match. He is no less responsive to new ideas than the Scotsman, only once he has perceived their intrinsic merit he is far more ready to embrace them.

A Briton who is a keen student of Czech civilization said: "As beautiful as Prague is, it always lacked what pre-war Paris and London possessed in so conspicuous a measure—places to which you could retreat and feast your eyes on sheer elegance," in dress, in manner, in taste. The Britisher may have been overcritical, but Czechs themselves would be the last to deny that, stemming as they do from a hardy peasantry, they have had neither the time nor the inclination to cultivate elegance for its own sake.

What lends a quality to the middle-class consciousness of the Czechs is the fact that since the collapse of their independence in the seventeenth century the molders and carriers of the folk tradition have been the intelligentsia. I use the word in the original sense—meaning the society of intelligence, which includes not only the man with a formal education like the school-teacher, the priest, the university professor, the publicist, the philosopher, but the *písmáci*—the self-educated peasant and worker. They all had a common origin—the peasantry. They rarely attained riches either through personal efforts or marriage. They lived off their earnings, which were never high. Always conscious of dangers to their people, always preoccupied with the problem of national survival, they never became money-minded nor particularly property-minded and never were obliged to lend their gifts or their energies to the defense and protection of personal property. It was as natural for them to be socially minded as to love books and music. It was as easy for them to strike a balance between the conflicting forces amid which they were living as to feel at home in the lowliest peasant cottage. They had no upper class to ape. They were the upper and the lower class—that is, really classless.

This is why the Communist and the Catholic, the Social Democrat and the National Socialist understand each other so well. Despite all their wrangling, which is often petty, even mean, they cannot possibly misunderstand one another, for they have only themselves from whom to learn, only themselves with whom to quarrel, only themselves with whom to compromise. Like the majestic willows and the sublime lindens that enhance the beauty of their landscape, they are rooted in their own soil, and however much it may be freshened and fertilized by outside fecundation, it is the native substance that gives them life and stature.

The healthy quality of this substance is attested by the fact that while Prague is only two hundred miles from the Austrian capital, Vienna's psychoanalysis has been of scarcely more than academic interest to Czechs. Freud, Stekel, and Jung are well known, but even in the pre-war days there were few practitioners of psychoanalysis. The maladies it is supposed to treat, the emotional derangements and nervous maladjustments it is intended to correct are too uncommon for lucrative practice. Nor has homosexuality been an affliction of serious magnitude. "It is no problem at all in our country," said Dr. Josef Vinař, a noted Prague psychiatrist. It has never been a theme to challenge the imagination of Czech playwright or novelist. Physically and emotionally the Czechs are one of the healthiest people in Europe.

This, then, is the social and intellectual background against which Czechoslovakia is proceeding with its stupendous historical experiment. It is stupendous in its promise and stupendous in the implications of failure. Calm and orderly as it may seem, it involves two worlds which are stacked with dynamite. The explosive quality of the one is symbolized by the specter of Communism which Karl Marx and Friedrich Engels evoked in 1847. The potential of the other was revealed by the blinding flash set off by scientists in Los Alamos, New Mexico, in July 1945.

The stern implications of both require more detailed discussion.

"A specter is haunting Europe—the specter of Communism." Thus reads the opening sentence of the *Communist Manifesto,* written one hundred years ago by Karl Marx and Friedrich Engels, as the platform of the conspiratorial Communist League, which was the first Communist party in the world.

Now a new specter is haunting not only Europe but the world, not only capitalism but Communism, the specter of the atomic bomb. Both the Communist revolution and the capitalist counter-revolution have to reckon with a force mightier than either, the omnipotent revolution of science. Marx and Engels had not envisaged it; Lenin and Stalin had not foreseen it. No revolutionary theorist anywhere had dreamed of it. In the Communist and Socialist theoretical discussions of plans of action, of techniques of revolution, there is no cognizance of the all-powerful monster science has conceived and incubated.

In their revolt in 1917, the Russian Bolsheviks followed the procedure prescribed by Marx and Engels. Class struggle, conspiratorial coup, civil war; liquidation of the bourgeois and of "all previous securities for and insurance of individual property," as the *Communist Manifesto* phrases it; dictatorship of the proletariat, supremacy of the Communist party; suppression of all other parties and of advocacy and discussion of ideas and doctrines antagonistic to the dictatorship—such has been the course of the Russian Bolshevik Revolution. Armies from foreign lands —England, France, Germany, Italy, Japan, America, other countries—joined the White Russian armies in the crusade against the Revolution. But the Revolution triumphed—in the absence of the atomic bomb!

Inevitably the question arises: Had this cosmic weapon of death been then in the possession of any of the foreign nations that strove for the extermination of Bolshevism, would it have been used in the achievement of that goal? Though a subject of speculation, the answer cannot be ignored.

I cannot imagine Woodrow Wilson sanctioning its discharge. In speaking of the Russian Revolution he once said: "Revolutions don't spring up overnight; revolutions gather through the ages; revolutions come from the suppression of the human spirit; revolutions come because men know that they have rights, and that they have been disregarded." Historian and humanist that he was, he did not appraise the Revolution, despite its excesses, in terms solely of evil and malevolence, as did so many of his contemporaries.

But what of Poincaré and Clemenceau, Winston Churchill and Lord Curzon, General von der Goltz and General Tanaka? Remembering the frenzy of hate the Bolsheviks—and especially their clamor for world revolution—had kindled in these men of

11

power, this writer is of the firm conviction that, one way or another, the atomic bomb would not have remained unexploited, if only in a final and desperate drive for victory. If none of the foreign armies had unleashed it on the Red fighting battalions, it would have been "slipped" to General Denikin or Wrangel, to Kornilov or Yudenitch, or to any of the other White Russian generals. The deed might have been executed quite anonymously and unofficially, with or without the provision that, as was the case of our own air force in Japan, it be tested on two or even one strategic Bolshevik stronghold, to impress Bolshevik leaders with the futility of their campaign and to terrorize them into submission. I cannot imagine Clemenceau and Poincairé, not to mention the Germans and the Japanese, refraining from the use of *any* weapon to win *that* war.

Now with World War II terminated, the specter of revolution is again floating over Europe, and once more the question arises —what price revolution? Supposing a Communist revolution accompanied by civil war and proletarian dictatorship impinges on British or American decisive positions or strategic spheres of influence? Will the atomic bomb be "slipped" to the armies we or the British may wish to win? Russia may not yet have perfected the nuclear weapon. But she will. If a Communist revolution, wherever it may break out, looms to her as paramount to her national security or necessary to her international aims, will she "slip" the bomb to the army she wishes to triumph? One thing is certain: Theorists and planners of revolution or counterrevolution must reckon with an affirmative answer to this question.

All the more pertinent are these reflections, because neither generals nor scientists cherish the illusion that nuclear explosives can long remain the exclusive property of the English-speaking nations, or that the creation of new types of atomic bombs, easy to plant or direct by air to faraway and specially chosen targets, is a remote contingency.

This writer makes no pretensions to being a Marxian scholar, a historian, a political scientist, or a philosopher. Solely as a student and reporter of the international scene, he cannot escape the conclusion that sooner or later there will be an official and an authoritative revaluation by Communist leaders of the century-old Marxian concept and technique of revolutionary engineering. To rely on the old formula, to pursue the course of the Russian Soviet Revolution, to invoke class war of serious magnitude is to gamble with doom and invite obliteration of revolutionary and counterrevolutionary alike. "Rifle bullets," writes Albert Einstein, "kill men, but atomic bombs kill cities."

A dictatorship, by the proletariat or any other class, can endure only so long as nuclear weapons remain unexploited by the opposition or by a power on the outside inimical to the dictatorship. The new specter of science has shrunk the stature of the Marxian specter. The proletarian dictatorship in the Marxian meaning of the phrase is, in this writer's judgment, as outmoded a weapon of social conflict as the tomahawk is in modern warfare. The age of the atom bomb has ended the age of the barricade.

No wonder that at a conference of the Central Committee of the Czechoslovakian Communist party, Klement Gottwald, leader of the party, who rose to the premiership after the election of May 1946, felt constrained to say: "Experience and the teachings of classical Marxism and Leninism tell us that dictatorship of the proletariat and the Soviets is not . . . the only road to socialism."[1]

I have gone into this lengthy discussion of the Marxian meaning and method of revolution because it bears intimately and suggestively on the Czech revolution, whose pattern is audaciously conceived. It is a bold revision if not a complete repudiation of the Marxian or Bolshevik pattern.

[1] *Rudé Právo,* organ of the Czech Communist party, September 26, 1946.

13

The Bright Passage

In his address to the Provisional Assembly on October 28, 1945, President Beneš solemnly declared: "Today we are entering the parting of the ways . . . we are betaking ourselves along a path which is to lead to the socialization of modern society." He was referring to the nationalization decree which he had signed only four days earlier and which *is* a parting of the ways, a break, bold and decisive, with the economic precepts and usages of pre-war Czechoslovakia. The decree makes this small Slav republic the most socialistic country in the world, after Russia.

Yet the concept out of which it stems differs radically from the Orthodox Marxian or Orthodox Bolshevik concept. It is revolution by evolution instead of evolution by revolution. Proudly Laušman, Minister of Industry, himself a left-wing Social Democrat and one of the youngest and most impressive of the new leaders, wrote in *Právo Lidu,* the official mouthpiece of his party: "Not a drop of blood was spilled over our nationalization decree; not a single strike took place." This is no empty boast. There is no proletarian or any other dictatorship. Not once have the Communists suggested it. There has been no physical "liquidation" of the bourgeois. There is no supremacy of the Communist or any other party. There are of course groups in the country who detest the decree. They moan and mourn and predict imminent collapse and chaos. But there have been no political murders. There have been no political executions. It has been as peaceful and orderly a revolution as the world has known.

Twice before in European history the Czechs have been in the vanguard of the human procession. After the burning of the patriot and reformist Jan Hus at the stake in 1415, they rose in rebellion against the Emperor of the Holy Roman Empire, who, by violating his pledge to bring their leader safely back home, caused his execution. The rebellion assumed the magnitude of a social revolt. The Czechs demanded a new way of life, new relationships of man to man, ruler to ruled, owner to worker. They

14

burned with a fierce hostility to German domination and German assumptions of superiority. Their revolt was smothered in blood, chiefly by the German-minded Emperor Sigismund and German armies.

On the conclusion of World War I in 1918, the Czechs set up a national state, their first in three hundred years, which despite its shortcomings and imperfections was abreast of all its neighbors in the democratic principles it promulgated, the social legislation it fostered, the educational level it attained. In treatment of minorities—German, Hungarian, Ruthenian, Polish, Jewish, which were allowed the use of their own language, their own schools, and the espousal of their own culture—no nation in Central Europe equaled the Czech Republic. The Czech state pioneered a new and advanced type of democracy in a part of the world that had been riddled with national rivalry, that had been drenched with racial hatred and had successfully beaten back the forces of democracy, dealing them blow upon blow.

Despite the multiplicity of political parties (at one time there were thirty-three) and the prevalence of political strife, the republic weathered, though not always with an easy grace, every internal tempest. At no time was it threatened with a *Putsch*. Unlike pre-war Poland, there was no Pilsudski to snap a military whip over the youthful democracy and bleed it so profusely that it could never recover from the bloodletting. There was no Admiral Horthy as in Hungary, King Alexander as in Yugoslavia, King Boris as in Bulgaria, Engelbert Dollfuss and Prince Stahremberg and his Heimwehr as in Austria, kings and queens and a Fascist "Iron Guard" as in Rumania, to subvert and macerate the will of the people. However imperfectly expressed, that will was always asserted. However inadequately heeded, it was always heard. But again the blow came from without. Again an alien power, once more German, extinguished the light that shone so luminously and so hopefully.

The Bright Passage

Now for the third time Czechs are pioneering in a new type of democracy, embracing the challenges of the times from East and West, from near-by Russia and faraway America. They are trying, as one Czech has expressed it, to "tame the storm instead of being overwhelmed by it." While in other lands political factions are fiercely feuding with one another, venting their energies on denunciation of Russia's collectivism or vilification of America's individualism, Czechoslovakia is peacefully and unobtrusively, with a calculated yet unthwarted audacity, proceeding to achieve a fusion of the two.

With singular perspicacity, its leaders, even while the war was raging, looked ahead, thought ahead, planned ahead. Long before the war had ended they knew what they wanted. Parties as diverse in viewpoint as Catholics and Communists had agreed on principles and policies that were to guide them in the re-creation of their national life. Thereby they averted the delays and dissensions that beset so many of the former war-ridden nations, including France.

Situated in the heart of Europe, age-old cockpit of clashing armies and clashing ideas, Czechoslovakia is building its new state and society on the ruins of the old. The old values which it deems operative are cherished and esteemed as ardently as new values which it deems necessary for survival and progress. Russian influence is strong, but the impact of Czechoslovakia's own century-old democracy, which embodies so much of Western democratic belief and practice, is no less impressive. While for the present imitating neither Russia nor America nor England, the little Slav republic is in its own fashion striving to reconcile the ideas and practices of all three, always mindful of its own stature and its own destiny, and the opportunities as well as the limitations that both impose.

The task is monumental, the difficulties are stupendous, the perils are incalculable. But if the venture in revolution by

16

evolution is crowned with success, Czechoslovakia may become a luminous beacon for others, particularly the smaller and more befuddled peoples of Europe. If it fails, anything may happen.

Failure would result from two circumstances now non-existent: internal disruption and foreign interference. If the political parties that rule the nation were to emphasize mutual hostilities instead of mutual agreements, violent and irreconcilable dissension would set the stage for hopeless internal disruption. If what Communists call "the reaction" were to succeed in sabotaging and smashing the nationalization program, disruption would be inescapable. Or if the Communists, who in the election of May 26, 1946, emerged as the strongest party, were to use their power to press the revolution into a proletarian instead of its present national pattern, the resulting conflict would be equally fatal.

But, as future chapters will demonstrate, "the reaction" is too feeble to assert itself effectively. The Communist party never would have won the vast following it has mustered had it campaigned, not on a Czech national, but on a proletarian or Marxian platform. It is because the Czech Communist party has accepted the formula of revolution by evolution that the other parties, particularly the Catholics, have found it possible to collaborate with it. Through this collaboration the nation has achieved phenomenal success in the program of reconversion and rehabilitation. Were the Communist party to reverse its position and flout its commitments to the other parties and to the people —were it seriously to encroach on civil liberties or in other ways to impose dictatorial rule—it would not only wreck the Czechoslovakian experiment; it would confront the nation, possibly all Europe and lands beyond, with the explosive dangers it has assiduously striven to avoid. Such a reversal would make a mockery of all the lessons of Czech history. It would rouse on itself the distrust and condemnation of the whole non-Communist democratic world. It would be tantamount to a declaration of war on collaboration between *any* Communists and *all* non-Communists, including those who favor nationalization and other policies which it espouses. It would heighten enormously the tension between Russia and the outside world. It might even be the *one* decisive instrument by which the Marxian specter would set off the Los Alamos flash and annihilate civilization.

Precisely because of the spirit of reasonableness and progressiveness which has been animating Czech national life, and because of Czechoslovakia's geographic position, the Czech Communist party is facing a test and a responsibility which transcends by far the destiny of their own country or Europe itself. Yet it must be emphasized that there is nothing on the Czechoslovakian scene now that remotely suggests a revolt of the Communist party against its own present self.

By far the greatest danger to the Czechoslovakian endeavor is the possibility of outside interference, such as has twice before wrecked the nation's independence and smashed its ventures into advanced modes of democracy. Because of the past and present course of its history, the unique position it holds in Europe and the world, Czechoslovakia, more than any other nation anywhere, is the acid test of the wisdom and the good faith, the tact and the tolerance and, in the long run, so it appears to this writer, the self-interest of America and England no less than Russia. America may frown on the nationalization decree, which is a renunciation of her concept of "free enterprise." In its heart the Kremlin may deprecate the Czech Coalition Government, which is a negation of its practice of Communist supremacy and "democratic dictatorship." But the election of May 1946 amply demonstrated that these are the principles and the forms to which the people are committed; they are *for* nationalization and against *any* dictatorship.

If Great Britain or America, or both, by direct economic strictures or by indirect political pressures, should at some future

Church of St. Týn, Prague

—*Hájek Photo, Prague*

St. Vitus Cathedral in Prague

date seek to draw Czechoslovakia into their orbit, they can only invite failure and perhaps bring calamity to the little nation. If Russia, with her newly won power and prestige and with her present favored position in Czechoslovakia, should strive to absorb the country into its own fold, it will shatter the experiment of revolution by evolution and plunge the people into a fratricidal strife. In either event the first sufferers will be the Czech and Slovak peoples. But the rest of the world cannot count on immunity from retribution, least of all those extreme leftists or extreme rightists to whom the Czechoslovakia of today may seem an anachronism and a menace. But if the big powers conscientiously observe the amenities of non-interference, something new and momentous is certain to come to life in the not-too-distant future within the confines of the little Slav republic.

If allowed to work out its own destiny in its own way it can within the next five years become one of the most envied countries in post-war Europe.

Fully to appreciate and evaluate the Czechoslovakian venture in revolution by evolution, we must first acquaint ourselves with the people and the country.

2. Paradise Regained

August, 1945. Seven years had fled since I had last been in the Czech capital. *Zlatá Praha,* "Golden Prague," "the city of one hundred spires" are favorite and affectionate expressions in the Czech language. "Rome of the north" was the famous Rodin's tribute to its semiclassic beauty, and the great Goethe glorified it as "the most precious jewel in the masoned crown of this earth." A city of great history and great drama, where an old culture dwells side by side with a youthful dispensation.

In the course of the centuries Prague has been captured and recaptured, tramped over and over by foreign and native legions. Yet friend and foe always loved it for its scenic beauty, its noble architecture, its magnificent churches, its sky-swept spires. It was all here now, the old charm and the old splendor, the old dignity and the old elevation, unmarred and unsullied by the latest invasions and occupations. The Gothic peaks, the baroque domes, as many as ever, were the first visible assurance of an unsacked and triumphant city. The Hradčany—the State Castle —and St. Vitus's loomed from their lofty heights as majestic and resplendent as in the old days. The gray and ornamental Charles

Bridge with its baroque statues of saints and heroes; St. Nicholas's and St. James's, with their austere exteriors and their reverently radiant interiors; the Týn Church and the Strahov Abbey; the gray-domed National Theatre, built by the pennies and nickels of the common man; the other memorable and cheering landmarks—all but the ancient and classical Town Hall, whose face had been blown off by German artillery, stood out as unscathed and untarnished as the broad and shimmering Vltava River. Again the city had won, this time against the meanest and fiercest foe.

No metropolis like New York or Paris, with neither the brittleness of the one nor the sophistication of the other, Prague, despite six and a half years of enemy subjugation, was alive with color and contrast. The war had been over less than four months, and not all the broken windows had been replaced. Blocks of once-flourishing shops were boarded up and darkened by paper curtains over the windows inside. Victory banners still floated from balconies and windows, the Russian Hammer and Sickle scarcely more in evidence than the American Stars and Stripes and the British Union Jack. Girls from villages, in pairs and foursomes, arms linked, paraded around in gay-hued costumes. Returned Czech soldiers in Russian-, British-, and German-style uniforms, but always with Czech insignia, heightened the liveliness of the street processions. From the four corners of the earth, from all the battlefields of the war, they were streaming home, hardy and unkempt, but jubilant with the spirit of victory, uplifted by the sentiment of liberation. An air of festivity, like the fragrance of vanished flowers, still lingered everywhere, as though the people wished to cling as long as they could to the joy and the glory of the long-hoped-for emancipation.

Out of long habit my eyes wandered toward the shoes of pedestrians. In my years of travel in foreign lands that had endured battle and stress, the quality and condition of footwear were a silent and unfailing guide to human welfare, to the rise or the fall in standard of living. Here the shoes were old, rarely flashing a gleam of newness, yet with scarcely a mark of dilapidation. None was barefooted. Nor was anyone in rags. The stamp of wretchedness such as I had observed in other lands was nowhere in sight, and neither on the crowded avenues nor on the tranquil side streets did I behold a single beggar. Men wore raincoats and frayed old hats and carried umbrellas as in London. Yet, save for some of the returned veterans and the girls from the villages, the dress of passing pedestrians was somber—dark blue, dark gray, black. Not even the women's hats, old in fashion, severe in design, beamed with the gay, many-hued ornateness of feminine headgear in America.

But then, except for the festive-minded in villages, Czechs have never been given to flashiness of style or color. Swank and extravagance have never held any allure for them—the very words seem synonymous with sin. Even among the rich, "conspicuous consumption," which, according to the late Thorstein Veblen, is as inseparable an attribute of middle-class vanity as the gaudy plumage of the strutting peacock, repels rather than flatters the Czech ego. Czechs have ever been mindful not of the vanities money may gratify but of the utility money commands. During the German occupation the flow of goods from the outside was as effectively dammed as the flow of new ideas. Rarely were people privileged to acquire new apparel or new footwear. All the more astounding was their presentable appearance in 1945.

"How have you managed it?" I asked a Czech friend.

"You know the kind of people we are," was the answer. "We make the most of what we have."

They do indeed! No people anywhere make more of old

dresses and old suits, turn them inside out so often, wear and handle them with such tender care. No matter how aged or ancient the garment, the deft and untiring hand of the Czech woman will contrive to hold it neatly and respectably together. In streetcars I often saw men standing when seats were available.

"Why do they do it?" I asked.

"Oh," came the answer, "some prefer standing; others don't want to wrinkle a newly remade or pressed suit." No wonder an American wit was constrained to remark that when an American buys a suit of clothes he is impatient to wear it out so he can buy another, but when a Czech buys a new suit he is impatient at the very thought of buying another.

Once while on a streetcar I plucked out of a paper-stuffed pocket a crumpled five-crown note with which to pay the fare. Indignantly the conductor refused to accept it. Grumbling audibly, he walked away. Presently he returned and chided me for my slovenly manner with money. Only when a Czech friend who was with me explained that I was a foreigner did he relent and accept the note I offered him. But before depositing it in his leather pouch, and as if to inspire in me a proper respect for money, he straightened out the note and with his long bony fingers pressed the creases out of it.

There were no busses and no taxis for street traffic, only trams, which on the main avenue were always overcrowded. Yet one only had to watch the people come off and get on to be impressed with their superb sense of orderliness. There was no pushing and no jostling, as in the New York and Moscow subways. When the conductor said, "No more room," none mistook his words for a challenge and sought to sneak or squeeze his way inside. When the tram gave a sudden lurch forward or jerked to an abrupt halt, the straphangers bumped and tumbled into one another. That was nature's protest against man's

23

infringement on its laws. But there was no wanton disregard of a neighbor's convenience. Discipline has ever been the slogan of the Czechs—almost the way of life. Whatever else the German siege may or may not have done, it had neither shattered nor degraded its hold on them; that is, on all but jaywalkers, who the world over are a law unto themselves and whose impulse toward waywardness is as much the despair of the policeman as schoolboy truancy is of the schoolmaster.

People were so starved for entertainment that they crowded theaters and motion-picture houses; that is, those which offered plays and films that made them forget the war and the occupation, political oratory and political sermonizing. The audiences were an actor's dream—scarcely a whisper or a shuffle; not a hint of the perverse propensity, so manifest in New York and Moscow playhouses, to tell one's neighbor what is good and what is faulty, what is coming or what is missing; the hush so intense it could almost be heard; the response to conflict and climax, to wit and irony, as hearty as it was spontaneous; the identification with the stage so complete and all-embracing that it heightened the zest of the performer and the allurement of the performance. This was more than discipline, more than decorum. It was testimony to intellectual earnestness and to a love and respect for art as humble as it was heartfelt. British and Russian artists who appeared before Czech audiences were enthralled with the attention and reception they were accorded.

Here and there at a doorway, on a street corner, or inside a many-windowed arcade nestled a little shrine in commemoration of someone who had fallen in the anti-German uprising of May 5, 1945. Nasturtiums and daisies, cornflowers and roses, intertwined with reeds and evergreen twigs, were neatly fashioned about a crucifix and the photograph of the victim, with a printed inscription of his name, the date of his birth and his death. Over the

24

flowers, like an ever-present guardian, floated a diminutive Czech tricolor.

The crucifix and the photograph gleamed with neatness. A wife, mother, sister, grandmother came on frequent pilgrimages, brushed the dust off the frames, watered the flowers, straightened the little flag, the reeds, the twigs, leaving it all as fresh and vivid as must have been the memory of the one who was no more. Pedestrians stopped and lingered. There was no exchange of comment, no talk at all, no sighing, and no mournful nodding of heads. Unlike other Slavs, Czechs, save when under violent provocation, are not given to public demonstrations of emotion. In the face of the tragedy which the ornate little shrines symbolized, they might be consumed with wrath for its perpetrators, or with grief for the departed. But the welled-up passion was suppressed, and their lips remained sealed. A tough people, seldom given to self-pity, though to plenty of self-castigation, a people who, as a Britisher once expressed himself, "think and think," they are as masterfully aware of their inner composure as they are of their outward appearance.

The city was awakening from its prolonged torpor. Gaiety was not only visible but audible. Cafés were crowded. Here and there on the sidewalk by a doorway was a luridly printed sign bearing in English the announcement: "Five o'clock tea dance." Dance halls, which the Germans had banned, were again resounding with the lilting tunes of the Czech polka or with the brash rhythm of modern jazz. Sports, which the Germans had outlawed, were once more enlivening the river, the tennis courts, the parks, the Sokol halls, the football fields, and of course the Masaryk Stadium, one of the largest and most beautiful in Europe.

Hardly a day but there was a "manifestation," which in Czech designates a public rally *for*—in distinction from a "demonstra-

tion," which is a public assemblage *against*—something or some-
body. Factory workers, Boy and Girl Scouts, the Sokol, the
Friends of the Soviet Union, the Friends of America, the Friends
of France, an endless array of societies championing as many
causes, with or without bands but always with a lavish assortment of bunting banners and slogans, marched through the
streets, including inevitably the many-laned Václavské Boulevard. "Why so much 'manifesting'?" I asked a political leader.
"Haven't you heard the latest saying in Prague?" he countered.
I shook my head. "Instead of working hard, let's 'manifest' hard.
Not bad, is it?"

The "manifestations" were too well organized, too easily
engineered, too luridly advertised this or that cause. The public
tired of them. Factory directors shrugged their shoulders and
fumed with indignation. What was the country coming to when,
instead of devoting themselves to constructive effort, people,
especially youths, were marching in the streets? The trade
unions were among the first to cry out against these excursions
into idleness. The press became more and more loud in its protests. Action followed. "Work and more work and still more
work," became the slogan of the day. The streets were presently
free again for the ever-swelling traffic.

Bookshop windows blazed with photographic displays of
athletic carnivals, and the eager-eyed crowds that paused to
survey and study them testified to a zest for physical contest and
outdoor adventure. In the pre-Munich days no people anywhere
on the Continent had made physical culture so buoyant though
unclamorous a part of national self-expression and personal edification as the Czechs. Physical fitness was gospel and glory and,
in the days of the Austrian Empire, a weapon of national emancipation. After the liberation every one of the ten daily newspapers, including the Communist *Rudé Právo* (Red Justice) and
the Catholic *Lidová Demokracie* (People's Democracy), dedi-

cated all or most of the back page to news and views of sports. Sitting in hotel lobbies or cafés over cups of ersatz tea or equally tasteless ersatz coffee, Czechs were perusing the sports columns with as rapt an eagerness as American fans. No doubt it heightened the sense of liberation. Confused as they might still be about their future and the interplay of national and international politics, here was something fresh and lively and theirs again; like the songs that had been banned, the books that had not escaped burning, the tricolor that had been banished, a bond with the past, a bridge to the future.

Again and again I sauntered up and down the Václavské Náměstí—Prague's leading avenue. Sloping upward to the ornate museum which stands mountain-like astride the flow of traffic along the many lanes, it is unlike any main street or any public square I know. It is one of the broadest avenues in the world and one of the shortest. Save for the museum, the architecture is modern and ultra-modern, with scarcely a glint of the grace, the nobility, the beauty, of churches and castles of past centuries. The trees that line the sidewalks appear as young and stunted as in the pre-war days. Drooping and listless with thin trunks and short limbs, they seem beyond hope of further growth and further florescence. Yet the avenue has something of the audacious sweep of Moscow's Red Square and the sedate grandeur of London's Trafalgar. Here are ample sky and space, with nothing to obstruct or halt the downpour of light and sun. Factories are far away, and no smoke dims or disfigures the low and translucent sky line. It is boulevard of the idle and the festive, thoroughfare of the hurrying and bustling, and here as nowhere else in the country the nation is on parade.

The very absence of lushness in architecture, of extravagance in the dress of pedestrians even on festive occasions is symbolic of frugality and self-effacement. Here and in the avenues that radiate in all directions are cafés and dance halls, theaters and

motion-picture palaces, mostly underground; here are intermi-
nable courtyards steeped with lore and winding arcades glistening with novelty; here are newspaper offices and bookshops; here
are crowds and more crowds and still more crowds, for the love
of promenading is innate in the Czechs, as in all Continentals.
Yet here is no tumult and no brashness, no glamor and no fever-
ishness, hardly even loud talk. Here there is nothing to rouse
envy or lust, to give even the humblest visitor from a faraway
mountain village a feeling of strangeness or frustration. Here
are no superiors and no inferiors. Rich and poor they may be,
but with scarcely anything in their manner to evince the quality
of the one or the condition of the other. Here everyone is as
aware of his dignity as of his humility, which strips the city of
the mystery and the awe that other cities, especially the metrop-
olises of the world, so often inspire in the newcomer. It is Main
Street with a difference; without frills and pretensions, without
a shadow of severity or a flicker of coquettishness; neither aloof
nor familiar, and with no hint in poster or advertising sign, in
business slogan or window display, of erotic sentiment or physical passion.

If only because it is one of the few truly beautiful cities in
Europe that has escaped serious molestation, Prague is certain to
be a mecca of the foreign visitor and the holiday seeker. But
unlike pre-war Berlin and Paris, it never did and never can
play up the blandishments of sex. Shrewd businessmen that the
Czechs are, sex is a commodity whose commercial rewards they
have never bothered to exploit. Never a puritanical people, nor
even austerely minded, they have been too rational, too practical,
too family-loving, too self-composed, to seek pleasure in the
pretensions or titillations of sex. In the years of greatest affluence,
good food, good wine, tuneful melodies, sprightly dances, hearty
conversation, or self-absorbed rumination have been the measure
and the limit of public self-indulgence. Women of easy virtue,

with or without commercial motivation, there were and there will be, yet, as in the past, not in the limelight but in the shadow. Neither café nor tavern, neither night club nor dance hall, has flaunted pulchritude as a bait to the pleasure seeker. Posters of nude or seminude and large-breasted females, such as glared at the passer-by in pre-war Berlin, have been neither fashion nor lure. The tourist sybarite with a thirst for erotic assuagement will find Prague as arid of appeal as a cow pasture.

It was on the Václavské Náměstí that I witnessed in 1938 two memorable events, one signalizing the glory, the other the doom, of Czech independence. The first was the parade of the Sokol, which once every six years holds a *slet,* a "flowing" together for a physical-culture carnival in the capital. The climax invariably is the Sokol parade. On this occasion it occurred on July 6. Across the border Hitler was thundering anathemas and threats, which heightened the emotional upsurge of the event.

The day had been clear and warm and the immense square was a flood of sunlight. Hope and dedication were as manifest a part of the festivities as the wreaths and banners that flowed river-like over the heads of the endless columns of marchers. Only the Czechs with their inner reserve and their outward dignity observed a semblance of decorum. Their posture was faultless, their tread was firm, and they were as silent as the trees they passed. Not so the other Slavs—the Ruthenians, the Slovaks, and the visitors from foreign lands—Slovenes, Serbs, Croats, Montenegrins, Bulgarians. They splashed the avenue with the gaudiness of their multicolored costumes. They shook the earth with the tumult of their rapture. Bursting with abandon, they sang and shouted for the sheer joy of making themselves heard. They broke ranks, hopped and whirled, jigged and pranced, singly and in groups, unmindful of anything but the gaiety of the moment, the rhythm and the wildness of their movements.

29

The crowds on the side lines were as swept away by the beauty and ecstasy of the spectacle as the participants. They, too, shouted, no words, no slogans, no salutes, save now and then the inevitable *na zdar*—only blasts of rapture, louder and louder, gayer and gayer, to the accompaniment of forests of hands, swarms of handkerchiefs waving a frantic and exalted response. It was all so simple and so innocent, so earnest and so heroic, man celebrating good will and good living and forgetting, if only for a fleeting moment, the evils and the sorrow of the world.

Then came the fateful Wednesday, September 21, the beginning of the end—not only of the Czechoslovakia that was, but of the Hungary and the Poland that were, the Hungary and the Poland that clamorously hastened to join hands and hearts with Hitler and to ravage the good earth of their Slav neighbor; the beginning of the end of the Germany that was, the England and the France that were, indeed the world that was. It was eight-forty in the evening, with the bluish-gray tints of twilight creeping over the city, when the explosion came.

"The Czechoslovak Government," blared the loud-speakers in the streets, "has been forced under irresistible pressure from both the British and the French governments to accept with pain the proposals worked out in London," proposals to placate Hitler and sever the Sudetenland from the Czechoslovakian domain.

I was in my hotel room when I heard shouting outside. I rushed down and found myself breasting a column of angry marchers. They were pedestrians who had stopped to hear the fateful announcement from the loud-speakers. Forgetting immediate tasks or pleasures, they shuffled together and in voices of wrath shook and cleaved the tranquillity of the square. As if by magic, the column broadened and deepened and, like rivers that empty into the same sea, other columns from near-by streets poured into the square until all of it surged and swelled with tumultuous humanity. From hotel and restaurant, from home and shop, from theater and motion-picture hall, rich and poor, men and women, boys and girls, here and there mothers with babies in their arms, all flung themselves into the street, into turbulence and rage.

"Pressure from the British and French governments . . . proposals worked out in London." The words were like dynamite exploding within every person in the street.

"Down with the British!"

"Down with the French!"

"Chamberlain has sold us out!"

"The French have betrayed us!"

Impassioned and bewildered, mad with agony and fury, the crowds swirled to and fro, shouting and shouting at the top of their voices, pausing only now and then to catch their breaths and, while they still had the right and the time to do so, to chant with tears and fervor the doleful strains of the national anthem, "Where is my home, Where is my home?" Never had the words sounded more defiant and more poignant!

"Give us arms, we want to fight," shouted the street. "Give us arms, we want to die!"

In fighting they perceived their only redemption, in dying their only absolution.

Now all was quiet on the Václavské. The enemy was prostrate. He was gone from the land, and his defeat was complete. The debasement was at an end. The terror was over. The darkness had lifted, and light made bare the mischief the foe had wrought in six years of ruthless rule. Nothing to buy, no shoes, no clothes, not even a handkerchief. Once Prague was a gourmet's paradise; now it was a pauper's kitchen. No world-renowned Prague ham, no savory goose, no fat-dripping sausage, not a glimpse of an apple or even an onion. In August 1945, three months after liberation, the food was worse than it had been in Moscow in the summer of 1942, when the Germans were hammering at the gateway of Stalingrad. In Moscow's market places, at inordinately high prices, it was always possible to buy openly and legally a head of cabbage, a handful of carrots, now and then an onion. But not in Prague. At the leading hotels there was no tea and no coffee, no cocoa and no *slivovice,* no butter and no sugar. I walked into a *výček*—beer tavern—where I often took my meals in 1938. No family parties now. No singing over fragrant goose and dumplings, no warmth and no comfort, not even the floor and the windows clean, almost no people; only the disheartened owner grown gray and wizened in the years of my absence, glad to meet an old customer and to reminisce with longing of the old days, the old pleasures, the old abundance.

The intellectual impoverishment of the city matched the collapse of its material welfare. Crowds swung in and out of bookshops, or gathered before the large windows to contemplate the displays of news photos and whatever reading matter the bookmen offered. Save for newly printed political pamphlets, there were scarcely any books. Once a rich repository of the greatest literary treasures of mankind, the old and the new, the ancient and the modern, in exquisite bindings for the connoisseur, in handsome paper covers for the man of small means, Prague was now empty of literature. The writings of France, England, Russia, and America the Gestapo had outlawed. All but the classics were banned, which excluded everything Russia or America had created because neither land, so the Gestapo proclaimed, could possibly have given the world any classics. Not even Mark Twain and Dickens were tolerated. Not even Hugo and Balzac were respected. Not even Tolstoy and Dostoyevsky were spared. All were anathema, all were evil, fit for the bonfire or the paper mill. The exceptions were three volumes of modern English fiction: Eric Linklater's *Juan in America,* A. J. Cronin's *The Stars Look Down,* Evelyn Waugh's *Vile Bodies.* To the

German mind these stories portrayed the hollowness and depravity of English and American life, and Czechs were to be discouraged from emulating either or from deeming them worthy of survival.

For a brief interval Bernard Shaw was tolerated, first because he was Irish—that is, the son of a people who were anti-British—secondly because he satirized British morals and manners. But he became too popular. Besides, while Ireland remained neutral in the war, too many Irish youths were enlisting in the British Army, and so Shaw, too, was anathema.

And so as I wandered the streets of Prague and rejoiced as does every visitor in the matchless beauty of "the most precious jewel in the masoned crown of this earth," in the grandeur of hills and river, of church and castle, with the Hradčany—Prague's Kremlin—lighted up after dark and rising out of the pall of night in a golden splendor that invokes the vision of a fairyland, I could not help reflecting on the vanished good life of the city, on a paradise lost.

"We have regained it again," said a Czech writer. "Prague is ours once more and it shall glow again with all the good things in life. Wait—give us time," and after a long reflective pause he added, "Of course it won't be the same as it was. It cannot, because we are not the same people; no one in Europe is. The old foundation is gone. Something new is coming up. But whatever it is, Prague is ours again, our Paradise regained."

A year later and what a change! Stalls, pushcarts, shops all over Prague gleamed with the choicest fruits and vegetables. UNRRA goods, chiefly with American labels, were everywhere on display. Food was still rationed, meats and fats were still scarce, but liquors, though from three to four times as costly as in pre-war times, were freely sold. Shops that had been boarded up or funereally darkened with black curtains were open and

33

aglow with merchandise, though more was on show than for sale except for such native specialties as china, glassware, and woodwork.

For once I became overwhelmingly aware of the rural quality of Prague. There were so many orchards and gardens in the city, especially in the newer residential districts. Only a brief space away from the State Castle were the seminary gardens, with the entire slope of the hill crowned with a magnificent orchard. Karel Čapek's *Gardener's Year* was both an expression of a folk urge for the land and an awakener of the urge in those in whom it had begun to atrophy. Fruit trees, flowers, vegetables had become as much a part of household economy as surcease from urban cares. The Prague statistical office supplied me with an impressive table of figures on the fruit trees in the city: apples, 179,932; pears, 135,911; cherries, 84,046; plums, 139,484; peaches, 6,674; apricots, 17,478; walnuts, 11,655. All of this lends special emphasis to Masaryk's saying: "Not one of us but has a grandfather or grandmother in the village."

As in the pre-war years, newsstands were neatly laid out with the latest editions of newspapers from foreign lands—from England, Russia, Sweden, Holland, Switzerland, Yugoslavia, Poland, even from Greece. Bookshops were liberally stocked with English books, though chiefly the low-priced paper-covered editions that boomed into popularity in England and America during the war years. Confusion had been replaced by confidence, except among those who felt disheartened and distraught by the stupendous move toward state ownership so vigorously endorsed by the results of the May elections.

"Mark my word," mourned an engineer who was frantically seeking means of fleeing the country. "It cannot last—it will all crash with a bang. It must, with all this new and fearful bureaucracy cluttering up the offices of the government and our once-famous industry. My country will become a wilderness, and

Russia will pounce on it and devour what is left. I want to run and I'm going to, anywhere at all; to South America, Africa, your country, Canada, and bid Prague and all this hellish Europe good-by forever." To him Prague was a paradise lost, never to be regained.

But cafés were crowded, jazz bands pouring jangling tunes out of open windows. The Václavské swarmed with promenaders, outwardly as orderly and cheerful as in the pre-war years.

3. Searching Hearts

While stopping in London on my first journey to Czechoslovakia after its liberation, I attended an exciting session of the House of Commons. The date was August 16, 1945, when Churchill made his impassioned address denouncing Russia's "iron curtain" over neighboring states. Among other things, Churchill said:

"The same conditions [of displaced persons] may reproduce themselves in more modified form in the expulsion of great numbers of Sudeten and other Germans from Czechoslovakia. Sparse and guarded accounts of what has happened and is happening have filtered through, but it is not impossible that tragedy on a prodigious scale is unfolding itself behind the iron curtain which at the moment divides Europe in twain." The charge of an iron curtain over Czechoslovakia was so new and so challenging that the moment I climbed out of the RAF plane at the Ruzyne airfield outside of Prague I started a diligent search for the all-enveloping and all-forbidding sequestration which the wartime Prime Minister had so movingly lamented.

The earnestness of my efforts was matched by their fruitlessness. Nothing at the airport suggested the remotest shadow of an enforced and impenetrable concealment from foreign eyes, or of the presence of an invisible and irresistible power imposing its will and authority on the Czech nation. Registration at the hotel, once I wrested a room from the overworked and overworried, overflattered and overscolded clerk, was no more taxing or devious a task than in London. The registration slip I filled out was as brief and as simple as the one I was given in the British capital. Nothing more was demanded of me, no photographs, no visit to the police station; no limit was placed on the length of my stay in the country. I might leave whenever I chose without benefit of an outgoing visa, precisely as in England. I might travel as freely as at home, with no need of applying to anyone for special permission. Best of all, there was no censorship, not even a request by anyone for a carbon copy of the stories I cabled to the New York *Herald Tribune*. I could not help asking myself what reason or motive had prompted Mr. Churchill to level the charge of an "iron curtain." But whatever the motive, with or without malice, the indictment was pure fantasy.

Nor was free and close association with Czechs barred any more than in Washington or London. Czechs were only too eager to talk about themselves, the revolution, the country, the Germans, above all about foreign lands from which they had been hermetically sealed off for over six years. They clamored for foreign literature, especially in the English language, magazines, books, catalogues, newspapers, anything fresh and informing from abroad. With an aching nostalgia they reveled in memories of travel in foreign countries, sights they had seen, people they had known, monuments they had loved, carousals they had enjoyed, levities they had indulged.

When they talked of themselves, and this regardless of religious faith or political persuasion, the one thought they never failed to impress on the listener was that whatever fate held in store for them they were determined above everything else to remain themselves—that is, Czech—in language, in tradition, in spirit, in failure, in achievement. Let Czechoslovakia remain a small country, a poor country, a humble country, so long as it was theirs and only theirs, like the homes in which they lived, the fields which they tilled, the churches in which they worshiped, the shops and offices in which they worked. Foreign occupation had stirred a fresh surge of national sentiment and a fresh suspicion of outside nations. Revolution was brewing in the land, and whether they welcomed or spurned it, they predicted its success or its failure by the measure and amplitude of its purely Czech content and coloration.

Here was Josef David, speaker of the Provisional Parliament. The boyish glow in his fine eyes, the sensitive expression of his face, the delicacy of his hands, the softness and the warmth of his voice bespoke the artist more than the politician. We talked of America, of England, of Czechoslovakia, and all of a sudden he asked if I remembered St. Wenceslaus Day in 1938. I nodded and said, "Yes." I remembered the stacks of floral wreaths on the monument of this prince of princes in Czech history, the noble who forswore his own class, picked fruit and cut wheat with his own hands so as to identify himself in sweat and toil with his people. Attached to the wreaths were cards with pleas and prayers to the leader who had ruled Bohemia for four eventful years, 925 to 929. One little girl had written, "Please, St. Wenceslaus, do not let anybody destroy our beautiful country." On that very day the Munich Agreement was signed.

For a lengthy interval David was silent. St. Wenceslaus Day and Munich—light and darkness, life and death! David's eyes grew shiny, his lids reddened, and he turned his face away until, Czech that he was, he subdued his emotion. Then, eying me once more, he said: "If you remember that day, then you know how *Czech* our people feel. Now they feel it even more strongly."

He was too highly educated, too widely traveled, too world-minded, to draw solace from a parochial and ingrowing nationalism. But to him the word Czech had meant something big in history, was crowned with martyrdom and glory, was a guiding star and a never-failing light. And now what? It was I who asked the question. "Truth conquers," the ancient Bohemian King, George of Poděbrady, had said. But which truth? With the old world gone and the new one slowly shuffling out of the ashes and agonies of the old, where was the prophet to proclaim the one and only truth that would stir all hearts and galvanize all minds? But Czechs were a thinking people—they would have to puzzle the answer out for themselves. Though it was not easy, it would be discovered; David was the supreme optimist.

Then there was the tall, broad-faced, big-boned peasant youth whom I knew well in 1938. He had grown thin and wrinkled and much too old for his age in the years that had since passed. Confused and tormented with uncertainty, he had begun to dream of a new nation and a new humanity. He said: "I am a good Czech. I feel Czech; I don't want to feel anything else. And I don't expect the German, the Englishman, the American, the Russian, the Chinese to feel other than what they are. Man cannot get away from his origin. But we must create a new religion, a universalist religion that will bind us all together in thought and in deed. The forces of evil are smashed, even though not dead. Fascism, Nazism, Prussianism are without vitality at the moment, have no physical pillars of support. The time is opportune in Europe, anyway, for a new brotherhood, for the words of the old prophets and of Jesus to transcend the words of living rulers and leaders, religious and secular. Even Communists don't talk and don't act as they did in the pre-war years. Something has happened to them too—they are not as vindictive and as exclusive, if you know what I mean." He paused and I said to him:

"Do many people feel as you do?"

"If they don't they should. The hearts of mankind in Asia, in Africa, in America, and in our prostrate and hate-drenched Europe must draw together into a bond of communal good will, without ritual, without pomp, without symbol, only with purity of motive, with the earnestness of dedication—not to idols, not to creeds, not to rivalries, but to the one and only goal of living and toiling together, the universal brotherhood of man."

Again he paused, eyed me fixedly, then smiled not with amusement but with pathetic sobriety, as does a patient in a doctor's office who hopes that his own outward good humor will mollify the verdict he is to hear.

"Oh, I know," he resumed. "You think I am a dreamer, a knight of King Arthur's court in search of an elusive Holy Grail. But why should it be elusive if man everywhere wanted it, sought it, suffered for it, was ready to glory in it, die for it?"

"There are obstacles," I ventured.

"Which obstacles?" he shot back. "Nazism is gone. The power of Germany is spent, and Communism is no longer what it was —wait until you meet and talk to our Communists."

"Economics," I said, "and nationalism."

"But what have economics and the old type of nationalism given us? Look at Europe—France, Germany, Poland, our own country. The time has come when in every nationalism the good must be sundered from the evil. Let us then play up this good. What other alternative is there?" Again he paused and looked at me, not in bafflement, but in resentment of possible disagreement with his words. "To continue with the economics and the politics of the old days," he resumed in a rising voice, "is to gather fuel for fresh conflagrations, to set fire to our own homes, our own beds, aye, lifting the knife to our own throats."

His big gray eyes dilated with a glow that was at once stern and solemn. I said nothing and waited for him to continue the discourse, the substance of which I had heard not only at home but in England and in Russia. His was the quest of the ever-searching heart, aching for tranquillity and goodness in all mankind.

"No," he resumed, his fingers twitching with energy, "only the recognition, once and for all and the world over, of the identity of man with man, white and yellow, brown and black, can lift us out of the bondage of our politics, our economics, our nationalism, and save us from the suicide they presage. Don't you agree?"

"A beautiful idea," I said.

"But don't misunderstand me. I don't mean religion in the old sense with church against church, faith against faith, priest against pastor, rabbi against mullah. All that is ancient and ruinous and, I tell you, ungodly." His cheeks flushed slightly with anger and his chin was taut with defiance.

"Think," he pursued, relaxing his expression and his voice, "of Loyola and the Jesuits and the brilliant inspiration they fathered. We need something like that and more, far more; something transcending Loyola's exclusiveness; something without the threat of pain or purgatory because of disagreement or difference in mode of worship and mystical faith. We need emphasis on man, all men everywhere, fighting the same battle, cherishing the same hope, the hope of security and peace, of reason and tolerance. The Quakers have something of that. They have grasped the imminence of human grace and human charity. But they, too, are exclusive and, above all, too reserved, too quiet, too content with their past, their good deeds, and themselves." He appeared the incarnation of misery and pity, like a man inspired yet tortured by the very magnitude of his inspiration.

"No," he continued firmly, shaking his sparsely haired head, "that won't do, neither Loyola as he was nor the Quakers as

41

they are. We need something new; something that will embrace and transcend Loyola and the Quakers, the Communists and the Socialists; something that will hold them together like the staves in a barrel, with new rings of human justice and human realism. Maybe the new Word will come from America, maybe it will come from Asia; it may even come from Germany, yes, yes. You should read Foerster's book on Germany. It was published in Prague before Hitler came, and then of course it was banned and I saved my copy and read it over and over in secret and pondered it. I am still pondering its meaning, which is that evil begets evil; and the evil in Germany, the evil that inspired her leaders and ruled their lives, gave them Hitler and the incarnation of Satan. Maybe they have had enough of evil. Maybe they, too, are ready for the good, or can be made to try the good and try it with as much passion as they again and again exulted in evil. I've been thinking a lot about it all, and I've scribbled a few pages of manuscript, setting forth my thoughts."

Suddenly he halted, straightened out as if struck by doubt. Then, slumping his shoulders, he added falteringly, "When you have gone for years without meat, without butter, without sugar, without good books, it's good to dream—it livens up the mind and cheers your restless soul. I am too Czech to seek consolation in drink and not Czech enough, I suppose, to find it in the everyday realities of our past and our present. I am so weary, so terribly weary—we all are in this beautiful land of ours. You in America will never know what it means to be as weary as we are. You are a lucky people, too lucky, too lucky. . . ." How often have I heard these words in the Europe of today!

Yet before he left he took heart again. "Everything must start with a dream. 'Behold this dreamer!' D'you remember the verse? If enough of us would dream of a transcendental brotherhood, we'd have it—perhaps we shall yet. I hope so; I cannot help hoping, otherwise . . ." And he never finished the sentence.

42

One day my telephone rang. I answered it, and over the wires came the halting, tremulous voice of a man too diffident to speak, or too disconsolate to collect his thoughts. He introduced himself as an American of Czech origin, with a letter of introduction from a mutual friend. I invited him to come over, and he did. He was tall, with a slight stoop in his broad shoulders and with thinning fair hair almost pasted to the scalp. Gaunt in body and with a youthful face, his expression was a blend of firmness and hesitancy, of hardness and compassion. His long fingers trembled visibly as he presented the letter of introduction. He smiled as he talked, a broad yet forced smile, like a man who is pained and angry yet wishes to appear composed and serene. He had lived in America a long time, he said, was an American citizen, and had only recently been demobilized from the American Army. He came to Prague like a pilgrim to an old and beloved shrine; Prague the city of his youth, his Jerusalem, and—he was disillusioned. Oh, he could understand why streets and buildings lacked the old luster, why food was so execrable, transport so shattered. Six years of cruel occupation and war were no jest to be dismissed with a shake of the head, but . . . He paused, reflected, pursed his lips, fumbled with his hands as though it were agony to utter the words that were storming inside of him. After a lengthy interval he resumed:

"The people are disappointing—the people—my people."

"Are they so changed?" I asked.

"Quite changed." With a nervous twitch of the shoulders he leaned forward and continued: "On my first day here I went for a ride in a streetcar just to observe the people. There were many boys and girls in the car, students, and they were so frivolous, so boisterous; their talk was trivial, pure nonsense. Young people were not like that in the old days."

"It's the privilege of youth," I said, "to be carefree and happy. Young people in America are no different."

43

"But America is America," he flashed back impatiently. "America can afford it. It fears and need fear nothing and no one. It is so vast, so rich, so powerful, and it has not suffered much in the war. But Czechoslovakia is a small country and it has always had powerful enemies at its doorway, powerful and brutal. Czech youth should realize it and should be thoughtful and well-mannered and ever aware of their responsibility to the country, its present, its future, yes, and its magnificent past, when it was in the vanguard of the human procession. They should never forget that they are Czech," he said, meaning among other things that they should maintain the discipline and decorum which are essentials of the Czech character.

"But you've been back only a short time, you say."

"The first impressions are the most memorable. And it is not only the young people who are disappointing. I meet friends, old friends, men and women I knew in my youth, and their language is harsh and bitter, sometimes even coarse. They are so preoccupied with themselves, with their today and their future. They seem stunned, almost depraved—not in their habits of life, but in their thoughts. Look here." He straightened in his seat, laid his clenched hand on the table, and again leaning forward as if to confide something solemn, continued: "I went to Plzeň the other day by train, and what a train—windows broken, wind and cinders whistling through the open holes, and so jammed with passengers they could hardly stir in their places. At one station a veteran got on, a legless man on crutches, and would you believe it, no one offered him a seat. I couldn't help saying to myself, 'What's happened to my people? Where are their good manners, their compassion for their own kind?' "

"Perhaps," I said, "you generalize too much. I have a contrary impression. It's quite a sight to see Czechs get on or off a street-car. They are so orderly, so disciplined, so considerate."

"Of course, of course. I don't mean to say they are all bad, and this is Prague, the home of the best the Czechs have ever attained. But those people on the train, refusing to offer a legless veteran a seat. It could never have happened in the old days. I tell you something has gone out of the Czech soul."

"They've had a hard time, a cruel time," I said.

Again he leaned back, half closed his eyes, and meditated in silence. Then with a sigh he resumed, as if continuing his interrupted discourse.

"They are so bewildered. What are the American and Russian troops doing here? What do they want of this poor country? The Americans say they'll go when the Russians leave. The Russians say nothing and are living off the land. The Americans, their pockets bulging with chocolates and cigarettes, loaf around with the German *Fräuleins,* make them feel they are sort of heroines, and are perpetrating a gigantic black market, converting worthless occupation crowns into American dollars which not Uncle Sam but the impoverished Czechs will have to make good, dollars that should buy food and machinery and help my people get on their feet. And look here"—his eyes lighted up with emotion as he raced on—"a friend told me that once he was walking along the street in Plzeň and two Americans, not too sober, stopped him and asked whether he was a Czech or a German. He said he was a Czech, and both struck him with their fists; yes, yes, they did. Of course he didn't complain. What's the use? That's what the German *Fräuleins* have done to the Americans here. . . . And—and—only last evening as I was sitting in the café of a hotel a party of Russian officers came in, and they were not any too sober either. They demanded *slivovice,* and the waiter told them there was none. They said they must have it. The waiter said he was sorry but none was available. One of the officers banged the table and shouted he must have *slivovice.* The waiter was frightened, the manager was frightened, the guests were frightened, and I—I was in a rage. But nobody did anything. People are scared. Can you imagine what would have happened to such louts if they had behaved like that in an American hotel—in New York, Chicago, San Francisco? But in Prague people have to put up with it. They are so scared of the Russians, the Americans, themselves. Allies, Allies, Allies!"

We smoked cigarettes. Turning his head to one side and crossing his legs, my companion kept puffing incessantly and peering into the wreath of smoke that was crawling over his face, his head, as if searching in its very dimness an answer to his aching perplexities.

"It's revolution," I said. "All Europe is passing through a cataclysmic change, and you must allow for the abnormal behavior of people. You shouldn't feel discouraged if at this moment Russians, Americans, and Czechs don't live up to your exalted opinions of them."

He nodded, murmured something under his breath, and was again silently watching the smoke curl up over his face. "I suppose," he said, "you wonder why I talk to you so openly; I am a Czech by blood and Czechs, as you know, don't spill their inner thoughts and feelings to strangers. You must excuse me if I seem brazen. But you see, I've read your two books on my people. I must tell you frankly I didn't care for your novel. It left me cold. But your other book, *We Shall Live Again*—what a prophetic title. My wife and I have read it aloud to each other, over and over. When we read your descriptions of the demonstration on the Václavské after the people learned England and France had betrayed them to Hitler, and they shouted for arms so they could fight and die, and how now and then someone would start singing 'Where is my home, Where is my home,' and the demonstration would halt and men would doff their hats and all would join in the stirring tune and the sorrowful words, we wept, we just wept, my wife and I, more with joy than grief, joy that our people were so strong in spirit. And your descrip-

46

tions of Tábor, town of lovely homes and spilling over with flowers—Tábor, where the Hussites with their blood purged the souls of their people—the Tábor my wife and I knew in our youth! When we read your description of the old town we were so thrilled that we said to each other, 'Thank God our people have a soul, and their soul is marching on.' *We Shall Live Again!* Our people will remember the faith you had in them—and, well, I came back hoping to find the soul of my people unsullied, but instead—they have grown so petty, so trivial-minded, and I am a sad man, I really am."

He rose, smiled affably, and extended his hand.

"Excuse me. I've taken too much of your time already. I had to talk to you, and now I must go." But even as he was standing I could perceive a glow rush into his eyes. "Maybe," he said, "I talk too much. Maybe I am misjudging my people. May I stay a while longer?"

"Please!"

He sat down again. His expression changed like that of a child that has been whipped and before whom a repentant parent is flaunting an enticing gift.

"I guess I am old-fashioned. I think too much of the past, want it back again, on my own terms, and who am I, anyway? After all, I am a gray-haired man and these young people of whom I complain—they may be loud and a bit coarse, but they are alive, there is joy in them, joy and strength, and that's really good, very good. You see how my mind works? Now I am groveling with despair and now I feel a sudden rush of exulta-tion—up and down—down and up—like the times we live in. So don't misunderstand me—I don't want to be a pessimist." He rose and left, a confused and tormented man, like many others especially in Prague in the early months after liberation, when foreign armies were still in the country, and when the nation was groping toward stability and toward a clarification of its immediate tasks and the eventual direction of its destiny.

A few weeks later we met again.

"How're you feeling? Still worried about the Czech soul?"

"Better, much better," he answered.

"Kind of getting used to things?"

"Getting used to myself. Are you busy?"

"Not especially."

He took me by the arm and we walked along the street, and as we walked he talked.

"I had an experience of which I must tell you, a wonderful experience. You know how Czechs love to honor their dead. The very second day after my return here I went to the village where my mother is buried to visit her grave. I felt happy, very happy. It was as though I would commune with my dear mother in the flesh—talk to her, embrace her, kiss her, and tell her how much I cared for her. But when I reached the cemetery the gate was locked. I called to the keeper and there was no response. There had been fighting in the neighborhood, and the keeper had evidently fled and had not yet returned. I felt quite distressed and thought first of climbing over the wall. I had to visit my mother's grave. Then I thought I'd walk around and perhaps there would be an opening somewhere in the wall. Sure enough, there was a hole, evidently blasted by a shell. I crawled through and found myself inside the cemetery. It was overgrown with weeds and no one was around. It was so unlike Czechs to neglect the home of the dead. But then—war is war. I walked past rows and rows of tombstones, knee-deep, shoulder-high in wild grass and weeds. Suddenly I heard a sound. I thought it was an animal fleeing or the approach of a man. But the sound continued, and it seemed to come from the same place and not from something in flight. I started in the direction from which it came, which was the same direction as my mother's grave. The sound grew louder and louder and more and more distinct. I recognized it for what it was—someone cutting grass. I hastened my steps and soon saw a woman on her knees cutting the grass over my mother's grave; I almost ran to her, and when she looked up I recognized her—our old housekeeper. She was as surprised to see me as I was to see her. We flung our arms around each other and kissed, and she said, 'I knew you'd come, I knew it, darling. I knew you wouldn't forget your *maminka,* and I made haste to cut the grass and pretty up the grave, so you'd feel you had really come home.'" He paused and swallowed and resumed with a fresh gush of ardor:

"I cannot tell you how deeply I was moved. Here she was, this old housekeeper, knowing in her heart that I would come back to the one place that was sacred to me—not out of duty but out of love and reverence—here she was on her knees, cleaning up the grave and making it look fresh and beautiful. . . . Ever since then I've felt better. Whenever I meet an old friend whose language annoys and pains me, I think of the old lady, this simple, hardy, tenderhearted peasant woman, and I say to myself: 'Not all Czechs have lost their souls. The little people who live on the land, close to trees and grass, flowers and birds, sun and skies, have preserved their souls. They are the salt and the glory of the good and beautiful Czech earth.'"

4. A Village Revisited

Going back to Strážnice, in the heart of sunny and fertile Moravia, was like going home. Not that I had ever spent any length of time in the village or had family roots there. But villages, like persons, often reveal on first approach an inner grace that evokes a spontaneous response and cements immediate acquaintance into lasting friendship. Such was the case of Strážnice and myself.

Mere accident took me there in the pre-Munich days. While loitering around the lobby of the Baťa Hotel in Zlín, my eyes were caught by a flamboyant poster announcing the annual three-day wine festival in Strážnice. That was the first time I had heard of the village, and the longer I lingered before the announcement, the more it captivated me. In colloquial and unboastful language it promised much: song and dances, display of ornate costumes and the enactment of the wedding ceremony of "the bartered bride"; gaieties for all, natives and strangers; and the sale without limit of home-grown wines of many vintages. It invited all who cared to come and assured them of a prodigal welcome.

I knew enough about Slav villages in other lands to appreciate

Slovak peasant woman

Slovak boy in festive attire

that on such an occasion, as on no other, one could glimpse fully
and intimately, as in a well-placed mirror, the life and the
character of the community; the pattern and the color and the
rhythm of its daily life, with past and present flowing side by
side, each making the other more luminous and vivid by contrast.

I had no sooner reached the village than I was aware of a
pictorial antiquity nestling within a well-ordered modernity. Here
were curving rows of ancient cottages with peaked tile roofs,
the walls aglow with fresh whitewash, side by side with stately
newly built apartment houses. Here were not only oxen but
cows doing the work of horses, and tractors trundling freight
vans and threshing machines. Here were city clothes and
ancestral costumes, paraded with equal pride. Here, instead of
clashing, the machine-age and century-old folkways coalesced
and made the spell of the old as alluring as the symbol of the new.

Overcast skies and a prickly drizzle neither halted nor marred
the festivities. The wine cellar was like a legend come to life.
Fairy queens might have held court there; goblins might have
gamboled there; saints might have sought refuge there and
felons salvation. Nor was it devoid of modern purpose beyond
its normal function. Over three hundred years old, deep underground, with thick brick walls and an arched brick ceiling, it
made an exemplary air-raid shelter, for the block-busters of
yesterday, perhaps for the solar explosives of tomorrow.

Ringed in hoops of iron, darkened with age and exuding a
fragrance of wine and wood, gigantic wooden casks leaned
against the old walls. The cellar was a winery and a festival
palace. Crowded to the doors, ablaze with lights and aglow with
many-hued costumes, it rocked with gaiety and comradeship.
Hospitality flowed as freely as wine. Friends were easy to make
and, once made, clung close and steadfast. Members of Parliament, lawyers, physicians, teachers, engineers, an author or two,
carpenters, farmers, cobblers, here and there a gypsy or Jew

mingled in unthwarted good-fellowship. Everyone was himself, and none paid homage to anyone else. None held himself aloof or beyond the spirit of the occasion. Antipathy and animosity, by whomever nurtured, were submerged in the swell and clamor of jollity, and, more than that, though faces were flushed and eyes beamed with the glow of wine and excitement, there were no altercations, no harsh words at all, only joy and comradeship. Hitler's fulminations across the border were growing increasingly thunderous, but the merry tumult in the wine cellar was like a mockery of the doom they boded. Hardy men and women, their nerves were as unfrayed as the ancestral costumes they paraded, and their trust in themselves was as unshaken as their faith in the God they devoutly worshiped.

I was so captivated by the village that a year later, when I set about planning my novel, *To Sing with the Angels,* I chose it for the locale of the story.

I timed my return with the wine feast, which the Germans had banned and which in 1945 was celebrated again for the first time in seven years.

It was close to midnight when I arrived in the village. The inn was crowded with visitors, and as in the pre-war days they sat around tables, reading newspapers and magazines, playing cards or chess and drinking, not *slivovice,* not wines, no liquors at all —none were as yet available—not even the deep-foamed and world-renowned Pilsener beer; only a mud-colored brew that bore the label of beer, ersatz coffee as black as coal, and a cherry-tinted beverage that passed for tea. Yet the pre-war atmosphere of amiability was unchanged. Here were composure and serenity, ease and self-assurance, though nowhere a glint of the one-time brightness. Only the black tuxedo and black tie of the headwaiter, shiny and spotted with wear, flaunted a ghostlike memory of yesterday.

I strolled around the streets, refreshing old memories and old sentiments, then looked up an old friend and continued the stroll with him. The streets were deserted and the footsteps of stray pedestrians resounded clear and loud over the cobbled pavements. The cottages, as if built in one piece, were, as ever, huddled together, and a full moon splashed the tiled roofs with a glazed brilliance. Here and there a light flickered in the windows, otherwise the village was asleep. On street after street there was no sign of destruction.

"You are lucky," I said, "to have escaped all war damage."

"Wait," said my companion, "I'll show you something."

We turned a corner and soon found ourselves on the bank of the deep-dug but now shallow canal which the Baťas had built to bring ships and barges direct from the Elbe River to their industrial empire. On the opposite bank sprawled a huge barn with the front ripped out; so slenderly was it held together by lone pillars and a broken back wall that a gale, it seemed, would tumble it into a heap of wreckage.

"A few days before the Germans left," explained my companion, "a partisan who lived here, acting on a radio signal from London, attempted to blow up a bridge. He was caught and shot. Then a squad of uniformed Germans commanded by a young lieutenant came over, rounded up all the men who lived on the same street as the partisan, and lined them up against this barn. Among them was a very old man, and he kept protesting: 'You aren't going to shoot me. It's so silly! I'm so old, you won't dare.' But they did dare; they shot him and nine others, whom they had picked out at random. Then they made those whose lives they had spared set fire to the home of the partisan and his neighbors, the entire block of houses. Let's go over and take a look."

We walked across the bridge over the canal and sauntered up to the burned homes. A few were already being rebuilt; others

53

were still heaps of charred ruins, neatly thrown together. Compared with the devastation I had witnessed in the Russian Ukraine or in the Tolstoy country, the scene before me was neither horrifying nor particularly impressive, if only because on neighboring streets houses, barns, trees were untouched. Yet to this village the memory of the shootings and the burnings must for generations to come fan an undying ember of hate for the enemy and for everything he symbolized.

We strolled on and presently came to the once-thriving and tumultuous Gypsy Town on the outskirts of the village. It had never been large, only of about a dozen families. But it had been a landmark in the community, bursting with the clang of tools, the bark of dogs, the screams of barefooted children. The first republic had weaned the residents from their distinctive garb and from vagabondage. They had settled into peaceful pursuits and no longer lived in hooded vans, but in whitewashed cottages. The men were carpenters, cobblers, butchers, day laborers, tinsmiths, and the women worked out in the fields, tended livestock, and brought into their homes more and more of the amenities of civilized living. Children, including girls, attended school and reached out for the worldly advantages the republic offered them.

Now all was dark and quiet in Gypsy Town, and not only because of deep night.

"Only a handful of them," explained my companion, "are alive. The others were slaughtered."

We stood around in silence and looked at the empty cottages drooping with neglect and dilapidation. Not a light in any of them, nowhere a sign of life, not a whine or howl of a dog, not a flicker of a cat's eye in the dark. They were like tombs, the very darkness and silence of which inspired a feeling of horror. We turned back and started walking again.

"What about the Jews in Strážnice?" I asked.

"I have the exact figures on the Jews. Out of the 180 who lived here before the war only twelve have survived."

We rambled on, and my companion related with gusto the adventures of the village during the German occupation. It was not all tragedy, he assured me. There were no little comedy and farce in the battle of wits by which Czechs sought to outsmart the enemy in big and in little things. It was fun to think up riddles and stratagems for the purpose of evading German law and German vigilance, to anticipate German snares and unravel them so neatly that nothing came of them. Everyone had to be a consummate liar and an actor: not only an actor, but a playwright, to think up new plots by which to mystify and bewilder the enemy and escape being ambushed by him. Only it was no comedy if one failed in the effort and found himself trapped. God, how dreadful it was then!

I asked if the village had suffered any unpleasant incidents when the Russian soldiers came.

My companion burst into a laugh and answered:

"Not at all," and he laughed again. "You see, stories had come to us that when Russian soldiers were sober they were jolly and likable and caused no one any trouble. But when they had too much to drink they were unmanageable. So you know what we did? We buried our *slivovice* and our wines—that is, those of us who had any left—where no one could even smell them out. When the Russians came we invited them to our homes and offered them milk instead of liquor. They drank milk and ate bread and bacon and pickles and we and they had a wonderful time, and after they left we had only pleasant memories of their stay."

Again bursting into a laugh, he continued:

"I must tell you something very amusing. One story had it that the first thing the Russians did when they came to a village

55

was to rape the women, and not in beds but in horse carts. So in a village around here several women decided that if they were going to be raped they might as well make a romantic adventure of it. They filled the carts with straw, trimmed them with flowers, and drew white sheets over them. The Russians arrived and—nothing happened. They never molested a single woman. There is romance for you!"

On reaching the inn, dark and deserted now, my companion and I parted. Through unlighted hallways and up dark stairs I groped my way not to my room but to the auditorium. I opened the window and leaned out. The moon was full and brilliant, and all was silence in the village. Not a soul in the street, not a dog barking. Dogs were tame and friendly here, with none of the violent temper their kind shows in Polish, Russian, or Ukrainian villages—good evidence of indulgent treatment of dogs and a comradely relationship with men.

All around were familiar landmarks—trees, shops, homes, gray and solid, old and undamaged. The highway that wound past the inn was as empty of traffic as the streets. The trees were shiny with gathering mist, and the air was raw and balmy with the scent of withering plants and drying hay. No armed guards stalked the sidewalks, for here was no danger of perverse deeds or of impulsive and unsocial performance. The old discipline and the old integrity had survived as unscathed as the window out of which I was leaning. Here was an old culture, its roots so deep in the fat Moravian soil that the last storm which had blown over it, like all the others in the past, had spent itself on the very strength the community had sucked up in the past centuries. It was not the person of the Czech but the culture he has created that overpowered the German. There was something haunting and beautiful about this culture, something as elusive as the night and as defiant of time and death as the moon that splashed the low cottages with a ravishing brilliance. . . .

As I wandered around the village renewing old friendships, what particularly impressed me now, even more than on my former visit, was the extraordinary quality of the women. Not one was illiterate; the high-school graduate was not uncommon. In the European more than the American sense of the term, they were magnificent helpmeets of the men. They milked the cows. They fed the geese, the hens, the pigs. They worked in the fields. They tended the gardens and cultivated the flowers. Skilled with needle and paintbrush, they were among the most consecrated homemakers in Europe. Small as were the cottages, of two or three more often than of four rooms, they were simply and tastefully furnished, with flowers in the windows, ornate spreads and quilts over the beds, embroidered towels on the walls, and the space over doors and windows enlivened with hand-painted designs, crowned with the inevitable figure of a rooster.

"But why a rooster?" I asked a young woman.

In reply came a melodious ditty:

> *"Sing Strážnice roosters,*
> *Sing me a gay song,*
> *So I may know no sorrow,*
> *So my heart may be merry."*

The young woman laughed and went on in a lyrical strain: "Is there a more majestic creature on a farm than a rooster, so dignified, so independent, so handsome of feather, so song-loving, so joy-giving? In the morning he wakes you with a song and all day he gladdens your heart with his singing." She chanted another ditty in praise of the object of her affection.

There are many folk tunes in the village in glorification of the virtues of this not-too-lowly barnyard bird.

The Sunday costumes of both sexes are the creation of women and defy the pen. There is not a hint of somberness in the color or the design, of anything reminiscent of the toil and the worries of a peasant, or suggestive of defeat and disenchantment. The colors are as rich and ornate as the flowers and fruit from which they were copied generations ago. Here are history and art, nature and science, love of beauty and joy.

Clearly here is no exclusive man's world, with woman subordinated in thought and in duty and cloistered within her own feminine seclusion. She is a person in her own right, with privileges in education and edification uncurtailed by man's whim or man's prerogative. Within the scheme of labor in the household and on the land, she commands her own income, derived from the care of poultry—hens, geese, ducks—and from her expert needlework. Illuminating is the Czech saying: "A man may be the head, but a woman is the neck that turns it."

Unremitting is the toil of the woman in the village, in some ways more so than of the man, though now amelioration is promised her by the introduction of more and more mechanized farming. Yet she is subject neither to the insults nor the abuses that are often the lot of women in peasant civilization. In pre-Soviet Russia, in the course of the wedding ceremony in the northern villages, the bride presented the groom with a whip which he lightly brandished over her as a reminder of the beating she would invite on herself if she disobeyed his will. In Strážnice to this day a mother or grandmother will be certain to instruct the bride not to fail to step on the groom's foot while the priest is marrying them, to remind him that if there is any henpecking in the household she will do it.

Here a woman's grace and femininity, as much as her work in the home and in the field, yield the reward of man's respect for her person, her judgment, her authority. If she is not queen of the household, neither is he king, which speaks for a democracy in home life in which the duties but not the rights are divided between men and women.

The wine cellar was still cluttered with humming presses and tubs of brewing juices. Grapes were late in ripening, and the making of wine took precedence over the celebration of its glories, so the festival was moved to the inn. It began solemnly enough with a blessing of the grape by a priest and a brief address of welcome by the mayor. The room was bright with grapevines, and clusters of choice grapes gleamed jewel-like from the vines.

Hedonistically the feast, the first in seven years, was a niggardly affair, almost a failure. There was hardly any wine, none at all for sale. The supplies people had managed to save from German looting they kept home for family use. The lone bottles that stuck out of the pockets of youths were more a symbol than a fulfillment. There was scarcely any goose or pork, not a glimmer of pastry. In the market place I saw no food carts and no food stalls offering, as in 1938, cakes with rich and ornate dressings, and large heart-shaped ginger snaps with tiny mirrors framed inside and embroidered with romantic legends, which boys and girls might send to one another. But the costumes were as resplendent, and the dancing and the singing, the laughing and the shouting even more merry and more tumultuous. . . . The old equalities were as pronounced, the old comradeships as ebullient, the old love of joy and lust for clamor as unrestrained.

As I watched it all it seemed to me that the occasion was more than a seasonal celebration. It partook of the spirit of a patriotic demonstration. The whirling and the hopping, the singing and the shouting, the banners and the bunting made it clear that love of country and of freedom, and all that these signify in custom and tradition, in individual identity and communal dedication, in the very costumes they were wearing, the very shouts of merriment that drowned out the playing of the orchestra, was

59

one of their most deep-felt emotions, all the more frenzied because so long repressed.

The more I glimpsed into the life of the peasantry, the more I marveled how they could live so well on such small acreages of land. Among a population of 6,000, only one family owned 120 acres; the others averaged from six to fifteen. Yet here was Martin Gajda, sixty-seven, with a bright twinkle in his shrewd dark eyes, hardly a stoop to his broad shoulders, and only a spray of grayness in his thick black hair. He is the father of eleven children, ten of whom are living. His oldest daughter fetched a pitcher of milk, home-baked bread, a platter of grapes, and set them on the table. As I talked to the father I could not help feeling that he was one of the most contented men I had known. Yet he cultivated only thirteen acres of land.

"How could you raise your large family on so small a farm?" I asked.

"And why not?" was the astounding reply.

Gajda is not rich. He has no automobile. His home is electrified but is innocent of the modern improvements that are a part of the American farm household. He does not even have a horse or a yoke of oxen. But he keeps three cows and a heifer calf. He fattens two hogs a year, raises a small flock of geese, chickens, and rabbits. He cultivates a vineyard, for in Strážnice wine is as much a food as it is a beverage. The combination of bread, bacon, and wine is regarded as the choicest of breakfasts.

"D'you do your plowing with cows?" I asked.

"I do everything with cows," the happy man answered.

I saw the cows plowing and hauling sugar beets to the railroad station, and I wondered how anyone could ever do planting and haying and harvesting on time with such dull-witted, slow-paced animals.

60

Yet in part the secret of the peasant's success in this village comes from the alertness with which he performs his field work. A Gajda has to be in tune with nature, else disaster overcomes him. He must take advantage of every hour of favorable weather. He must be intelligent and calculating and highly industrious to whip out of the land all the bounty it can yield.

He can afford no wasteland such as one sees along the fields and highways in Russia and America. Every span of soil must grow something—grain, sugar beets, potatoes, tobacco, clover, corn, fruit. Though the labor is arduous because performed chiefly by hand and largely with tools that belong to an older era, the care of crops is so expert that the yield is rarely disappointing. There is, of course, no pasture for livestock. Not even the richest farmer deems it profitable to take land out of cultivation and turn it into pasturage. The year-round livestock are housed in the barn, and the increased amounts of manure help to keep the land rich and fertile. . . .

"How about the peasant who cultivates only six acres of land," I asked a schoolteacher. "How does he make ends meet?"

"Maybe the swallows help him," he said with a reflective shrug. "Our people believe in swallows. They bring good luck. That's why you see flocks of them in the barns. They flit and twitter around and alight on the cows' backs, and the bossies do not even bother to swish them off with their tails. Good luck is good luck, isn't it?" He laughed aloud, then continued soberly:

"Unless he leases the land of a shopkeeper or professional man, the farmer with six acres has a tough time. By January or February his food gives out and he works around by the day or goes off to the Baťa factories in Zlín. He is a real problem all over our country. Now many of them will move to the Sudetenland and settle on the lands that belonged to Germans. The others will struggle along as they have always done, unless the government does something for them. It's one of the things the new government cannot ignore. Of course the co-operatives are a great help."

They are indeed. They are one reason for the absence in rural Czechoslovakia of the antagonism to nationalization that one often encounters in middle-class circles in Prague. The very streets of Strážnice attest to the communal spirit of the people. They are lined with fruit trees—cherry, apple, plum, pear, walnut, apricot. In spring when they are in bloom, the village presents an extraordinary sight: wave after wave of white alternates with rose and purple and invest the cobbled streets and whitewashed cottages with beauty and festiveness that dazzle the eye. But the trees are a communal affair. The community has set them out, cares for them, and only the residents whose homes they are facing are, on payment of a small fee, permitted to pick the fruit. Though the trees are unfenced, stealing is rare, and when they are in bloom children would no more think of breaking an apple or cherry twig than of throwing a stone into a neighbor's window. Respect for public property and a neighbor's rights is a part of the discipline of daily living.

Hardly a service the farmer requires in his everyday life and work but is rendered by the co-operatives. At nominal cost he may make use of a purebred bull, boar, or ram that is the possession of a livestock co-operative. The savings bank and the loan association are co-operative enterprises. Wholesale and retail establishments, dispensing cement, grains, agricultural implements, seeds, fertilizers, everything else a farmer must purchase, are co-operatively owned. There is no creamery and no sugar factory in the village, but both are within easy reach, and both are the property of co-operative societies. The village itself owns and operates a slaughterhouse, a brickyard, a distillery, the motion-picture theater—or did until the film industry was nationalized—and is likewise the owner of the only heavy scales. Even the wine cellar, the pride and joy of the village, modern with its electric lights and plumbing, and its dance floor large enough to accommodate several hundred couples, is a co-operative institution. At its own expense the village is now enlarging and mechanizing the brickyard and plans to do the same with the distillery, both of which have been profitable public enterprises. The village has built four apartment houses, the most modern in the community, and rents them just as a private landlord would and with the same motive in mind, to obtain profits from the investment. The peaceful dissolution of feudalism yielded the village a grant of 867 acres of forest and thirty-eight acres of arable land which residents who have no gardens of their own rent in small plots for a nominal fee.

There are private traders in the village, and the competition between them and the co-operatives makes for the increased efficiency of both.

The striking feature of this inclusive program of public and co-operative ownership is that most of it was achieved during the years of the first republic. This testifies to the fact that the institution of private enterprise in business never attained the magnitude and the power that it had in the United States, or even in England and France. It never had become as important and firmly rooted a component of the folk mind as in those countries. Only if an effort were made to collectivize the land in the Russian manner, with Russian speed and with Russian disregard for immediate results, would there be a violent protest. But the revolution, however ambitious in its plans of nationalization, is not encroaching on the privately owned farms of the peasantry. No one ever mentions the word "kolkhoz." The fact is that the nationalization program impinges but lightly on the economic life of the village. It intends no such violent upheavals in the countryside as were a part of the first Soviet Five-Year Plan, and for the reason that Czechoslovakia has not the heritage of squalor and poverty, of illiteracy and backwardness that characterized the pre-Soviet village, nor the violent dislike of innovation and the violent emotion against the outside world which rural Russia had for centuries been harboring.

Only in China, with its cult of ancestor worship and individual responsibility for the family group, is the family more closely knit than in this village. Small as the farm may be, it rarely passes out of family ownership. There is always a son or daughter to remain on the homestead, to maintain old family traditions, to hold together the family heirlooms, from old Bibles and prayer books to old costumes or old family albums, and to keep alive the memory of the dead. Neither this nor any village in the country knows the institution of the abandoned farm. The family homestead is too hallowed to be deserted or, save under irrepressible urgency, to be allowed to pass into the possession of strangers.

One Sunday afternoon the daughter of a shopkeeper whose guest I was for midday dinner invited me to go with her to the cemetery. We walked over to the graves of her mother and brother, both of whom had been dead for some years. Tenderly and reverently the young woman brushed the dust off the tombstone, watered the flowers, smoothed the grass with her hands. Then she stood before the graves in prayerful contemplation.

"How often," I said, when she turned to go, "do you visit the cemetery?"

"Every Sunday," was her reply, "unless I am away from home."

"Summer and winter?"

"Summer and winter."

Not only she but her father and other members of the family make such pilgrimages to the dead on Sundays. A Sunday is never complete without solemn homage to those who have passed away.

Karel Mastný, a schoolteacher, invited me to a party in his home. I had no more than entered his courtyard than I realized that in this village a teacher is more than a pedagogue. In front of the house stood a huge wagon loaded with tubs of grapes.

"What is that for?" I asked.

"Wine," was his jovial reply.

Mastný does more than make his own wine. He cultivates a vegetable garden and fruit trees. He raises two pigs a year, a few geese, a small flock of hens, and of course rabbits. He and his wife do all the work, and their sunburned faces attested to long hours of outdoor toil with spade and hoe.

Guests came. The schoolmaster's wife set the table with wine, milk, grapes, homemade bread and cakes. Suddenly I heard music outside.

"What is that?" I asked.

"You shall soon see," replied the schoolmaster's wife, smiling.

Presently a village orchestra, five youths of high-school age, bounded into the house. At once the guests arose and the living room shook with lively singing and boisterous dancing. It was all in honor of the "American guest," though all but he participated with zeal in the impromptu entertainment.

After the musicians departed all returned to the table, ate, drank, talked, jested, and laughed uproariously. Every now and then someone would start a song and again everybody joined in the singing but the American, to whom the songs were new and alien. The songs were so lively and melodious, so gay and so lilting, that I asked my neighbor at the table if the people in Strážnice ever sang solemn or sorrowful songs. "You see," came the enlightening answer, "we take our sorrows philosophically," and to demonstrate the meaning of her words, she started a folk melody about a youth who is jilted in love, yet who sings:

> *"I shall tip my hat to one side,*
> *For another girl I shall search,*
> *Not I to hold a grudge against all girls."*

Here was a spirit of reasonableness and equanimity which I have observed among no other Slav peasants, be they Poles, Ukrainians, Russians, or Yugoslavs. Generalizations on the basis of songs, however popular, may lead to faulty conclusions. Yet it was not only this and other songs but all I had observed and heard in the village that reinforced an old conviction that in his mental and emotional make-up the Czech is unlike other Slavs. Mature, he abhors explosive rhetoric, melodramatic gestures, violent action. Reason controls impulse. Thought mellows emotion. Purpose rules judgment. Neither in his personal life nor in his political thinking is he disposed to swerve into an irrational or extreme position. That is why murder and other violent crimes are such rare occurrences. However shaken by immediate travail or catastrophe, his is essentially an optimistic mood. The world neither ends nor begins with the cloudburst of today. There is always a tomorrow bright with warmth and sun. He neither wails nor rails at fate, for he never deems himself a helpless victim of its powers and its caprices. He has too much faith in himself to be swayed by oracles of despair. He will demand change, fight for favors, but in his own fashion. Reason has ever been a guide and a hope, a source of strength and deliverance.

I cannot conceive of a Czech Tolstoy composing so terrifying a tale of peasant degradation as *Power of Darkness,* a Czech Ivan Bunin penning so melancholy a story of peasant life, all the more moving because so beautifully written, as *The Village,* nor a Czech Chekhov painting so shattering a picture of peasant desolation as *The Peasants.* Neither do I know anything in Russian literature to rival the Czech classic tale, *Grandmother,* by Božena Němcová, an idyllic story of peasant serenity and good humor, of peasant simplicity and nobility. Nor do I know of any Czech who so passionately glories in this literary gem in Czech literature as does Professor Zdeněk Nejedlý, one of the most voluble exponents of Communist doctrine.

In appraising the meaning and scope of the Czech revolution it is well to emphasize the differences in the history, the culture, the temperament of the Russian and the Czech peasantry. To ignore these differences would falsify the event, especially in these turbulent times when the very word revolution conjures forth in so many a reader the picture of all the worst that has happened in Russia since the advent of Sovietism, and impels him to associate with it any and all revolutionary situations in other countries.

5. Middle-Class Proletarians

Pre-war Zlín was the fulfillment of an audacious dream and a world-renowned monument to the village cobbler who had conceived it and clothed it in the flesh and blood of reality. His was one of the most spectacular success stories of the twentieth century. More in the nature of an American than a European saga, it singles out pre-war Czechoslovakia as neither too old nor too small, neither too petrified with authority nor too stratified with tradition, to halt the rise of a humble craftsman to fabulous triumph.

Today Zlín is an idea and a challenge, a dream unfulfilled and a goal to be attained. No other city in Czechoslovakia, perhaps none in all non-Russian Europe, is more certain than this remote town in the hilly and wooded Moravian countryside to draw on itself the attention of capitalist and Communist, of social philosopher and industrial planner. The principal forge in which the key to success or failure of the new and revolutionary Czechoslovakia is being hammered out is Zlín. For here, as in no other community, are the facts and the realities, the machines and the men, the traditions and the talents, the ideas and the policies to subject the revolution to the sternest and most searching trials. To appreciate the Zlín of today and of tomorrow we must glance back into the history of the town, looking particularly at the career of the cobbler who lifted it to one of the most grandiose industrial enterprises in the world.

The name of the cobbler was Thomas Baťa, and for over three centuries his ancestors had lived in Zlín and had pursued the craft of shoemaking. Thomas followed in their footsteps. In his youth Zlín was the trading center for an unprosperous peasantry, holding out no promise of deliverance from the routine of his ancestors.

At the age of fifteen, already a skilled craftsman, Thomas Baťa went to Vienna in quest of fresh opportunities. He sold shoes, but sophisticated, joy-loving Vienna was unimpressed by the offerings of the peasant cobbler. After losing what little capital he had invested in his Viennese venture, he returned home. Undaunted by failure, he went to Prague to try his luck there as salesman of his father's shoes. Success was instantaneous and surpassed all Thomas's expectations. Encouraged by the good fortune, he formed a partnership with his brother and sister and built a shoe factory in Zlín. The daily output was fifty pairs, a supreme achievement for Zlín but of no worldly consequence. Realizing that he did not know enough about shoemaking to fulfill his ambition, he journeyed to America and worked in a shoe factory in Lynn, Massachusetts. The American machine and the American system of rationalization of labor and raw materials were a revelation and an inspiration. On his return to Zlín, young Baťa proceeded to revolutionize his shoe industry.

Opportunity for sensational growth came with the severance of Czechoslovakia from Austria and the founding of the first republic. Zlín boomed and boomed, in size, in riches, in glory. Between 1894 and 1938 the population rose from 2,894 to 43,660; daily output of shoes soared from 3,000 pairs in 1920 to 180,000 pairs in 1938; the retail price fell from 220 crowns for the average pair in 1920 to 99 crowns for the choicest pair in 1938. Baťa not only made shoes but sold them and repaired them in his own retail shops, of which there were 2,084 in Czechoslovakia alone. A Baťa shoe store was as much a national institution as a post office or a village inn.

Not content with home markets, Baťa cast his eyes over the map for new fields of conquest. Shoes to him were not only a business but a mission, and with a crusader's zeal he prowled into the most faraway corners of the world: into the depths of Asia and Africa, into regions where shoes were unknown or a luxury, and which other shoe manufacturers had not deemed worthy of exploration. With charts and graphs, with words and figures, he preached the gospel of shoes everywhere he went. His slogan was: "Two pairs of shoes a year for every human being everywhere." Within less than a generation he girdled the globe with shoe factories and shoe shops and became not only the world's leading exponent of "shoes for everybody," including the most backward natives in deepest Africa, but the "shoe king of the world." He studied the climate, the habits, the income of the countries he penetrated, and made shoes to meet all pocketbooks, all tastes, all other contingencies. Always he catered not to the man of wealth but to the man of modest or low earnings. Germany, France, England, Holland, Switzerland, the Balkans, Poland, India, Egypt, Arabia, Turkey, all succumbed to the Baťa gospel, the Baťa advertiser, the Baťa salesman. Thomas Baťa had carved for himself an empire unrivaled by any of his competitors and on which, like the British Empire, the sun never set.

In 1932 Thomas Baťa was killed in an airplane accident. But his brother Jan and his son Thomas Junior, aided by a corps of trained and skilled executives, carried on with undiminished energy, hewing fast to the ideas and the patterns Thomas Senior had evolved.

This much I had learned about Zlín before starting on my first journey there in the summer of 1938. As I was leaving for the town, a court clerk from Zlín whom I had met in Prague said to me, "When you get to my home town you'll think you're back in America."

Nor were his words a flagrant exaggeration. Billboards along highways were as garish as in America and as brief and terse in appeal. The tall red buildings with enormous window space were precisely what one would expect in the newest and most advanced American industrial community. Traffic was as thick and boisterous. Restaurants, dance halls, lunchrooms with automatic devices, open all hours of day and night, served not only choice sandwiches, milk foods, fruit, pastry, and other delicacies but, of all things and the only place in the country to do so, iced tea and iced coffee. The service was faultless—quick and courteous response to all demands and whims. Here was peace. Here was service supreme. Here was "business vision," as consummate as anywhere in America.

From the vast amount of publicity, neatly and eminently displayed at every turn, it was apparent that Baťa took no chances on native and foreign visitors failing to be impressed with the name Baťa, the supremacy of Baťa, the stupendousness of Baťa, the glories of Baťa. This, too, was strikingly and exuberantly American. Lynn made Zlín, but Zlín had outvied Lynn in self-glorification. Baťa's genius for publicity was exceeded only by his genius in production and salesmanship. Not only in Czechoslovakia, but all over Europe, all over the far-flung Baťa empire, Zlín was acclaimed as "Little America."

Nor was Baťa behind American exponents of paternalism. Few if any Americans espoused it with greater stubbornness or greater efficiency. He fought labor unions and would permit none in his shoe factories. He had lifted Zlín from obscurity and indigence to eminence and affluence, and only he knew what was best for the men who worked for him and whose destiny was tied up with his. So he never ceased to proclaim. He paid the highest wages in the country. He introduced the five-day, forty-hour week. The lunch period lasted one and three quarter hours so workers could go home for a family meal, potter around their Baťa-built, Baťa-owned homes, or, in the case of young people, indulge in tennis, football, or other games on a Baťa athletic field, a swim in the Baťa pool, a stroll in the tree-shaded, flower-brightened Baťa parks, a dance in a Baťa dance hall, a movie in a Baťa motion-picture theater.

Baťa believed in sun and space, in trees and grass, in open skies and faraway horizons, not only for himself but for the men and women who were in his employ. He was no real estate penny-pincher. He loathed slums and would have none in Zlín. The houses he built and rented but never sold to workers, while devoid of architectural distinction, were bright and large, with tall windows and modern plumbing, with spacious kitchens and ample living rooms, with grounds for lawns and shrubs, for trees and flowers, and with as much privacy, a supreme requisite for a Czech, as anyone might care to indulge. Zlín had become the garden city Baťa had set out to build. Between 1931 and 1937, in the workers' district alone, 40,075 trees were set out and 182,575 shrubs. Not even the tall factory buildings obscured from workers' homes the view of near-by hills and forests, of overhead skies and sun. However taxing the speed of the assembly line, however onerous the task of keeping up with ever-rolling belts of leather—once the day's labor was over, the worker had no reason to feel cramped for space and never was shut off from sun and light.

Baťa believed in work, in extracting from every man and woman all the production his ingeniously contrived assembly line and his ever-modernized machines permitted. But he also believed in play and diversion, especially for young people. He felt it his mission to minister not only to the material wants of his workers but to their social thinking and their personal morals. He banned alcoholic beverages from nearly all the eating places and amusement resorts he owned. Young people had to be on guard against trespassing conventional proprieties. Baťa had "eyes" that saw everything. "Loose living" he flagrantly discouraged and unceremoniously penalized. Apostle of simple living, he preached by means of chart and statistical tabulation, slogan and admonition, the virtues of amply caloried meals for office employees, for factory workers, for adults and adolescents. With special eloquence he boosted the glories of milk foods. "The more milk, the better your health," read the legend on one poster. "Milk foods make a good and cheap supper," was the advice of another. In the restaurants I visited, boys and girls were sipping milk from glasses and bottles with the relish of American boys and girls sipping Coca-Colas or ice-cream sodas. I drank a pint bottle, and the cost in American money was the equivalent of three cents. It was Baťa's boast that nowhere else in Czechoslovakia was the individual consumption of milk as high as in Zlín.

Property-minded, immensely successful, the richest man in his own land and one of the richest in Europe, with bank balances in all the leading industrial nations of the world, inordinately proud of his fabulous rise from "rags to riches," Baťa espoused the philosophy of economic individualism with as impassioned a zeal as the gospel of "shoes for everybody." Yet like Henry Ford, he nurtured a fierce contempt for bankers. Polonius's creed, "Neither a lender nor a borrower be," was a principle from which he never swerved in all his gigantic business operations. "A bank loan," he once said, "is like an umbrella. When things go well and the sun shines, they let you keep it, but when things go badly and it rains, they take it away from you."

His own philosophy of life and his economic individualism he sought to inculcate in his workers not only with words but with deeds. The thousands of apprentices who annually flocked to Zlín, chiefly from villages, were required to conform not only to prescribed rules of diet, hygiene, physical culture, curfew hours, schooling, and factory discipline, but also to lay up a "nest egg" for the future, which to Thomas Baťa was the supreme goal in all human endeavor. The apprentices were given accounting books and instructed to budget earnings and expenses so as to maintain a weekly balance which, left with the Baťa treasury, yielded ten per cent annual interest. An indomitable foe of all forms of collectivism—Socialism, Communism, statism, trade unionism—he evoked the fury of all labor parties and labor leaders, especially the Social Democrats and the Communists.

As I wandered around the Baťa kingdom in Zlín and the surrounding countryside I could not help marveling at the energy, the single-mindedness, the foresight, the efficiency, yet the arbitrariness with which the once-lowly cobbler had piloted his little ship of state. Autocratic as he was in his social thinking, arrogating unto himself all authority and all wisdom as to the way men and women in his employ should order their lives, he was one of the foremost industrial geniuses and planners of all Europe, not omitting plan-impassioned, plan-inspired Soviet Russia. No Soviet leader reverenced the machine more than he and, despite difference in motivation, viewed it with more fanatical faith as the instrument of mankind's ultimate deliverance from all want and all stagnation. Long before the Russians had dramatized the word plan, Baťa had made it the cornerstone of his own far-flung business empire. That was what his system of "shop autonomy" meant. Every six months each and all of his shoe shops and all other enterprises worked out a detailed plan of production, distribution, sales, costs, and profits. Nor could any Marxist or Bolshevik hurl at him the usual Marxist indictment that in the interest of personal accumulation he was blocking the advance of science and the elevation of the machine to new heights of output. His slogans, "The machine is eternally unfinished," and "Let the machine sweat so man can think," might have been uttered by Karl Marx or Josef Stalin. In his own laboratories and machine shops he was continually inventing new machines which, once their applicability and feasibility were demonstrated, were quickly installed, regardless of immediate cost. "Buy cheap, sell cheap," was the key to his financial success; and new inventions, by facilitating production and increasing output, enabled him to garner ever-increasing fortunes.

Baťa, the technical engineer, was as revolutionary as Baťa, the social philosopher, was orthodox. In its technical aspects his "shop autonomy" brings to mind Russian "Socialist competition." By pitting factory against factory, department against department, office against office, Russian industrialists are seeking to attain the fulfillment and overfulfillment of the periodic schedules of production. "Shop autonomy" aimed at the same objective, and to give it a fresh and unfailing stimulation Baťa evolved a special system of bookkeeping by means of which every unit in his vastly ramified business enterprises ascertained at the end of each work week, and in minutest detail, success or failure in the fulfillment of its own particular plan, not only in production, but in income and expense, in profit or loss. Baťa deemed his bookkeeping system one of his most cherished trade secrets. Other industrialists sought to buy or worm it out of him, but he never would listen to their bids or pleas. It was his invention and only he would reap the rewards it assured.

In the Zlín of today, engineers and executives, as well as political leaders and government officials, regard the Baťa bookkeeping system as one of the most brilliant aids to production that has ever been invented anywhere. By enabling a shop or office to uncover flaws quickly—any flaws, however minute in detail, whether technical or psychological—it makes possible the immediate discovery of their cause and the instantaneous application of measures for their removal. So enthusiastic are the new executives over its virtues that they are advocating its installation in every nationalized industry.

Zlín and all that it symbolizes in technical attainment is the most precious single asset of post-war Czechoslovakia. It would be priceless to any nation anywhere, especially in time of crisis and readjustment. Shoes were not the only commodity in which Bařa achieved fame. He branched out into a multitude of subsidiary and unrelated industries, and everything to which he lent his prodigious talents bloomed and flowered into breathtaking success. "He was one of the greatest industrial geniuses of all time," remarked a stern-minded Communist leader in Zlín, "and he has left us a priceless heritage." All the more significant are these words because they come from a person who was revolted by Bařa's social philosophy.

Textiles, hosiery, tanneries, chemicals, machine tools, cardboard, woodwork, artificial silk, rubber and tires, airplanes, bricks, publishing, building, all these became a part of the Zlín or Bařa industrial empire. What was more, Czech that he was, with a contempt for aristocratic usage, with no aspiration to social swank, he eschewed the least suggestion of social exclusiveness. Though a company town if ever there was one, Zlín boasted no special residential section for owners and executives. Their homes were scattered over the district in which workers lived. There was no elite society in the town. There were no exclusive clubs or select restaurants. The Bařa children entertained themselves and their friends in the same places to which workers went for their pleasure. The ten-story Bařa hotel, one of the most modern and comfortable in Europe and the cheapest anywhere, operated one of the largest roof gardens in Europe; prices were so moderate that waitresses in the Bařa restaurants, clerks in the

Baťa offices could afford to patronize it. "And it was all profitable," said Jan Baťa. "We never put our hands to anything that did not make us money."

Zlín was a strange combination of dictatorial capitalism and social simplicity; of a highly ramified paternalism and a highly mechanized efficiency. The grounds and the buildings in which the thousands of apprentices lived conveyed no hint of shoemaking or any industrial pursuit. They made me think of a magnificent American college campus; that was how clean and green and spacious and refreshing it all was.

Yet everything—buildings, homes, furniture, grounds—bore almost as much the stamp of standardization as the assembly belts in the factories. I could not help thinking that Zlín might have been the inspiration for *R.U.R.,* the late Karel Čapek's famous robot play. No other community in Czechoslovakia or Europe could have afforded a better pattern for the play. Superb materialist that Baťa was, art and intellect in and of themselves hardly held any place in his scheme of things. Zlín was proud of its schools; and in equipment, much of which Baťa had contributed, they had not their equal in the country. But, save for the Zlín Art School, one of the best known in the country, the emphasis was always on vocational pursuits, on utilitarian objectives, on preparing students for executive positions in modern industry and modern business. Culture as such held scarcely any meaning for Baťa. In this one respect he was the antithesis of the Soviet industrialist to whom theater, even if expressed only in local amateur performances, or music, even if played only by an amateur orchestra, is as much a part of the factory system as machines and other installations.

In August 1945 I went back to Zlín, and I had no more than alighted from the train than I perceived a stupendous change in the appearance of the town. The glow of fresh paint, red and white, which had given pre-war Zlín an aspect of gaiety, almost hilarity, was nowhere in evidence. Since 1940 there had been no repainting of buildings or anything else—the Germans had forbidden it. Not a factory, not a dormitory on the once-gleaming "campus" for apprentices but had windows pasted with cardboard or nailed up with boards. It seemed ironic that Zlín, which had once known the most highly mechanized building industry in Europe, should be without glass for bomb-blasted windows, without lumber for bomb-shattered doors, without paint for anything. The town looked as though an evil hand had malevolently scraped it clean of color and brightness. Only the trees and grass reminded the visitor of its pre-war glory.

Within a few steps of the now-unkempt railroad station a shoe factory seemed turned upside down—a sprawling mass of broken brick and twisted steel. This was my first glimpse of the effects of the American air raid of November 20, 1944. Citizens of the town still speak with emotion compounded of wonder and terror of American daylight precision bombing. The air raid lasted only four minutes and demolished seven five-story shoe factories, a ten-story warehouse, and wrecked and damaged not a few other buildings.

Like Prague, Zlín was emptied of the sumptuous living it had enjoyed in the pre-Munich days—no coffee, no tea, scanty supplies of meat and sugar, not a glass of milk anywhere, not a sight of an apple or pear. In outward appearance there was nothing save the surviving buildings, now lusterless and bleak, and the crowds of workers, gray and somber, to bring to mind the "Little America" that was so profligately on display in 1938.

Yet the town was tranquil. In the midst of a social revolution it maintained a stout composure. I sensed at once the basic contrast between the Russian and the Czechoslovak revolution. The destructive phase incident to the transition from one system to another was achieved here with none of the fury which marked the advent of Sovietism in Russia. Disruption incident to the war and the revolution was as visible as the neglected lawns and parks, but nowhere was there any evidence of revolutionary violence against property or life.

There had been no end of violent and vindictive talk, and no little rough treatment of former executives. Dominik Čipera, the general director of the Baťa enterprises and a Minister in the Cabinet of the second republic, though not of the Protektorat Government, was arrested as a collaborator and locked in a cell with a German Gestapo officer. He was in poor health at the time, and this was the only cell with only one inmate. All the others were overcrowded. There were Communists in Zlín who by virtue of their eminence in the partisan movement imagined that Czechoslovakia was to be sovietized at once and proceeded with more zeal than tact to prepare for the change. People were jailed, held without trial, without indictment other than the charge that they had been collaborators. Because of the acute housing shortage the Communist-dominated National Council started a campaign to evict childless couples from homes to provide accommodation for families with children. Once they came to the home of a minor businessman and told him to vacate his house. "On whose orders?" he demanded. "The people's," was the reply. "Well," he countered, "I too am the people." They left and never came back.

The Red Army which was in Zlín at the time held aloof from the internal strife. It had even permitted the old Baťa management to remain in authority for fourteen days. With no little emotion non-Communists complained that "the moral terror" which the Communists had unleashed in the early weeks of liberation was as confusing as it was frightening. "What next?" people were asking themselves. The program laid down in Košice, to which the Communist leaders had subscribed, was of no moment in Zlín. The local leaders proceeded to realize the revolution in their own way. Afraid lest Baťa supporters and under-cover men undermine their authority, they proclaimed an immediate twenty-five-per-cent increase in wages and re-enforced the manning of the ever-rolling belt line with additional hands. In every way they could they sought to gain more and more power and use it recklessly, non-Communists charged.

When I spoke of these complaints to Josef Kionka, the wiry little Communist leader in the Baťa industry, his reply was: "Our enemies like to exaggerate. I deny that anybody was beaten. Mr. Čipera has long been out of jail. A sick man, he is now in a sanatorium and nobody bothers him, and don't forget he was Minister in the second and already German-dominated republic. Besides, remember that during the six years of German occupation not a single Baťa executive was jailed by the Gestapo or sent to a concentration camp or put to death. But think how many workers were seized and hounded and tortured."

After listening to complaints and denunciations of Communist action during the early weeks of liberation, I still wondered where the "proletarian revolution" was in this most proletarian of all Czechoslovakia's industrial cities. I heard of not a single murder or execution of "class enemies." Only twenty of the Baťa executives were dismissed, and several were expected to be re-admitted.

The very tranquillity of Zlín three months after liberation signalized a spirit of moderation which one would associate not with proletarian combativeness but with middle-class caution. "Quite true," said the Communist mayor of the city, "we're a middle-class people, even our workers." It was obvious that, in spite of Communist domination, the revolution of which everybody was speaking was interlarded with more Czech reasonableness than with revolutionary class-consciousness. Having observed real class-consciousness and class struggle in the early years of Sovietism, I could not help asking myself where was the class-consciousness of the Czech proletarian. Even the vocabulary of workers and leaders did not suggest it. Their speech was as simple and hearty and folksy as in the old days. The period of "critical thinking," which came in the wake of the early "ebullience," as a Zlín woman expressed herself, had restored calm and equanimity and had swung the revolution from a local to a national discipline. The Prague Government, with the consent of Communist leaders, "cracked down" on local authority, and even the twenty-five-per-cent increase in wages was rescinded because the industry could not afford it, though lump sums were advanced to workers out of factory profits in order to enable them to meet the immediate economic crisis.

The sharp contrast with Russia was even more glaringly manifest when I went to see František Mráz, secretary of the Communist party of the province of Zlín. A man in his late thirties, with a broad open face and deep-sunk blue eyes, of a calm demeanor and reflective manner of speech, he made me think more of a business executive than of a revolutionary crusader. His office was crowded with functionaries, young people from all over the province, animated and friendly and ready, indeed eager, to talk to an American writer. The most impressive feature of the conversation was the insistence I had heard everywhere else I had been that Czechoslovakia is a small country and wants to remain Czech above everything else and to become a "model republic." I could think of no enemy of the Communists who would take exception to such pronouncements, however violently they might disagree on the meaning of the language, especially the adjectives which Communists used. Nationalism and patriotism were strong here, as strong as everywhere else, though all the men in the room were committed to "the classless society according to Marx and Lenin." The benighted proletarian of whom Marx and Engels speak in the *Communist Manifesto,* he whom "modern industrial labor . . . had stripped of every trace of national character," and to whom "law, morality, religion are so many bourgeois prejudices," was present—if he was present at all—only as a ghost, conceived in theory if not in fantasy, with no breath of life in him. When the question of the classless society was under discussion I said:

"Without a proletarian dictatorship?"

"We don't need it in this country," someone replied, "unless reactionaries and Fascists start a fight and want to kill our nationalization program."

"If reaction raises its fist against us," said the meditative František Mráz, "we shall not sit with folded arms and let them have their way."

"Is there any danger of that?" I asked.

"Not at present, but we aren't taking chances and we shall always be prepared to meet it effectively."

"D'you take anybody but factory workers into the party?"

"We take anybody who can qualify and who wants to join."

"Even businessmen?"

"Everybody who is a good patriotic Czech and supports nationalization may join the Communist party. One fourth of our members are business and professional folk."

"D'you exclude factory owners?"

"Of course not. One of our members has a factory of his own and employs 250 workers. All we demand of such men is that they live up to their agreements with the trade unions."

"What about peasants?"

"They are welcome to our ranks."

"Kulaks too?"

"Kulaks are no problem here—our peasants are overwhelmingly small landholders."

"In Russia," I said, "kulaks and businessmen, of whom there are no more now, were regarded as 'enemies of the people.'"

"We're different. We're a small nation; our history is different;

Zlín, peasant woman painting rubber dolls

Zlín, seat of the Baťa Industries

our conditions are different. We must work out our revolution in our own way, unless the reactionaries revolt and try to stop us."

"Are Catholics eligible to membership?"

"We do not indulge in religious discrimination. Religion is a private affair, and we do not interfere in strictly private affairs. Zlín is eighty per cent Catholic, and about half our members are of the Catholic faith."

"Haven't leaders of the Church warned members against joining the Communist party?"

"Not in our country, I haven't heard of any," and as the speaker looked around, one after another of those present shook his head and repeated, "We have not heard of any."

"Are priests eligible?"

"Of course."

"Even bishops and archbishops," someone exclaimed. The words caused a burst of laughter and were followed by the further explanation from the youth who had spoken last: "We Czechs are an independent people; we do our own political thinking. Priests don't tell Catholics to stay away from the party, and the party does not tell its members to stay away from the church."

"But what of the materialist philosophy of history with its accent on atheism?" I asked.

"We study the materialist philosophy. We shall study it more and more. But if members wish to remain practicing Catholics or Evangelicals it's their affair."

I asked to see the application blank for membership to the party. A girl secretary hastened to fetch one. It was an ordinary-sized sheet of paper with a mere sprinkling of questions and with blank space on the reverse side for a brief biographical sketch—nothing like the encyclopedic dissection of an applicant's private life which the Russian Communist party makes obligatory. No preliminary examination into a person's knowledge of the Communist creed or philosophy, no half year of probation or candidacy before membership is conferred, none of the other severe restrictions which are a part of the Russian Communist party policy.

"All we demand of an applicant is that he be a good patriotic Czech," said the secretary.

"What do you mean by that?"

"That he be of decent personal habits, not given to alcoholism, to sex laxity, and that he pledge himself to the promotion of our new democracy."

"That's all?"

"That's all."[1]

Further discussion elicited the firm reiteration that unless reactionaries contrived or conspired to thwart the revolution, especially if they resorted to violence, Communists, like other good Czechs, would devote themselves not to ripping things apart but to building them up together and to boosting production, which is "the lifeblood of any people and any society."

"We're a small nation. We must conserve and make use of all our resources, human and natural," said the secretary.

Slav consciousness; devotion to Russia; hatred of Germany and Germans, except the proven anti-Fascists; keen awareness that a small nation must strive for socialist salvation without civil war, avoiding political maneuvers which might incite it; supreme consciousness of the difference between Czech and Russian history and conditions of living; extraordinary national pride; unshakable faith in the inevitability and imminence of socialist triumph the world over—these were the main motivations and driving powers of the Communists in the most proletarian city in the country.

[1]Since the above conversation took place party members are obliged to attend a brief series of lectures on Marxism and Leninism.

A new era has opened for Zlín. Gone is the old paternalism. Gone is the old battle against trade unions and the old acclaim of the superiorities of private enterprise. The Communists who were mocked and hounded in the old days are now in the ascendancy. They are wielding their power with none of the exclusiveness which is so marked in Russian factories; their growing reasonableness which, even if distrusted, is yet welcomed by the other parties.

None of the Baťas are in Zlín any more. Jan Baťa, the brother of Thomas, has been charged with being a collaborator—than which there is no more malevolent sin in the new Czechoslovakia. He is not likely to be granted the privilege of returning to his homeland soon, if ever. The widow of Thomas Baťa, who spent the years of occupation in Czechoslovakia, has left for Switzerland; whether permanently or not, only she knows. Thomas Baťa, Jr., only son and only child of the founder of the Zlín empire, has moved to Canada, built up a shoe business there, and has become a naturalized Canadian citizen. Thus the Baťa family, which made Zlín famous and which bequeathed to the new Czechoslovakia its most precious industrial asset, is now completely divorced from Zlín itself and from all that the word implies.

Late in the summer of 1946 I revisited Zlín, and as I strolled around the streets, the factory grounds, the athletic fields I marveled at the changes that had taken place in the outward appearance of the town. Gone were the disorder and untidiness of the previous year. Only a few of the buildings had been repainted, but there were no broken windows any more in factories and homes, no unhinged doors, no rubbish-strewn courtyards. The rubble of bombed buildings and all other war wreckage were carted away. Flowers again brightened the scene; hedges were neatly trimmed; the trees, especially the lush poplars and the majestic weeping willows, added to the beauty and the cheerfulness of the town. Evenings, cafés were brilliantly lighted and crowds of factory workers, as in the pre-war days, were dancing rather sedately to the lively tunes of American jazz. Zlín was again beginning to sparkle with its one-time color and gaiety.

The political strife for the control of the nationalized Baťa empire had simmered down to a scarcely audible grumble. There was no more national custodian, as the provisional supervising manager was called. Now there was a director general, as in the old days, except that this time he was a member of the Communist party. The first three assistants, all Baťa-trained executives, were members of the other three political parties—the Czech National Socialist, the Catholic, and the Social Democratic. The immediate supervision of the many departments into which the Zlín and affiliated enterprises are divided were under their direction. The Factory Council, dominated by Communists, had gained in prestige but had lost none of its power. After talking to the chairman and to other personages of importance in the factory it was clear to this writer that the factory councils all over the country were still in an experimental stage. It was most likely that Zlín, more than any other industrial community, would eventually evolve the pattern of their final relationship to the management, whether embodied in written statute or in unwritten practice. Yet whatever their future, they would be stripped of authority that might in any way hinder or endanger the fulfillment of the prescribed program of production. On this subject all parties and all industrial and economic experts are unanimous.

Production in the shoe factories was still only 560,000 pairs a week, which is slightly over half of what it had been under private ownership. While decreased workers' productivity was a definite cause of the diminished output, the American four-minute bombing of November 20, 1946, which reduced to rubble quite a few of the factories, and the difficulties the management was experiencing in the procurement of raw materials, either because of a lack of foreign exchange or shattered transport or any of the other predicaments incident to the derangement of the business community all over the world, were equally responsible for the stupendous drop in production. Only the machinery shops, unhurt by the war, and hardly troubled by the vicissitudes incident to political rivalry, have experienced no significant setbacks in their manufacturing schedules.

Two new factory buildings, each five stories high, taller and broader than the old ones, were in process of construction, and plans were ready for the erection of other shops—as many as are required for maximum production. By the end of 1948, on the conclusion of the Two-Year Plan, the management hopes to equal and perhaps exceed the former output of shoes and stockings and all the other products for which the late Baťa industries have always been noted.

While the new management lags behind the old in production, its social and cultural program is striking a new note in the life of Zlín. Under Baťa, Zlín had neither drama theater nor philharmonic orchestra, and its Baťa-owned motion-picture house, immense, airy, with broad aisles and comfortable seats, had neither architectural nor artistic distinction. Now Zlín already has an acting company and is soon to start building a theater with modern stage equipment and a seating capacity of fifteen hundred. It has its own philharmonic orchestra under the direction of Rudolf Kvasnica, who is not unknown in America. It has drawn up plans for the construction of a new motion-picture theater, to be modeled after the Gaumont in Paris. Its scheme of adult education outrivals anything Zlín had known in the old days. Professor Hubert Slouka, an eminent educator who is also a distinguished astronomer, is to head the new school. The one subject that has not yet been fully settled is the type of political education. That there will be courses in Marxism and Leninism for those who might choose to attend them goes without saying. But that there will be emphasis on science and the humanities, particularly Czech history, from which the present revolution has drawn so much precedent and inspiration, is equally without doubt.

Most illuminating are the social ministrations which the new regime is sponsoring. Because of the occupation and the consequent undernourishment there is more tuberculosis in the community than in the pre-war years. Two new pavilions for the treatment of sufferers from the disease have been built. Zlín's birth rate has risen to the highest rate it has ever known. It was still rising in 1946. But quite a few of the newly born children needed special medical care. To meet the need a new hospital has been opened, which also operates a training school for nurses and midwives. Six new kindergartens have been started to augment those the Baťas had always maintained. Nurseries for the children of working mothers have already been established, though as yet on a modest scale. Plans are ready for the construction of a new health home with a thousand beds for the treatment of sick workers. The Baťas had always maintained a highly efficient medical service, and the new institution is to supplement the old one and is to be equipped with the latest medical discoveries for the diagnosis and treatment of disease.

One of the liveliest towns in the country, Zlín was always noted for its love of sports and athletics. The Baťas had generously encouraged both, and the Zlín football team could always be depended on for a spirited and often spectacular performance. Some of the old athletic fields have already been restored, and a new and ambitious recreation center is to be built in the southern part of the town, on the hills that rise abruptly from the valley in which the factories and office buildings are located. It will cater not only to sports, but to concerts, dancing, singing, other diversions. Modeled somewhat after Russia's "Parks of Culture and Rest," it will yet bear a purely Czech name, "The Zlín Playground," testifying to the long-cherished and deep-seated Czech love of their own language and their urge to keep it, when possible, free of foreign terminology.

The building plans of Zlín envision the development of two residence communities, likewise on southern sites which are still pasture and farmlands. One of these communities will be built by co-operative effort, the other by private funds and for private ownership. Aside from schools and other indispensable social institutions, the plans call for no communal services that would in any way infringe on the highly cultivated sense of privacy of the residents. No family apartment will be less than three rooms, exclusive of kitchen and bathroom. . . . The fulfillment of all these ambitious projects for which funds are available is contingent only on the supplies of labor and building materials.

A new Zlín is in process of being born, as bright and gay as the old, with as great a passion for science and the machine, but with a new accent on art and culture and social elevation.

Zlín, more than any other industrial community, is the acid test of the nationalization program and of all the other political and cultural innovations which have come to the land since liberation. Whatever Baťa's failings as a social thinker, he was the supreme and matchless industrial engineer. Can the new administration perform as well or better than he with the superb and gigantic inheritance it has acquired? Whatever the blessings the new system may be holding forth, unless output is at least as high in quantity, as meritorious in quality, and as proportionately low in cost as under Baťa, Zlín will be a failure. On this subject all, including Communists, are agreed. If Socialism fails to meet the test of capitalism in production, it will crash into catastrophe in Zlín and elsewhere.

Throughout the five-year plans in Russia the slogan was and still is: "catch up with and surpass" capitalism first and foremost in production. But Russia had inherited from the czars a backward and shattered national economy and was harassed by a deep-rooted feudalism, especially in the village. Russia is still in the throes of a never-ending struggle to match capitalism in quantity and quality output. Since the beginning of the plans, she has had to dedicate a major portion of her energies to building factories, training staffs of executives and skilled workers, from administrator and director down to mechanics and bookkeepers. Russia is still shaken with the pangs of pioneering.

Zlín faces none of these problems. It has long since finished with mere pioneering. It is in the vanguard of modern production and the modern machine age. Nazi occupation has seriously impaired its technical progress. Zlín experts say it will take them at least five years to make up for lost time. But Zlín is its own great teacher and must continue to learn from its own accumulated knowledge, traditions, and triumphs. In its own field and in its own land, it is the last word in mechanization, rationalization, efficiency. Nowhere else has the Detroit assembly belt or conveyor system, as it is known in Europe, attained such high fulfillment—and it knows, as perhaps no other industry in Czechoslovakia, that, as Thomas Baťa said, "the machine is eternally unfinished." To the shoe manufacturers of the world Baťa or Zlín always spelled audacity, imagination, challenge, and the fiercest of competition, precisely because Baťa was so brilliant a master of production and salesmanship. Whatever its shortcomings in social relations, Zlín under Baťa was an example, unparalleled in Europe, of constant and eloquent emphasis of service to the public. The Baťa shoe stores, over two thousand of them in Czechoslovakia alone, were models not only in efficiency but in courtesy and salesmanship.

Can Zlín make good under the new dispensation?

The Two-Year Plan should supply the indisputable answer to the question.

6. The Monster

As I walked the streets of Zlín and talked to the people, the Nazi occupation with its accompanying terrors and havoc seemed remote and unreal. Yet it was in Zlín that I again came face to face with the Nazi monster.

One evening as Dr. Luboš Nondek, chairman of the Provincial Council, and I were sitting in his office discussing Czech-German animosities he said: "You must talk to Raschka."

"Who is he?"

"A Sudeten German, a former Gestapo officer in Zlín, now a prisoner in our jail."

I shook my head. I had talked to too many Germans, war prisoners in Russia, civilians in the Sudetenland and in Prague, to feel confident of further enlightenment from an interview with one more of them. I did not expect to hear anything more original than that they had been victims of a malevolent power and were therefore as blameless for their evil deeds as is the lightning that strikes down plowman or wayfarer.

"But you must talk to Raschka," insisted Dr. Nondek. "He is unique."

92

Though only thirty-five years old, the doctor is a scholar of parts, a specialist in the Slav literatures of Europe, with a fluent command of German, Russian, and Polish. He holds the degree of doctor of philosophy from Prague University. Despite three years in a German concentration camp, the frequent beatings to which he had been subjected, and the loss of his teeth at the hands of the Gestapo, he was singularly unemotional in his discussion of Germans. The high position he was holding, the judicious language he was using, the utter lack of venom in his pronouncements on the Germans broke down my reluctance to interview the former Gestapo official.

"Raschka," he said, "is exceptionally intelligent and is gifted with a phenomenal memory. He remembers dates, names, places, events, to the minutest detail—an encyclopedia of information—and he spills it all like a child that is trying to show off. Besides, you'll learn something new about Nazi psychology, perhaps sensationally new. Come along."

Accompanied by an executive of the Baťa factories, we went to the town jail. The military commandant guided us down an underground hallway, dimly lighted and lined with a double row of cells. He unlocked one of the cells and instantly, on the snappy command of the monitor inside, the six German inmates leaped to their feet, clicked their heels, and, facing about so that their backs were toward us, lifted their arms overhead. The jailer called Raschka's name and asked him to step outside. About forty years of age, Raschka had the build and the manner of a man who had known hard physical labor. He was short and stocky, with an enormous back and large head; only his gray flashing eyes livened up his broad and sharp-featured face. He was visibly pleased to be singled out for special attention, even if it was only for one more interrogation. His large mouth was half open and he was blandly at ease, like a self-confident pupil poised for an examination.

"I wish," said Dr. Nondek, "you'd tell the American writer how you in the Gestapo here treated Czech prisoners; I mean the methods of torture you used."

Without a moment's hesitation, the flow of rhetoric accompanied by swift and constantly changing postures, Raschka proceeded to demonstrate one form of torture after another. He might have been a salesman demonstrating sporting equipment, so agile were his movements; so ebullient his words; so eager, almost frantic, his manner. His face twitched and his eyes gathered glow. "I'm hiding nothing," he interpolated. "I'm showing everything. I believe in telling the truth." With no further prompting from any of the Czechs, he re-enacted one mode of torture after another. It was obvious that he had done it before, many times, and was merely rehearsing a part he had learned to play with skill and enthusiasm. His zeal was astonishing, almost comical, yet none smiled, none interrupted.

"But I always felt sorry for Czechs," he said. "I was moderate. I never shot anyone, I never caused anyone's death; you can't prove that I did."

"Tell the American," said Dr. Nondek, "what you beat Czechs with."

A shadow swept Raschka's broad bony face, and he was lost for words. His eagerness vanished and he kept flashing his eyes from one bystander to another, finally fixing them on the doctor in supplication, it seemed, to be excused from answering the question. The change in the man's manner was as sudden as it was startling. He was not frightened, only self-conscious and annoyed.

"Don't hesitate," said the doctor.

Again silence.

"Go on, Raschka," prompted the jailer with good humor. "It isn't like you to be stuck for words."

"With the usual thing," the German blurted out.

94

"What was it? Quick, be yourself," the jailer prompted with facetious flattery.

"With a bull's penis." The words flew out of Raschka's lips. Here was something new in Gestapo warfare on prisoners. I had been in Poland's Majdanek, had walked through the gas chambers where tens of thousands of prisoners were asphyxiated. I had seen the furnaces in which the dead bodies were burned and the stacks of ashes that were used as fertilizer on a near-by cabbage field. In Minsk, the capital of White Russia, I had seen a basement equipped with all manner of electrical and mechanical appliances with which to twist and rack, to shock and scorch prisoners. But I never before had heard of Gestapo jailers bludgeoning prisoners with a bull's sexual organ.

"Why such a weapon?" I asked.

"It's very effective."

"Did you use it?"

"Yes, but I never killed anyone. I never beat anyone to death, I swear I didn't."

"Does it hurt more than a rubber truncheon?"

"It hurts plenty; it's very powerful."

"Was that why you killed so many of our bulls and oxen?" the jailer asked.

"We had plenty of bulls' penises."

"Did you feel any revulsion in using it?"

"It didn't make any difference."

"Did you get any pleasure out of it?"

"I was under orders, but I never beat anyone to death; no one can prove that I did."

"Who thought of it?"

"The Gestapo, of course."

"Who? Himmler?"

"I don't think so; it must have been someone here in the Protektorat."

"It wasn't your idea, was it?"

"No, no, no, I swear it wasn't."

"A steel rod would have been more effective, wouldn't it?"

A shrug and silence.

"Come, Raschka, speak up."

"With a steel rod you can quickly kill a man—and I never wanted to kill anyone, and never did."

"What else did you do to Czech prisoners?" asked Dr. Nondek.

"When they were thirsty we'd give them a bottle to drink from, but instead of water there was kerosene in the bottle."

"How would you like to have it done to you?"

Silence.

"What else—what else?" the Baťa executive asked a little impatiently.

"We'd spit on the floor and make Czechs lick up the spittle!"

"What else?"

"We'd order them to stretch out on a table, bind their hands and feet, and twist and squeeze their testicles."

"Did you do it?"

"Yes, but I was always careful; I knew how it hurt."

"You were merciful?"

"Yes, as much as I could be. I never shot anyone, never beat anyone to death."

"What did you do to the two priests from Hostýn?" Hostýn is a Catholic shrine near Zlín.

"They hid several million crowns and we found it. They said they'd put away the money to repair their church. But we didn't believe them and arrested them and brought them to Zlín and made them get on the top of a table and run around like they were having a race, and as they ran we beat them."

"With what?"

"With the usual thing—bulls' penises."

"Did they scream?"

"Yes, terribly."

"Did you twist their testicles too?"

"Yes."

"But they were priests, didn't that make any difference to you?"

"Orders were orders, but I never killed anyone, no one ever died from my beatings, and don't forget I spared Father Laciga." He turned to Dr. Nondek. "I knew all about his partisan work; he was a dangerous man, he spied on us all the time, and I was ordered again and again to get him, but I never did."

"Why not?"

"I didn't want to."

"Wasn't it because the Russians were already in Slovakia and you didn't want to make your record blacker than it was?" asked the Baťa executive.

"I never laid my hands on him, you know it's the truth. He might have been shot for being a partisan."

"And you wanted to spare his life?"

"I wanted to spare every Czech's life, you know I did; no one can prove I killed anyone." He made me think of a sinner pleading for exculpation not because of virtues fulfilled but because of sins which it was within his power to commit but which he did not.

The interview was over. The jailer ushered his charge back into the cell, and we made our way out of the thick-walled and dim-lighted basement into the cool and bracing night air.

"Didn't I tell you Raschka is unique?" said Dr. Nondek.

"Quite unique," I replied. More than any German I had talked with during the war years in Russia and since then in other parts of Europe, Raschka dramatized the two primary passions and obsessions that motivated so much of Gestapo behavior—sex and death. They gloated in death when they had the power to inflict it on others with impunity. They reveled in sex, normal and abnormal, so long as their might shielded them from retribution and from the barbs of public obloquy. Hence their zest for whole-sale public executions and for photographing the forests of gal-lows with dangling corpses which often enough darkened the streets and squares of Russian towns and villages. Under Hitler the Raschkas were happy enough to divest themselves of the decencies and decorums they may have acquired in their homes, in church, in school, in their daily association with friends and neighbors—and to flaunt their superiority by indulgences which mankind had long ago outlawed and from which the ordinary man in ordinary life shrinks with loathing and dread. Here was cruelty heightened by imagination, carnality spiced with per-version.

Now that they were deprived of the environment in which the road to glory was paved with evil deeds, the Raschkas were as abject in acknowledging their iniquities as they were once defiant in perpetrating them. They dreaded death as hysterically as they had once gloried in it. The law and convention they had flouted, the morality and magnanimity they had cast away, they now strove to invoke in their own behalf with an abasement and servility that were as fervid as they were repellent.

"A case for a psychologist," Dr. Nondek went on. "Sex degen-erates, that's what so many of them were, especially the Sudeten Germans. Himmler favored them here because they could speak our language. How can anyone reform such people now that they are grown up and their habits are fixed; now that their minds are corrupted and all decency and compassion are gone out of them? You must start with the new generation, with children as soon as they're born—that's the only way to humanize the Germans. Do you see now why we Czechs want them to leave our country? We can never hope for peace if they remain, and go they must."

7. The Village Priest

When I first met Father Josef Laciga I was struck by his close resemblance to the late Wendell Willkie. He was as tall as Willkie, as breezy in manner, as frank and talkative, with the same shape of eyes, the same color and abundance of hair, and the same forelock dangling over his right temple. When I mentioned the resemblance the priest gave a lively toss of the head, laughed, and said, "A good man to resemble."

Dr. Nondek, who is a member of the Communist party and who introduced me to Father Laciga, had already spoken to me of him in words of admiration and eulogy. The son of a peasant, Laciga studied in the Olomouc Theological Seminary and now had his parish in the village of Jasenná, which is in the province of Zlín. During the war he had done yeoman work for the partisan movement. He had been a one-man intelligence service, a one-man bank, a one-man drugstore, a one-man supply depot, a one-man everything for the partisans. Now he was an active member of the Zlín National Council over which Dr. Nondek was presiding.

The priest invited me to come to his home, and late one afternoon I drove to Jasenná to spend the night with him. The population of Jasenná is only one thousand, but it dates its origin to the fifteenth century and bears its age with a robust and dignified stateliness. Save for an occasional new house, spoken of as a Baťa house because built with money earned in the Baťa factories, there is nowhere a glint or a spurt of modernity. The sky line is low, accentuating the air and the spirit of antiquity that brood over the village. All around are mountains, high and wooded, and the low, neatly whitewashed cottages with tiled roofs seem as if grown into the earth like the trees around them. Here is none of the lushness of the Moravian plain, none of the stir and the color of its rich and cheerful countryside. The streets are so void of traffic and so tranquil that the shout of a child, the bark of a dog, the bellow of a´ cow rouse a homey and joyful sensation.

From the patches of rock-ribbed land on the surrounding hillsides, one marked off from the other by a dead furrow or a scarcely perceptible grass-grown ridge, it was evident that the family allotments were small and the tillage arduous. In winter the frost heaves the rocks to the surface and in spring after the melted snows wash down the topsoil, these have to be picked and lugged away before the plow can cut fresh furrows in the land. Only the luxurious fruit trees—apple, plum, cherry—hold out the promise of lavish reward for unending toil. Yet nowhere was there a suggestion of squalor or poverty, nowhere a hint of disorder or slovenliness.

The war had swept over the village like a passing storm, with a crash of thunder, a blaze of lightning, but had left it with scarcely a mark of molestation. An air of ease and contentment hovered over homes and people. It was the sort of village where —within the walls of the old white church, or inside the near-by parish house set back from the street on a steep and tree-sheltered incline—partisan plots might be conceived and executed without a stir of excitement, without the participation or the knowledge of the neighbors. Its very age and sedateness would be a shield against the prying eyes and the eavesdropping ears of the enemy.

The priest welcomed me with a flow of warm words and invited me into his study. As I glanced around I held my breath. I had already become accustomed to paradoxical situations in the country, but nothing had prepared me for what I now beheld. Over the door of the study, nailed to a black wooden cross, was a brown-bodied statue of Jesus. Some space away, high above a little altar, was a beautifully framed image of the Virgin and the Son, and on top of the bookcases that lined the walls were the framed photographs of President Beneš, Monsignor Šrámek, leader of the Catholic party, and Josef Stalin! I said nothing at the moment, but the pictures and the statuary, the Christ and the Mother side by side with Šrámek, Beneš, and Stalin, so strained my credulity that I kept shifting my eyes from the one to the other to make certain it was all real.

Refreshments appeared on the table, topped with what the priest spoke of as "American" but which was only UNRRA coffee, served with special pride by the smiling and trimly clad peasant housekeeper. After we had our refreshments the priest arose and said: "You must see something of the village and meet some of the people. Many of them have relatives in America and they want to meet you. I told them you were coming."

We left the house and first walked to the outskirts of the village. Here out of a rain-packed, flower-strewn mound of earth rose a high wooden obelisk painted red and mounted with the Russian Hammer and Sickle.

"A remarkable man is buried here," said the priest, "a Russian partisan. I knew him well. Once while chased by the Gestapo he found refuge in a creek and lay there for eighteen hours, constantly ducking his head in and out of the water. Afterward he fell ill with galloping consumption and died in the mountains.

We brought his body down and buried it with solemn honors and with speeches by the Evangelical pastor and myself."

For some moments we contemplated the grave in silence, then taking me by the arm and without saying a word, the priest led me back to the village. Night was upon us, and as we walked the priest kept talking of the Russians in the partisan army in which he had served. Of the twelve hundred men and women in the outfit, four hundred were Russians. The leader was a Russian, Siberian, a captain in aviation. "We became fast friends," said the priest, "and what a man he was—warrior and boy, as ready to sing and laugh as to fight and die. I shall always remember him, and when we return home I'll tell you his story, one of the weirdest and most moving you've ever heard. You may want to write it—you really should."

The physician in the partisan army, the priest continued, was a Russian girl who had walked alone through forest and mountain all the way from Slovakia. The radio operator was also a Russian girl who had parachuted down into the mountains. Two other Russian girls had come down by parachute but were blown into a clearing, and there the Gestapo shot them. They were an amazing crowd, these Russians, utterly without fear of death and always thinking up spectacular ways of saving themselves from the ever-hunting Gestapo. One Russian he knew, whom the Gestapo was pursuing, flung himself into the turning wheel of a water mill and fastened himself on one of the spokes. The wheel kept splashing him in and out of the water, but he never budged from his place. He clung there for hours and after dark made his way to the parish house. "We built a fire for him," said the priest, "gave him medicine, fed him, dried and mended his clothes, and would you believe it, not a bone in his body was broken. An inventive, desperate people, these Russian partisans were."

Presently we came to a little cottage set back from the street, and the priest knocked on the door. A woman opened it and with a gush of hospitality invited us inside. We walked into the living room, in the center of which, in a broad and shiny wooden bed high with feather pillows and feather covers, lay the man of the house. "Only a cold," he said, and invited us to sit down.

Instantly the family gathered around us, and we had no more than exchanged salutations when the woman of the house set before us a pitcher of milk and a platter of sliced home-baked bread. "Help yourselves," she urged. "It's fresh, this evening's milking." She remained beside us, coaxing the priest and myself to drink more and more of the milk and eat more and more of the bread. . . . The children stood around, silent and smiling and big-eyed with attention and curiosity. They had relatives in America, said the man of the house, as what Czech has not? Theirs were in Texas. Had I ever been there? They had been gone many years, these relatives of theirs, having left before World War I. It was a long time since they had received letters from Texas, and they did not know what might have happened to their kin there.

"Czech farmers in Texas," I said, "are very prosperous."

"That's good," said the host. "They must have lots of land there?"

Land—the beginning and the end of all joy and all sorrow, all reward and all failure to the European peasant.

"Yes," I said, "there's lots of land in Texas, more than is cultivated."

"Is that so?"

The children, too, looked excited. That there should be any place on the globe with more land than is tilled was legend and miracle.

Our hostess invited us to see her kitchen, which adjoined the living room. As low-ceilinged as the living room and as bright with whitewash, it was no less clean. There was not a fly in sight.

"Have you anything like it in America?" she said, pointing with pride at the gigantic brick oven.

I shook my head.

"In America you do everything with machines, yes?—cooking washing, baking—but here we are old-fashioned country folk." Drawing close to the hearth, she lifted the shutter and motioned for me to come over.

"Look inside," she said, her eyes sparkling with triumph. A wave of heat blew into my face as I stooped down and peered into the oven. Rising out over the bricks were loaves of bread turning brown and shiny with a satiny luster.

"Machines can't bake bread like this, can they, Father?" she said, turning to the priest and smiling with girlish delight.

"No, they cannot," said the priest, and I hastened to confirm his words. Nowhere in Prague had I tasted such luscious bread as I had eaten in this house.

"We're simple people," the hostess said, "but we make a go of things, don't we, Father?"

"Quite so, quite so," said the priest.

No complaints against destiny here. Dignified humility leavened with pride in personal accomplishment; sturdy self-confidence and lucidity of purpose; sober comprehension of the surrounding world and joyful acceptance of the stern responsibilities it presents. Meeting such people reinforces one's faith in their competence to grapple coolly and wisely with the exacting tasks before them.

We visited other homes and finally returned to the parish house and sat down in the priest's study, warm now with the coal fire in the bellied little stove, and bright with the shiny covers of books and the galaxy of secular pictures and sacred images.

"Now," said the priest, "I'll tell you the story of my Siberian friend. His name was Peter Butko and he was quite a wit. Often he teased me by saying, 'Remember, Father, my name is Peter and I hold the keys to heaven.' As I told you, he was a captain of aviation and while flying in a fighter plane he was shot at and had to bail out. A bullet struck him in the abdomen and he fell to the ground, twisted with pain and almost unconscious. Germans picked him up and carried him to a field hospital. While there the Gestapo and the *Reichswehr,* jealous of each other, started a battle for his possession, and that's what saved him. The *Reichswehr* wanted him so he could explain the nature of the new equipment on his fighter plane, which was all but wrecked; the Gestapo wanted him for purposes of its own. Luckily for him the hospital staff was on the side of the *Reichswehr,* and one evening when another Russian in the hospital was dying they transferred him to Butko's bed and Butko to his. The man died and officially it was Butko who had passed away. He was transferred to another place, and when he recovered the *Reichswehr* took him to the woods where his wrecked plane was lying and questioned him about its new equipment. Butko talked calmly, evasively, improvising, falsifying, and all the time his mind was in a whirl, for he was feverishly thinking of running away. At an opportune moment he made a dash into the forest. A Siberian, he knew the forest like a wild animal, and though the Germans instantly gave chase and kept firing and firing, they never caught him. Think of the spirit of a man like that—courting death, gambling with death, indeed contemptuous of death!" The priest halted and fixed his wide-opened eyes on me, still marveling, it seemed, at the sheer audacity and rashness of a man like Butko. He gave a shrug and a deep sigh and resumed:

"He wandered for days, living on what he could find—berries, mushrooms, edible plants and leaves, and finally came to this part of our mountains. I was among the first to meet him, and we became close friends, very close. He was a Bolshevik and I a Catholic priest. Ideologically there was an unbridgeable chasm between us, but we were brother Slavs, face to face with a common threat, and our ideological differences never obtruded into our comradeship. Meanwhile, the partisan army around here was growing larger and more and more powerful. Russians were coming over from Slovakia and Czechs from around here were going up to the mountains. I was the go-between, linking the partisans and the outside world. I gathered information about the Germans, where their garrisons were, how large they were, what their equipment was, what they were doing. I listened to the BBC, in secret of course, and learned all the war news, and everything I knew I passed on to Butko and he transmitted it by wireless to the Red Army. I lived a double life. Daytimes I was priest; nights I was a partisan. Every morning I celebrated Mass, and evenings after dark, no matter how wild and stormy the weather, I made my way to the mountains, loaded with packs of clothing, food, medicine, ammunition, other things, and my pockets bulging with money. Once I carried a sewing machine up there; another time a tooth extractor and other surgical instruments. Anything the partisans needed I got for them." He paused, lowered his head, and grew reflective, as though reliving the experiences of which he had talked. Locks of hair tumbled over his forehead and, brushing them back, he lifted his head and resumed:

"Every now and then, late in the night, I'd hear a rap at the window—quiet and deliberate, never rapid or loud, almost like the scratching of a kitten—and I knew it was Butko. Often when he entered he was soaked with rain or heavy with snow. But he was always cheerful, always ready with a jest, and always with a tommy gun like an inseparable companion under his jacket, and hand grenades in his pouches. 'Don't worry, Father,' he'd say to me. 'If the Germans come I'll take care of them. I've got a little arsenal with me. I'll do away with them, and you and

I will run off to the woods.' He didn't know the meaning of fear and nothing ever tired him, though he was still a very sick man, and twice or three times a week he'd double up with terrible pain. His abdominal wounds had not healed, and he was not giving himself a chance to get healed because he was always on the hunt for the enemy. The Germans were searching for him more than for any other partisan, and I took chances when I let him come to the house and spend the night here. But—a partisan is a partisan—he must always take risks, however great, and Butko always was so jovial and so good-humored that in his presence one forgot the meaning of risk or danger. My housekeeper washed his linen, mended his clothes, darned his socks; this house was like home to him. Again and again we stayed up together into the early hours of dawn, planning things. Though there were several hundred German soldiers in the village, they never knew when Butko was staying with me." Again the priest paused, stirred the coal in the fire, and then, fixing his eyes on me, continued:

"And now I'll tell you something quite terrible. Has anyone in Zlín told you what happened to the village of Ploština?" I nodded. Dr. Nondek had related to me the story of Ploština, fifteen miles away from Zlín. A Czech from London had parachuted down in the vicinity and found refuge for several days in the village. The Gestapo heard of it and raided the village. The parachutist was no longer there. The people denied they had ever seen him. Infuriated, the Gestapo seized a crowd of villagers, drove them into one house, and set it afire, burning the house and the people within. "It was another Lidice," said the priest, "and when Butko heard of it he vowed vengeance. He'd have a reckoning with the men who perpetrated the outrage. I'd never seen Butko so white with rage, and I was fearful that in his zeal to capture the offenders he'd commit an indiscretion which would cost him his own life. I warned him against being reckless, but he wasn't the man to heed warnings. He told me not to worry. He'd have his revenge on the Gestapo cost what it might. . . . He started hunting for the enemy and finally found one of them loitering about the very village he'd helped sack. How he did it I never learned; Butko didn't go into details. He leaped on the German, felled him to the ground, bound his hands and feet, and, lying on top of him, pressed him with all his great power deeper and deeper into the earth. Then he took a knife and made deep gashes in the murderer's body and after every gash he sprinkled salt over the wound and said: 'This for Ploština, you bandit, and this is for Ploština, you savage.' Finally, with a swift stroke of the knife, he finished off the Gestapo agent."

The priest halted and lowered his head. A long interval passed and neither of us said a word. Somewhere a dog was barking, a car drove by in the street, and it was good to hear these signs of life outside.

"Yet Butko was a kindly soul," the priest resumed. "He always shared everything he had with his men. He did heroic work, and now he is a legend in these parts. When the war was over he came down for a little celebration. Then he returned to Russia and went to a hospital. He should've gone earlier because he was so sick. But he wanted to stay and fight until victory was won. An amazing man. Knowing him as I did, I can understand why the Russians fought with such fury in Stalingrad, yes, my friend, I can." He rose, poured *slivovice* into two little tumblers, and said, "Let's have a drink, yes?"

We drank *slivovice* and toasted the partisans and all the fighting armies, and all the Allies, and the village and the priest of Jasenná. It was like being back in Russia again, rousing and drowning emotions with toasts, except that here the flow in rhetoric transcended the flow of *slivovice*.

We sat down again. The moment was opportune for the

question which had lurked in my mind from the moment I first glanced around the priest's study.

"Father," I said, "I have a personal question to ask you."

"Please, please, go ahead," and he smiled benevolently in assurance that he could not possibly resent any question I might put to him, however personal.

"It is about that photograph of Stalin right here in your study. I cannot imagine an American priest of your faith bestowing such an honor on the foremost Bolshevik in the world."

"America!" he began somewhat ruefully. "America is so far away, so very far from our unfortunate Europe. But we Czechs live in the heart of the continent, and we are Slavs. I feel very Slav, so do all the men and women of my faith and of other faiths too. Of the one thousand population here, only one hundred and twenty are Catholics. The others are Protestants, Evangelicals. But we are Slavs, all of us, and we all know the Germans. We have lived with and among them for a thousand years. We've had plenty of time to know them. With some exceptions they were always our enemies, always seeking to dominate, despoil, and degrade us. Only a short time ago"—his voice dropped and his face grew somber—"I went with a friend of mine, an engineer from Prague, to Lidice. What did I see? Emptiness, dread emptiness. Trees gone, houses gone, the school gone, the church gone, the stream turned away, and a cross over the mass grave! It was too heartbreaking, and I found myself weeping. I could not say a word and neither could my friend. I prayed, my friend prayed, and we left. . . . Our chauffeur told us he was a Communist, yet every time he came to Lidice he felt like kneeling down and praying. . . . You have to be a Czech to realize what Lidice means to us, and if the Germans come again they'll turn all Czechoslovakia into a Lidice. Don't underestimate their lust for revenge. But who can stop them? We're a small nation—only ten and a half millions of us. You know how the French and the British betrayed us in Munich. Can we trust them again? We dare not. Only a powerful Slav army can protect us, and he"—pointing to Stalin's photograph—"is commander in chief of that army, the most powerful Slav army in the world. Only he and his army can save us."

"But Stalin," I said, "is the apostle of materialism."

"Right, and as such he is my opponent and I am his, one hundred per cent his opponent, as is every practicing Catholic. But Stalin, the commander in chief of the Red Army, is something else again, a symbol of our security, a guarantee of our survival. That's why I honor him."

He looked fixedly at me as though expecting comment on his words. I offered none. It was his explanation that mattered and it was as challenging as it was illuminating.

The hour was past midnight, and the father suggested that we retire. He arose and led me into a small, brightly decorated room and, pointing to a narrow, shiny brass bed, high with feather pillows and feather covers, he said:

"D'you know who slept in this bed?"

"I have no idea."

"Peter Butko. He liked to tuck himself into the feather bedding, with his hand grenades and tommy gun beside him. . . . Sleep well and good night."

He left and shut the door. I looked around the room. The walls were hung with pictures, sacred and secular. Near the bed was a washstand with pitcher and bowl and clean towels over the bowl. Set against the wall was a small organ and on the top a neatly folded white robe with gleaming yellow lining. A violin case rested against the foot of the bed. The most imposing piece of furniture was a dresser, stacked with ceramics and in the center a cross with the body of Jesus. . . . Yet over it all floated the image of Butko and it was long before sleep came to me.

110

8. The Poet and the Cow

"He's more than likely to slam the door in your face than to open it to you," said an editor in Zlín when I told him I was leaving for a visit to Peter Bezruč, the seventy-eight-year-old poet on whom a short time earlier the Prague Government had conferred the title of "National Poet."

Others had given more severe warnings. "He loathes visitors," said a young poet in Prague. "You'll be wasting your time to make the trip."

Only a few weeks earlier Professor Zdeněk Nejedlý, the Minister of Education, had journeyed to the village of Ostravica, where Bezruč lives in summer, to award him in public the honor the government had bestowed on him. But on Nejedlý's arrival in the mountain village there was no Bezruč. The thought of a public ceremony had dismayed him so that he vanished from the scene.

This time he reckoned without his neighbors. To them the arrival of the Minister from Prague was an exalted event and, knowing Bezruč's haunts, they went in search of him and persuaded him to go through with the public function. Instead of returning by way of the main road he meandered his way back along a hidden mountain trail so his approach would not be visible to the assembled audience. No sooner was the celebration over than he again disappeared.

Despite discouraging warnings I resolved to make the trip, for though Bezruč is remote from the political scene, aloof from the new groupings of the Czech intelligentsia, and especially from literary people, he is one of the most extraordinary figures in the country. Recluse he is and always has been, preferring the solitude of wood and mountain to the blandishments of society. But he has left an imperishable mark on the mind and the culture of his people. A rebel supreme, he grew up with the generation of liberators who gathered around Masaryk, and from behind the shield of isolation and anonymity he wakened the national sentiments of his people with no less fervor than did Masaryk himself, though with less power.

Withal there is something buoyantly juvenile and dramatically perverse about his person—a wild flower lurking in the shadow of wood and mountain and folding up as if in caprice on the approach of man. From a perusal of his biographies I learned that the figure *one* is a symbol and summary of his character, his life, his achievements. His real name is Vašek. Bezruč is a pseudonym meaning "without an arm"; that is, a man with *one* arm. He has written only one volume of verse and for nearly half a century it has been published and republished, often without either his knowledge or approval. Only *one* photograph of the man is in existence, taken when he was already a gray-haired savant. His summer home in the mountains and his winter abode in the Moravian valley are inhabited by only *one* person, himself. He will have no one else, not even a servant to aid in his cooking and housekeeping. He loved only *one* woman, and his biographer, Adolf Veselý, is authority for the statement that the girl's surname was Bezruč. Hence his pseu-

donym. It was an unhappy affair, as is testified by the following
verse:

> *Yonder in Těšín, where the Lučina roars,*
> *Grew up the little girl who smashed into ruins*
> *Somebody's life. How sad to remember;*
> *I gave only my heart and a song now and then*
> *But the other proffered a castle in Frýdek and*
> *jewels galore.*
> *Whom did she choose? Why ask the question?*

Famous as he is, his verses sung in chorus and recited by
elocutionists all over the land; streets, towns, educational institutions, the very region of which he writes named after
him—he is *one* and alone in all that he does and contemplates,
all that he suffers and fulfills. He is the apotheosis of the somewhat dour but highly integrated Czech hardiness of character
and individual self-sufficiency.

When he started publishing his verses he insisted on absolute
anonymity, and when they were first brought out in a thin
volume in 1903 no name was affixed. Hana Kvapilová, a famous
actress in her day, had scheduled an evening's recital of his
poems, but Bezruč was not invited for the simple reason that no
one knew where and how to reach him—none but his editors,
and they were pledged to inviolable secrecy. Yet Bezruč slipped
into the hall, incognito, and when the recital was over he slipped
away as mysteriously as he had entered.

For nearly two generations young and old have sorrowed
and wept over the tragic life and the catastrophic end of his
village heroine, Maryčka Magdonova, whose name is the title
of his most celebrated poem. Because she was supposed to have
lived in Staré Hamry, the people of the little town decided to
immortalize her memory in a marble relief on the cemetery
gateway. Bezruč was invited to the unveiling of the memorial,

113

but he never appeared. Some days later he wandered up to the cemetery alone and contemplated the tribute to his literary heroine.

Charles University in Prague awarded him an honorary degree. He never came to receive it. That is the way he has been all his life, as somber and sturdy, as aloof and self-contained as the Beskydy Mountains in whose wilds he spends so much of his time.

The strange behavior of a man so accomplished has elicited varied interpretations, from the banal and the ludicrous to the solemn and the tragic. There have been those who have charged that Bezruč's passion for hiding is no more than a theatrical trick to further his own popularity, while others have held that it is a matter of temperament and nothing more; still others have ventured the opinion that it is the consequence of his tragic love affair. For a long time Bezruč paid no heed to the controversy. Neither odium nor plaudits evoked a word of explanation from him. Only when, despite himself, his anonymity was disclosed did he feel impelled to declare himself on the subject, and his words are remarkable for the revelation of the spirit of the man and the mind of the artist he is. "All I said," he wrote, "could be uttered only by a man without a name; when human curiosity began to peep through my mask I had nothing more to say."

These words were penned in 1919, and since then the only verses Bezruč has composed are the bits of fancy he has now and then set down on postal cards in reply to admirers and in greeting to the very few friends he has, despite himself, acquired. Not always does he affix his pseudonym to these impulsive efforts. Instead he draws a picture of a crocodile—a creature that is hard and powerful and exclusive. So long as he was a voice unknown and unheralded he wrote with passion and tenderness of the things that stirred his imagination. The moment he ceased to be a voice and became an individual the

Thomas G. Masaryk (1850–1937), first President of the
Czechoslovak Republic

Jaromír Vejvoda, composer of the "Beer-Barrel Polka"

creative fire, while unextinguished, lost its one-time power. He is destined to remain a one-book man.

It must be said that the subject which preoccupied him in his ardently creative years is not unrelated to his lifelong passion for isolation. Though he has made a religion of aloneness, he rarely speaks of himself. He is no flaming lyricist. He is not preoccupied with his own inner, purely human experience. He has penned only a few love poems, tender and moving, but with grudging expansiveness. He has never sought to dramatize personal emotion. Not for him Turgenev's invocation of a love "which is stronger than death and the fear of death." Nor for him Lermontov's brooding over "the heart that loves much and sorrows much." Bezruč's main theme, almost his only theme, is his people: the Czech miner, the Czech peasant, the Czech lumberman in his native Silesia. He is a regional poet, as is testified by the only title of his one volume of verse, *Songs of Silesia*. These are hymns of pity and compassion for his people, bursts of scorn and wrath for the enemy who is seeking their subjugation, not only as human beings but as Czechs. He is the poet of his little brother, of the man who lives by unremitting toil with but few joys in life and from whom the enemy, out of greed or vanity, is conspiring to drain his national identity and all the inner satisfactions it yields.

The enemy may be the Pole who migrates from Galicia in the wake of the industrial upsurge of Těšín and brings with him his habit of superiority to other Slavs, his passion for imposing his nationality, his language, his mode of worship on others. Chiefly the enemy is the German who swoops over the ancient domain of the Bohemian crown, exploits the mines, puts up factories, and shackles the doughty and helpless Czech native and sucks the very substance of his Czech spirit and Czech personality out of him.

"I am Peter Bezruč from Těšín," he wrote, "the bard of an

enslaved nation." A folk poet with a robust folk-consciousness, he has no plan of reform, no program of emancipation. He espouses neither political doctrine nor social dispensation. Crusader for the purely human rights of his people, for the salvation of their purely Czech souls, he hurls anathemas at the enemy who deprives them of the one and stultifies the other. He appeals for no mercy to the German invader or the Polish interloper. He knows the futility and cannot suffer the indignity of such appeals. He is too proud to beg but not too meek to curse and to commiserate. He broods over the woes of his smitten folk and seeks to stir them into the passion and dignity of revolt. He is a rebel to whom nothing is more precious than the preservation of personal identity and the freedom with which to fulfill its innate divinations, however few and simple. To him the Czech laborer and peasant of the country are as if a part of the forests and mountains, the rivers and the low-lands which they inhabit. Ousted or alienated from these, they, like uprooted plants and trees, wither away and die, and such a death imposed from without transcends tragedy and sacrilege. "I was like a torch," he writes, "burning from both ends . . . one named hate, the other love. . . . Often I ask myself how I could survive it all." He wants neither grandeur nor fame for his people. He seeks neither glory nor empire for his nation. He cares not for the lands that lie beyond its borders and covets none of the wealth within them. All he cherishes, all he cries out for, is salvation within one's own person. Czech self-conscious-ness is to him an end in itself, a condition of living and being transcending all other values and attributes, and no enemy the Czech faces is so grim and so ruthless as the one who seeks forcibly to deny him his own mode of self-expression. His poems are an echo of Hus's outcry against the alien, the German in particular, whose faith in his own supremacy blinds and hardens him to the inner yearning of others. Reading the poems, one is

overpowered by the richness of the content, the beauty of the
spirit with which Bezruč invests the very word Czech.

All the more eager was I to talk to Bezruč because I was
fresh from a journey to Těšín, the place of his origin, which he
loved and made the one cause to which he dedicated his supreme talents. His poems held more meaning for me than any
and all the historical and geographical documents which Czechs
and Poles had adduced in proof of their respective claims to
the already partitioned and still hotly contested little land. The
very word Těšín Bezruč has clothed with a sentiment and a sanctity which no Pole, however loud his protestations, has ever encompassed in song, story, or legal argument. Unlike the Czech,
the Pole, with but rare exceptions, is a quite recent migrant to
Těšín, and however numerous he may be there now, it never
can hold for him the historical meaning, the passionate appeal,
the lure of motherland that it exercises on Bezruč and his countrymen.

I journeyed to Moravská Ostrava and from there, together
with a young Moravian woman and a lawyer from the city, drove
to Ostravica, where Bezruč lived. The distance is only twenty
miles, and the road winds along rolling and magnificently cultivated countryside. All around are forest and mountains where
rises the bare summit of the famed Lisa Hora, Bezruč's favorite
hide-out. Clouds hung low over forest and mountain, not in a
dense mass, but in floating waves, with here and there the peaks
of evergreens peeping in playful splendor out of the gray-blue
mists. Cottages were trim and neat with the dense verdure
heightening the brilliance of their fresh white paint—islands of
white in a heaving sea of green.

We passed the roaring and pellucid Ostrava River in which
Maryčka Magdonova was supposed to have drowned herself.

It tore down from the mountains with a frenzied swiftness, and to look down over the bridge railing made our heads spin.

The lawyer, who had met Bezruč, went ahead to ascertain whether he was disposed to receive an American caller. The young Moravian woman and I stood under the trees and waited. A long interval elapsed, and our emissary failed to return. We thought it an evil omen, all the more portentous because we knew that only a few days earlier a distinguished Swedish literary critic had journeyed to Ostravica only to discover that his trip had been in vain—Bezruč would not open the door to him.

Finally the lawyer returned, smiling.

"Come along," he called cheerfully.

We walked through a neighbor's courtyard and came upon a large and beautifully renovated barn with tall windows and a gable roof. This was Bezruč's home. In the rear, flowing into a strip of woodland, was a luxurious meadow with grass nipped close by a huge gray cow tied to a post only a few steps away from the house. As we passed she lifted her head and stared with wide-opened friendly eyes. She evinced no fear, not even when I drew close and began to caress her smooth and spacious face. When we left she followed us as far as the stout rope would allow.

"What a friendly cow," I said. "Is it his?"

The lawyer shrugged his shoulders and said, "I doubt it. He likes aloneness too much to bother with anyone, even a cow."

We came to an enclosed veranda, and as we walked up the few wooden steps I saw a card nailed to the door. A verse penned in longhand stated Bezruč's admonition to callers:

> *Welcome visitor*
> *but even if you're an innocent angel,*
> *longer than half an hour*
> *you needn't stay*
> *just arise and drift away.*

We walked into a tiny dark vestibule and, following a hallway, came to an open door that led into the kitchen. As in all Czech country homes, the kitchen was large and bright with many windows, but instead of smelling of food it was redolent with the scent of the freshly planed and shiny wood paneling on the walls. The little table by the window was stacked high with piles of letters. Clearly this was more than kitchen; it was workroom, study, lounge, and guest room. Presently Bezruč appeared, a mountain of a man in slippers, flannel shirt open at the collar, and a broad smile on his full, finely curved lips. Tall and as upright as a young pine, with powerful neck, broad chest, and no trace of a bulge at the waistline, he made me think of a lumberman rather than a poet. The ruggedness of his person explained much of the rugged quality of his verse. His massive, shapely head, with no suggestion of baldness, was cropped short; his face, unshaved, was shiny with needlelike stubble.

"Please," he said in English and in a remarkably resonant voice, "sit down in my kitchen." He smiled and took a seat beside me.

"How well you speak English," I said.

Again he smiled and answered in English: "I don't speak the language." His voice was astonishingly young and melodious, more tenor than baritone, and with buoyant inflection. His small, half-shut merry eyes, as clear as the torrential waters in the near-by river, radiated a joviality and eagerness that was in strange contrast to the picture of sullenness, almost fierceness, I had formed of him.

"Your English diction is excellent," I said.

"I know only a few words," he answered.

I knew that Shakespeare and Shelley were his favorite poets and that he read both in the original, even as he did Tolstoy, who was his favorite novelist. Because of constant exposure to sun or because of some ailment, he had the habit when he was silent of shutting his eyes, and as I observed him closely I was struck by his resemblance to Gorky and Mark Twain. The upper part of his face, prominent and furrowed, reminded me of the Russian; the lower part, especially when he smiled, brought to mind the American.

"What are you doing nowadays," I asked, "writing new poems?"

Puffing at his pipe and nodding toward the piles of letters on the table, he said:

"Look at these! Seven hundred of them!"

"Are you going to answer them all?"

He gave a shrug and smiled but made no answer to the question. Then as an afterthought he remarked:

"Much work, very much."

Remembering the highly publicized story of the title he had been awarded and the gift of a hundred thousand crowns that went with the honor, and which I knew he had given away to needy villagers in Těšín, I said:

"I suppose people write you all the time and ask for money?"

"Yes, some ask for money, others just write."

Moved by sudden impulse, he arose, excused himself, and left the room. Soon he returned, holding in one hand a bottle of *borovička*—Slovak vodka—and in the other an open box of cigarettes with a Hungarian band label.

"Please," he said, extending the box to me, then to the lawyer, then turning to the young woman, he paused an instant, shook his head, and said, "None for you. You're a woman; you shouldn't indulge in this."

We lighted the cigarettes and smoked and, becoming aware of the bottle in his hand, he gave a start, walked over to a closet, brought out little tumblers, and filled them. He passed one to me, one to the lawyer, filled a third and, turning to the woman, surveyed her with a merry twinkle and, shaking his head, said:

"None for you—a woman is a woman; you shouldn't indulge."
Instead he gave her an apple.

We drank the *borovička* and he refilled the glasses.

"You live all alone," I said.

"Of course."

"And do your own work in the house?"

"Of course."

As if to impress us with the quality of his housekeeping, he
invited us to go through the house. Not a room, not a window
but gleamed with cleanliness, and every nook was flooded with
light.

"I like the sun," he said. "I like the outdoors. I like the indoors to be close to the outdoors, that's why I have all these
windows."

"A wonderful home," I said.

"Good enough," he answered, and ushered us back into the
kitchen.

"Another drink," he said, and we drank another *borovička,*
all but the young woman.

"Another smoke?" And once more he passed around the cigarettes, but not to the young woman.

I recalled the poem he had once written in the guest book of
a young girl:

> *Both as alike as an unerring straight line:*
> *the book and the pipe.*
> *Hey, little sweethearts, how much longer*
> *will you be by my side?*
> *Until my body*
> *is carried out.*
> *Then the book shall close, the pipe shall go out.*

It was now obvious that *borovička* was a companion no less
welcome than the pipe and the book.

Conversation lapsed. There was much I wished to discuss with him—Těšín, politics, literature, life—but remembering the admonition on the door, I refrained. There was no time for serious discussion of anything. Yet it was impressive to see in person, and in his native haunt of forest, mountain and roaring river, the man who had written such stirring tributes to the lowly people who had been his neighbors and whom he sought to rouse to protest and rebellion against the efforts to throttle their human dignity and their Czech identity. I said:

"That's a fine cow you have."

"I have no cow. I have nothing. I have only myself," he said, his ponderous body shaking with laughter.

"There is a cow outside in your meadow," I said.

"It isn't mine. It belongs to my neighbor. She owns the cow. I own the meadow. Her cow eats my grass. She gives me her milk."

"A beautiful cow," I said.

"A nice cow."

"She must give a lot of milk."

He puffed away without answering, and I took it as a signal that our time had run out. I rose to go, but to my surprise he said politely:

"Don't be in a hurry." I glanced at the lawyer, and he seemed to hold his breath. Bezruč was actually saying to a caller, "Don't be in a hurry." That was a violation of every canon in his social creed.

"We've been here half an hour already," I said.

"No," he said in Czech, and hastened to add in English, "Not yet," and again he laughed a jovial boyish laugh. There was nothing stern about the man, neither in his manner, his language, nor his voice. He proved so companionable a host that I said:

"You really love to be alone?"

"Oh yes, oh yes." But he laughed no more.

He started to pour another *borovička,* but I shook my head, and he desisted. Instead he once more passed the Hungarian cigarettes. He talked of the mountains, the weather, the beautiful scenery of Ostravica. He asked a few questions about America, England, nothing with any bearing on the turmoil or the hope of the world or of immediate consequence to him as a Czech or a literary figure. It was obvious he was living in a world of his own, far removed from the clashing forces of mankind, but whether it was a world of calm or of commotion, he never disclosed.

Having overstayed our time, we rose to go. He escorted us to the door, warmly shook our hands, and said:

"Take my greetings to America."

Outside the young woman said: "He didn't say, 'Call again.' "

The cow was still in the meadow, as friendly and as curious as when we first passed her. Again I drew close and caressed her face, and she sniffed my hand and licked it and in no way indicated that the owner of the field in which she was feeding had been querulous or even aloof or had habituated her to shy away from the world even as he was doing.

The one living thing the recluse poet liked having close was the cow.

9. The Beer-Barrel Polka

American and British war correspondents who were in Clyde, Scotland, on the day a Swedish ship brought the first boatload of exchanged war prisoners will long remember the scene. On the pier were friends and relatives of the incoming passengers; on the ship were men fresh from captivity: wounded men, some totally blind, others hopelessly maimed. There were suspense and tension as the ship was brought into dock. There were silent tears and unspoken grief. It was almost as though Britishers had gathered for a funeral.

Of a sudden the band struck up the "Beer-Barrel Polka," and all felt as if purged of pain and gloom. The wounded men came off the ship, smiling; the crowds on the pier greeted them with bursts of cheers. The change of mood was as electrifying as it was salutary. Funeral solemnity gave way to buoyant liveliness. Such was the magic power of the lilting polka tune.

During the war years I had heard it in Natal, Brazil, in Khartoum and Accra, Africa, in Cairo and Teheran, in many other faraway places where the British and American armies maintained camps and bases, and at gatherings of the small foreign

124

colony in Moscow. Throughout the fighting years it gave great joy to Allied and enemy armies. Soldiers sang it, danced to it, thrilled to its merry lilt and its heart-warming witchery. It had been a theme song, a fight song, a marching tune; the "Tipperary" of World War II. The most moving incident in Noel Coward's war film, *In Which We Serve,* at least to this writer, is of the wrecked sailors and their captain clinging in a surging sea to a rubber raft and singing the "Beer-Barrel Polka."

Yet it was not until I reached Prague, some months after the war ended, that I learned the composer of the song was a Czech. Nor was he a noted or even a professional musician. He was only a village innkeeper and band leader. His name was Jaromír Vejvoda.

That a Czech should compose a tuneful polka was no surprise. It was in the village Labská Týnice, in 1830, that a gay-hearted housemaid named Ann Slezak first improvised the deft steps that caught the fancy, first of her own countrymen, then of dance-loving people the world over. But that an obscure village band leader should be the creator of a tune which in a moment of great crisis and great tragedy stirred the imagination of mankind, and especially the fighting armies of all lands, was more than a tribute to the composer's personal gifts. It testified to an innate love of gay melody in Czech folk everywhere and to a fond preoccupation with new variations of the old and ever-alluring theme.

I learned more. During the war years Vejvoda had heard of the popularity of his song in certain parts of Europe, but it was not until the black-out had been lifted from his native land that he first learned of its sensational success all over the world. He was a rich man now, richer perhaps than any present-day Czech. For there was no way the Germans could loot the pounds and dollars that had been accumulating for him abroad, particularly in the two great English-speaking countries. A world celebrity, still living in the village, still an innkeeper and band leader—what manner of man was he, and Czech that he was, how was he reacting to the dreamlike discovery of wealth and fame?

I journeyed to Vrané, or "Vrané on the Vltava," as Czech speak of the village, to see Vejvoda in his native surroundings.

The river separates the village from highway and railroad, and I ferried across in a lumbering and ancient raft piloted by an old man with massive hair and a sun-scorched face, and a young girl with fat legs and seductive eyes. After crossing the river I walked up a sloping bank and found myself on the main street, only a few steps from the gray concrete two-story building which is the inn in which Vejvoda lives.

All around were mountains thatched with wild grass and scrub trees, which, together with the river, gave the village a rugged splendor. Shade and fruit trees, chiefly apple and pear, shadowed the cozy cottages; an old paper mill in the heart of the village might have been a hospital or a church, for all the intrusion it made on the tranquillity of the place. Hens strutted in and out of courtyards; here and there a cat leaped over a fence; children were quietly playing under the trees. Otherwise the village was deserted and so silent that the clang of hammer and anvil in the blacksmith shop resounded high and shrill, the lingering echoes adding to the rustic flavor of the place.

Here were ease and seclusion, with river and mountains shielding the mind and emotions of man from the harsh discords of the modern city. Here the imagination might spill over with melody as naturally as the earth did with the ever-present and ever-glowing wild flowers. Vejvoda's band was made up of villagers like himself, friends and neighbors with whom he had grown up. One was an electrician, another a textile salesman, a third a metalworker, four were clerks, four were music teachers in near-by villages. Vejvoda was no more than an amateur himself, music being incidental to the administration of a beer tavern, an inn, a bowling alley. Though small, with only a population of one thousand, the village abounded in musical talent.

I walked into the inn and was met by a short, stocky old man with a face as wrinkled as a withered leaf and enlivened by gay blue eyes. He introduced himself as Vejvoda's father-in-law and invited me into the taproom where, when not leading his band, Vejvoda was dispensing schooners of beer to visiting customers. Yes, said the old man, Vejvoda lived in the inn with his wife, three children, and the in-laws. And why not? He himself had passed the bloom of life; it was time for a younger man to take over the duties of innkeeper, and who was more entitled to do so than the husband of his own daughter? No trouble at all between Vejvoda and the in-laws. Why should there be, when people were as closely drawn to one another as parents and children and their life mates?

Here was peasant logic, or what Tolstoy would term peasant simplicity, unshaken by city restlessness, unspoiled by urban sophistication.

Slowly and soberly the old man spoke of Jaromír's career. His great-grandfather, his grandfather, his father had kept inns and had led village bands. From his own father Jaromír learned to play the violin when a very young boy. Though he also played the cornet and the piano, the violin was his real love. But Jaromír was more than a musician, more than a bartender and innkeeper. He was a sportsman of parts, an honored member of the local Sokol society. He was chess champion of the village, an unexcelled bowler, a skilled hand in card games—especially in "marriage," a gay and boisterous game popular in Vrané. His favorite opponent in chess was the pensioned local policeman; his customary partners in card games were the village butcher, the village mechanic, and a retired army lieutenant. On and on the old man talked, with pride yet with modesty, avoiding as might other Slavs in his place extravagant rhetoric and a lavish show of self-esteem.

Then Jaromír came. He looked much younger than his forty-three years. He was of medium height, wiry, slender, with sharp irregular features; it was his fine mouth and his astonishingly handsome eyes that dominated not only his face but his person. Dark and large and wide open, his eyes set everything about him—his smile, his gestures, his nods and nays—aglow with a boyish ardor, and he displayed a boyish diffidence in the presence of strangers. Unlike his father-in-law, he was slow of speech and reluctant, indeed embarrassed, to speak of himself.

"Have you ever played in Prague?" I asked.

"No."

This was an astonishing and revealing reply. The fact is that Prague knows little about him, nor does the rest of the country. Despite the world renown he has attained, he is no celebrity to his own countrymen. In a land that teems with melody, his compositions have created no stir, and the acclaim he has received in the outside world has scarcely been publicized in the press. The only official recognition he has been accorded was the invitation by President Beneš to stand beside him on the reviewing stand during a military parade when an army band passed by playing "Modřanská Polka," which was the song's original title and which is named after a village in the neighborhood of the composer's home.

Not that Czechs take no pride in the achievements of their countrymen. But a polka is no more than a polka. It is nothing to get excited about. It is no outstanding achievement, nothing like the plays of Karel Čapek or a novel like *The Good Soldier Švejk*. It may or may not advertise the country, but even if it does, it is no national triumph, adds little or nothing to its culture, is only one more blossom on a tree already rich with bloom.

"Would you like to go to England and America?" I asked.

"Of course I'd love to travel," Vejvoda answered with no visible enthusiasm. For a musician he seemed singularly lacking in animation, or perhaps it was only his innate Czech reserve.

"And settle abroad?" I asked.

"Oh no." He firmly shook his head. "Everybody I know is here, everything I like is here, and it's nice to live here."

"You are a rich man now," I said. "What are you going to do when you collect your money from England and America?"

"The same as I've always done."

"Play at village dances and weddings?"

"And at funerals," he added with a smile.

Of the thirty tunes he has composed, two are elegies; the others are polkas and waltzes, testifying to the overwhelming popularity of old-fashioned dancing in the Czech countryside. He was still composing, he said, but only polkas and waltzes. Modern jazz was too alien to his ears to tempt him into imitating it. "I must content myself with the musical language I know," he said. Invariably he does his composing in the back room of the bowling alley, where visitors are served beer and sandwiches. He composes on the piano or on the violin, strumming the strings as on a guitar and taking up the bow only when a good tune begins to form.

"What do you do if people are bowling when you get the urge to compose?"

"That's no trouble at all," he said. "I tell them to clear out."

"Don't they resent it?"

"No, they are my friends. Why should they resent it?"

His diffidence was abating and speech came more easily, though still reluctantly.

I asked him how he came to write the "Beer-Barrel Polka." At once his tongue seemed as if frozen. He looked at me questioningly, his wide-open and brilliant eyes reflecting bafflement and concern. Yet after a lengthy pause he replied:

"That was a special occasion."

"Quite special?"

He nodded and mumbled, "Yes," and from the suffusion of his cheeks it was clear that the occasion was related to an uncommon experience.

"What moved you to compose it?" I asked.

He kept looking at me diffidently but not resentfully, then gave a little laugh.

"I was feeling good, very good," he finally said. "I couldn't help composing it." He halted, smiling, and I waited for him to continue and when he did not I asked what made him feel so good.

"Well," he began hesitantly, "I'd been drinking quite a bit of wine—my head was giddy—and——" He paused, pursed his lips as if to hold back the words.

"And then?" I prompted.

He looked confused and yet elated, obviously reliving a memorable experience of which he felt embarrassed to speak. Again I prompted him, and slowly, haltingly, yet never turning his eyes away, he said:

"It happened this way. One evening I was leading my band in the Sokolovna Inn in this village a few blocks away from here. Suddenly I saw a girl. She had just come in and she was so beautiful I could not take my eyes off her. But I was leading my band and she was dancing and dancing. I made up my mind I'd meet her, and I did. I danced with her. The next time I played there she came again, and I decided I'd get to know her better. So when the dance was over I invited her to stay and have a drink of wine with me. Well, we sat and drank wine and talked." He paused, gave a toss of the head, and smiled and remained silent. I could not help reflecting how difficult it was for him, a Czech, to speak of a personal experience, of which with but little encouragement Russians or Poles I had known would have delivered themselves with unabated fervor as of a personal triumph. After much prodding on my part and much hesitancy on his, and perhaps only out of courtesy to an American visitor, Vejvoda finished the story.

"You see—we both felt good—the girl and I—we'd had quite a bit of wine—and she kissed me for the first time. I took her home, and when I got back to my room I couldn't sleep—my head swam with happiness, so I sat down at the piano and started to play, nothing in particular, just improvising—and the polka rolled out of the keys. I played it over and over, and the more I played it, the better I liked it, so I set it down on paper and put it away in a drawer. I wanted to play it again with a clear and—well, sobered mind. When I did play it again I liked it so much I started featuring it in village dances."

"What year was that?"

"Nineteen-thirty."

It seemed incredible that like a seed in arid soil the melody had lain virtually unknown for almost a decade, and that only catastrophe had drenched it with the fertility to give it the lusty bloom it had subsequently acquired.

"Yes," Vejvoda explained with no show of regret, "I composed it a long time ago, and it was the most successful polka tune my band played. Other band leaders in surrounding villages heard it and wanted to play it, but I wouldn't allow them. Then a music publisher in Prague heard of it and invited me to come to see her—it was a woman. She talked to me at length but showed no enthusiasm and asked me to come again, and when I did we signed a contract for its publication."

"Did she pay you much in advance?"

"One hundred and fifty crowns." This is the equivalent of less than five dollars.

"No more?"

"Not a crown more. But by 1939 I had collected one hundred

thousand crowns." The equivalent of over three thousand dollars.

"Were you surprised when you learned of its sensational success during the war years?"

"I never expected it. I'd composed it only for my band, and as you know I had named it after one of our neighboring villages."

"By the way," I asked, "did you marry the girl?"

"Of course—she is his daughter"—pointing at his father-in-law—"that's how I came to live in this inn." He laughed uproariously, and his father-in-law joined in the laughter.

"And you'd rather remain here in Vrané than live in England or America?"

"He'd miss his birthday parties," interjected the father-in-law.

"Are they so exciting?" I asked.

"He gets his *hobl* all right."

"What's a *hobl*?"

Thereupon the few guests who had straggled into the inn flung themselves on the band leader, seized him by the arms and legs, and started to swing him up and down and sideways, to the right and the left, now and then deliberately bumping his behind against the floor and shouting at the top of their voices, with Jaromír, as though enjoying not only the excitement but the bumping, shouting as lustily as they.

I could not help comparing Bezruč, the poet, and Jaromír, the composer of the "Beer-Barrel Polka"—not as persons, but as products of the same civilization, as sons of the same people. Bezruč is the impassioned crusader. There is something grim and heroic in his manner and in his stature. He is overcome with *Weltschmerz* and with the problem of good and evil. He is a superlative hater, with scarcely a note of gaiety in him. A folk poet, he has created his own tradition, his own rhythm, if not his own language.

Vejvoda has neither the education nor the passion of Bezruč. He is not literary at all, not even in his own field. Yet he, too, is a folk poet, but he lives within the tradition and the spirit of his people. He has created nothing new, nor did he attempt it; he has only enlivened an old theme, an old form of folk art. There is nothing grim or heroic in anything he has done, in anything he hopes to achieve. He is not concerned with struggle and conflict, any more than is a bird, but only with harmony and festiveness. He is the real amateur, so much the lover of his art that though he has lived all his life within the shadow of Prague, within sight and sound of the machine age, he has remained untouched by urban harshness or urban restlessness. He is the gay lyricist, happy with his environment, both human and natural, spilling over with joy and with a wish to impart it to the people among whom he lives. He has sought neither success nor fame, and he lives in a society which is neither burdened nor harassed by the professionalism which would exploit his talent or his notoriety to the inevitable debasement of his art, perhaps of his person. He does not think of himself as an artist, but as a band leader who wants to make good within his own milieu and in his own media of self-expression.

If Bezruč is the impersonation of the somber mood of the Czech with his excessive self-criticism and his unquenched ardor to keep his soul his own, Vevjoda is the expression of Czech love of gaiety and festiveness and sheer delight in living.

10. The Great Heritage

In summer the Tábor I knew in the pre-war years would be a feast for anyone's eyes. A town of intelligentsia, officials, pensioners, small shopkeepers, artisans, factory workers, it commands a natural beauty hardly rivaled by any other community. When I visited it in the summer of 1938 it was ablaze with flowers. In an array of colors as resplendent as the spectrum, they beckoned to the pedestrian at every turn, from parks and playgrounds, from doorways and windows, from front and back yards. Outdoors and indoors, in sun and storm, day and night, flowers were an ever-present testimony to a love of brightness and cheer. They softened the harshness of the architecture in the new part of the town and enhanced the charm of the zigzagging antiquity of the old, perched like a gigantic nest on top of a high hill.

When I came back in 1945, early winter shrouded the place. Trees were bare of foliage; flowers were nowhere in sight. I sauntered up the hill to the Žižka Square. The sixteenth-century Gothic church loomed as large though not as white as formerly out of a sparse row of majestic chestnut trees. The Town Hall with its Renaissance gables made the Finance Building with its

134

ultra-modern façade no less an anachronism now than in former years. The spacious square was silent and almost deserted. Once it had teemed with people and donkeys, with sturdy dogs and well-groomed horses hitched to carts laden with produce. Washed and polished, fruits and vegetables gleamed with freshness. Anything and everything the country produced, even fish swimming in deep vats of translucent water, was at the disposal of shoppers. Now the square was empty of teams and carts, of stalls and crowds, and only a few moribund old women were crouching on ragged quilts and tattered sacks spread over the cobbles, displaying wilted onions, small potatoes, a few strings of dried mushrooms, and nothing more. Not only winter had obscured the luster of Tábor; war and the Nazis had passed over it like a soiled hand across a radiant face.

Yet the monuments of the two men, General Jan Žižka and Master Jan Hus, with whose names the history and the glory of the town are identified, rose no less sublimely above the poverty of today than above the affluence of yesterday. Sword in one hand, dagger in the other, helmet on head, cloth over his blind eye, his immense mustaches winding like ripe ears of wheat beyond his cheeks, an expression of sturdy reserve in his sharp features, such was Žižka in the square which bears his name. Bible clasped to his breast, head held high, eyes lifted heavenward, the long hair swept back, the thin broad face bright with compassion, such was Master Jan Hus in the park in the lower part of the town.

As I walked around the streets and parks, the hills and valleys of this historic town, I could not help remembering the frock-coated, stripe-trousered businessman with whom I had shared a train compartment on my earlier journey. "To us Czechs," he had said, "Tábor is not a town but an idea, the core of which is truth, freedom, democracy." Prosperous and self-confident, he assured me that no matter what the Germans might do, even if they came and razed it, they never could annihilate the idea of Tábor. I had thought of his words when I stepped out of the train and glanced around the square that fronts the railroad station. The first thing that caught my eyes, gleaming in letters of many-hued flower heads, was Masaryk's enunciation, "Tábor is our program."

Tábor is the great milestone in Czech history and Czech life.

In a brochure which I had picked up in Prague I read: "The name of the city of Tábor heads the most famous chapter in our national history during the fifteenth century. It was the cradle of medieval Czech democracy, the district where in the year 1420 was proclaimed the Czech dream of a Kingdom of God on earth, a place where all men would be brothers and would not be beholden to one another. It was here that the great legacy of Master Jan Hus was guarded against all enemies by the 'Warriors of God,' under the leadership of Jan Žižka of Trocnov."

The paragraph is brief but it tells much. It gives concrete meaning to the words my traveling companion had spoken and to Masaryk's flower-headed enunciation. Though small in size, only twenty-three thousand in population, no other town in Czechoslovakia is so glowing a monument to the struggle for religious reform and social liberation. The very name of the place, Tábor, associated with the Mount of Transfiguration, speaks for its transcendent place in Czech history. It was the seat of a revolution not only in manners but in morals, not only in intellect but in usage, and out of it have sprung ideas and inspirations which have galvanized the thinking not only of Czechs but of peoples beyond their frontier.

The central figure of the movement was Jan Hus. The son of a poor peasant, he manifested from earliest days a love of learning, which his father and mother were happy to encourage. He made his way to Prague University and helped support himself

136

by singing in the streets and in churches. He was so poor that he could not afford to buy a spoon for himself. He fashioned a spoon out of bread, ate with it peas, and finished his meal by eating the spoon. He was not a particularly brilliant student, and the only hobby besides singing in which he indulged (and which he subsequently repented) was chess, which he played with no little skill, often winning small sums of money from his opponents. But teachers and students admired him for his piety and the purity of his character. When he was 20 years of age, he was awarded the degree of master of arts. Four years later he won another degree—bachelor of divinity. Soon afterward he was appointed dean of the faculty of philosophy, in which he had studied, and the following year was elevated to the position of rector. His personal charm and his devoutness aroused the affection of the Queen, and for some years he was her personal confessor. His eloquent sermons won him a pastorate in Bethlehem Chapel, built by a wealthy citizen to encourage preaching in the native tongue.

Appalled by the corruption of the clergy of his day, Hus launched a crusade against the greed and the immoralities of the priesthood. Stimulated by the teachings of John Wycliffe of England, he also advocated reform in the church, in dogma and in discipline. For him the Law of Christ or the Word of God as revealed in the Scriptures transcended the law of man. This was a defiance not only of the Church but of the temporal authority of his day. Nor did he confine his zeal for reform to the clergy and the Church. Vexed by the low state of education among his people and aroused by the tyrannical domination of Germans over them, he struck out for the regeneration of the one and for the removal of the other. The idea of ridding the Czech lands of Germans is no outgrowth of Munich and the Nazi occupation. It dates back to Hus, who said in a sermon: "The Bohemians [Czechs] are more wretched than dogs or snakes, for a dog defends the couch on which he lies, and if another dog tries to drive him away he fights and a snake does the same. But the Germans oppress us, seize all the offices of the state, while we are silent. . . . Of what use would it be if a Bohemian became a priest or a bishop in Germany? He assuredly would be as useful as a dumb dog who cannot bark at a herd. Equally useless to us Bohemians is a German. . . . The Germans who are in Bohemia should go to their King [Wenceslaus] and swear that they will be faithful to him and to the country. But this will come to pass only when a serpent warms itself on ice."[1] Hus cherished no racial hate of Germans. "A good German," he said, "is dearer to me than a bad Bohemian." But he denounced their abuse of power, their misuse of privilege.

No less passionately did he deplore the condition of the underprivileged of his day. Unlike Luther, who spoke of himself as a pupil of Hus, but who in 1525 abandoned the peasantry in their revolt against the nobility, Hus to the end championed the common man. Unlike Luther, he subjected all mortal authority to the Law of Christ, including the authority of kings, the nobility, and other political rulers. For him Christ was the King of all men, and Christ's Word was the only law by which man, whatever his position, was to guide himself in his daily life. His, therefore, was a crusade against evils in clericalism, in education, in politics, in social life.

His contribution to Czech civilization was enormous, not only in the body of ideas which he enunciated, but in methods of applying them. He simplified the spelling of the Czech language. He enriched its literary quality. He taught and preached in the native tongue, the language of the laborer and the peasant. He called on teachers and priests to emulate his example and to rid education and public speech of the Latin scholasticism that had denatured them. Gifted with a love of music which is the inborn

[1]Count Lützou, *Life of Jan Hus.*

heritage of his people, he wrote hymns, opened a music school, and made congregational singing a special feature of his chapel. In his book *Dcera* [*Daughter*] he advocated the moral and religious education of women, which resulted in giving them the same education as men, so that they too could read the Word of God. Let the reader remember, all this happened in the early part of the fifteenth century. Modern nationalism, modern democracy were then unknown, and the word "socialism" was yet to become a part of man's vocabulary. Yet much of what Hus taught was in later years to stimulate the political and social thinking of men not only in his native land but in other countries.

His teachings and his sermons brought on him the charge of heresy, and he was summoned for trial before the Council of Constance. Against the advice of friends who urged him to ignore the summons, he trusted Emperor Sigismund, who had promised him safe conduct to Constance and back home. But Sigismund betrayed him. Condemned for heresy, Hus was burned at the stake on July 6, 1415, and his ashes were scattered to the winds. He went to his death singing a hymn to the Holy Mother.

The betrayal and execution of Hus brought to a climax the social rebellion his teachings had inspired. Religious sentiment fused with national aspiration and the desire for social liberation. It was then that Tábor came into being. Excepting an old fort and a few houses, there was no town; there was only a wooded wilderness. But it was some distance away from Prague, which was the capital of the Holy Roman Empire, whose Emperor Sigismund had caused the great man's death. It was near Hrad Kozi, the village to which Hus had fled from the capital when his life was endangered. It was near Sezimovo Usti, where the first Hussite parish was founded. Above all, its steep hills, swift-flowing river, and wooded spaces lent themselves superbly to military fortifications. Tábor became the citadel of the more irreconcilable, or what we should now term the leftist wing, of the movement. To the poorer shopkeepers, artisans, peasants, and to the patriotic lower nobility, Hus was more than the man who had preached the true gospel of Jesus. He was their martyr and emancipator. He had inspired a new faith in them as Czechs and as human beings. They were all "brothers and sisters," equal before one another and before all rulers. The folk saying, *"Ja pan, ty pan* [I am lord, you are lord]," could only have stemmed from the Hussite gospel of equality.

Under the leadership of Jan Žižka, a blind general, and one of Hus's stanchest disciples, they formed themselves into an army of the "Warriors of God." They went into battle singing hymns, and the fervor and desperation which animated them are brilliantly reflected in all their war songs.

Emperor Sigismund had mobilized a large part of Europe for a war of annihilation against the Táborites. But so long as Žižka was alive the vengeful Emperor suffered defeat after defeat. Brilliant strategy, new weapons—chief of which was a horse-drawn, wood-constructed cart loaded with cannon, precursor of the tank—always turned the numerically superior enemy to flight. After Žižka's death from the plague a priest named Prokop Holj—"The Beardless"—took over command. He, too, was a brilliant soldier and for ten years kept up the fight against Tábor's enemies. With manpower depleted, with the country exhausted, with the nobility and the University of Prague frightened by the radicalism of Tábor, joining in the battle against them, the Táborites went down to defeat in 1434.

But the cause which Hus preached and for which Tábor fought survived through the ages. In the nineteenth century Czech intellectuals, stirred by the gusts of rebellion which were blowing over Europe, turned to the past for guidance and inspiration. František Palacký (1798–1876), the eminent historian, was among the first to reinterpret Hus and the Hussite movement in modern terms and give them a modern meaning. In his summary of Palacký's teachings Professor Hans Kohn writes: "The Czech people in the Hussite Wars pioneered for the whole of humanity in a spiritual struggle for freedom of conscience, for the equality of men against authority and hierarchy. Of course the Hussites were in no way modern man, but their fight contained the seeds out of which later a freer and more human Europe grew up. The Hussite Revolution not only started the Protestant Reformation but carried the germs for the future growth of rationalism and of freedom of thought, of democracy and of socialism, founded on religious idealism, of nationalism and of the new spirit of activity pervading the masses. In the Hussite movement with its ethical rigorism and its chiliastic enthusiasm, he saw the forerunner of the Puritan revolution which in its turn heralded the American and the French revolutions. The fact that the Czechs could fulfill this function in history Palacký explained by pointing out that the level of education had been higher in Bohemia, especially under Charles IV, than in any of the surrounding countries, that feudalism and serfdom had not yet fully been established among the Czechs. . . . The old opposition of Slav democracy and German aristocracy was resumed on a higher level under the religious inspiration of Hussitism and became of world-wide importance."[2]

Tábor and all that it symbolizes, more than any circumstance in life and in history, is the reason for the ideological gulf that separates Czech from Slovak, from Pole, from Hungarian, from Rumanian, from all other peoples in central and eastern Europe who were tardy in shaking off the ancient social dogma as embodied in feudalism, with its sharp social cleavages, its neglect of the machine age, its contempt for humanistic enlightenment, its loathing of popular democracy. The historic hurdle the

[2]*Czechoslovakia,* edited by Robert J. Kerner, University of California Press.

Czechs surmounted five centuries ago has made it easy for them to keep up with the advance in modern science, politics, education. Not having to clear the hurdle at this belated date, they are saved from the turbulences and vexations which make the re-creation of neighboring states so painful a process, so distressing an ordeal.

I went to the Žižka Museum to look up an old friend, Dr. František Kroupa, the director. He is a lifelong student of the history of Tábor and of the Hussite movement. I found him in a small, chilly office, bent over a smoking, pudgy little stove, shoveling coal inside. Seven years had passed since I had last seen him, and that he survived the German occupation was a tribute to his courage and his diplomacy. Nobody could have been more abhorrent to the Nazis than a scholar who had given his life to the study of the most violent anti-totalitarian and anti-German struggle in Czech history and to the preservation and perpetuation of the relics and monuments of that struggle.

Dr. Kroupa looked much thinner and paler than when I had last seen him. His mass of dark chestnut hair, neatly brushed back and as thick as ever, was only slightly tinged with gray. Hardy and upright, with an athletic alertness in his movements, he was his old cheerful, optimistic self. Now that the German minorities were being made to leave the country, he said, the one perpetual source of internal turmoil would be plucked out by the roots. Czechs could be themselves again, and despite difficulties with food and national impoverishment the country had a "positive future." Tábor had been a Masaryk town. Now it was a Beneš town. Beneš had his country home in Sezimovo Usti, where the Tábor movement had first begun, and his presence there only enhanced the influence of old Tábor on the Tábor of today. That is why Tábor accepted the new dispensation as embodied in the nationalization program. Tábor was, of course, middle class, which did not necessarily mean antagonism to change. Tábor knew that growth and change were implicit in civilization even as in nature, and that to survive at all democracy needed to be redefined and reshuffled, else it could only perish from stagnation. No, he, Kroupa, cherished no misgivings about the future, now that the ancient and irrepressible enemy was leaving the country. He suggested that I see the new mayor of the town, a man who had spent five and a half years in concentration camps, had been five times under sentence of death, and had miraculously eluded the gallows and the firing squad. "A man of principles and conviction," said Dr. Kroupa. He telephoned the mayor and we were invited to come over.

The Town Hall, where the mayor has his office, is only a few doors away from the museum. The mayor's name is Franz Sivera, a man in his early forties. Stocky, well-built, with a powerful back, an energetic handshake, and flashing blue eyes, he gestured profusely as he talked. In outward appearance there was scarcely anything to distinguish him from a go-getting mayor in an American Western town. Expansive and voluble, he was as proud of his town, as fervent in his local patriotism as would be his American counterpart. But the intensity of the emotion with which he spoke, the ethical concepts with which he punctuated his pronouncements were distinctively Táborite. It was as though he had an inner compulsion to reassert and reaffirm a faith long cherished but forcibly subdued during the German occupation, and all the more hallowed because so long under ban. Business and evangelism intertwined, like the words and the melody in a song.

"By blood," he said, "we Czechs are drawn east to the Russians, our brother Slavs. Our hearts and our sentiments are with them. But America is also close to us. We have much in common with America. Many of our people live there, and we shall always remember Woodrow Wilson's friendship with Masaryk and the help he gave us in starting our first republic. Right, Doctor?"

"Quite right," answered Dr. Kroupa.

"I personally," the mayor continued, "am particularly indebted to the Americans. They liberated me from a concentration camp in Germany. I remember the date, April 23, 1945, and the hour, yes, and the minute—eleven-fourteen in the morning, when the Americans came and said: 'You're free to go home.' Can you imagine what the words meant to us? Sixteen thousand of us had for three days been on a forced march, which only seven thousand had survived. Hungry and sick, we were wondering what would happen to us, and suddenly the Americans came and said: 'Go, you're free.' " He leaned back in his chair and sighed in relief, almost in exultation, like a man recalling a sorrow that ended in a joy.

"What a trip home we had," he resumed. "We came to a German town and asked the mayor for bread. 'I have no bread,' said the mayor. 'Have you flour?' we asked. 'I have no flour either,' he answered. 'I only have wheat.' 'If you have wheat you can grind it into flour,' we told him. 'I can't. The mill is broken and there is no one to repair it; the mechanics have fled.' 'We'll repair the mill,' we told him. 'Come and show us where it is.' He went with us and we got busy and"—throwing out his hands and scanning them appreciatively—"these blessed hands, skilled sweating hands, that's what the Lord has given us Czechs, hands that love to feel their way to trouble in watches, engines, tools, any piece of machinery, and bring the gift of life to them. We're like your people, like the new Russians. We love the feel, the look, the sound of tools, the joy and the challenge of the machine. Nothing is difficult or impossible for our hands. So we repaired the mill and ground the flour and baked the bread and ate it."

He paused, puffed energetically at a newly lighted cigarette, and blew the smoke overhead with a vigor that denoted an

inner restlessness in marked contrast with the blithe repose of
Dr. Kroupa.

"How do you look on the future of Tábor?" I asked.

"With faith and hope."

"Do your people accept nationalization as a way of life?"

"Of course. I am a Socialist; nearly all of us in this town are,
aren't we, Doctor?"

"We are, indeed," nodded the director of the museum.

"Middle-class Socialists?"

He shrugged, smiled, exchanged a half-amused glance with
Dr. Kroupa.

"Put it that way if you choose," he answered, "but Socialists
in the real sense of the word." Swiftly he swung out of his chair
and beckoned to me to follow him to the window, which looked
out on the spacious square. With a quick thrust of the hand he
pointed to the cobbles outside and continued: "See how round
the cobbles are? That's the way they were five hundred years
ago, when in their war against absolutism our ancestors drenched
them with their blood. That's the way they have remained
through the centuries, and that's the way they shall always
remain, sacred reminders of the past and the cause for which
our ancestors gave their lives. Every time I glance at these cobbles I say to myself, 'Tábor means freedom, and absolutism
means death to freedom.' But what is freedom? You may think
of it one way, I another. Every people must interpret it in the
light of its own history, its own needs, its own conscience. But
freedom has to be flexible enough to benefit all the people, all
the time. People's freedom, that's what we here want, enlightened freedom, reasonable freedom, that will grow and bloom
like our flowers in summer."

He paused and looked contemplatively at the square outside.
Two boys, followed by a dog, were chasing each other around
the chestnut tree by the old church. An old woman was enter-

ing the church; an old man was coming out. The sky was cloudy, and a fog was rolling over the tops of the tall buildings on the square. There was nothing spectacular or unusual in the scene outside. Yet the mayor's eyes seemed as if entranced with the sight before him. Once more thrusting his hand in the direction of the square, he said: "There are those cobbles, and we know what they mean. To us they speak an ancient and ever-living language." And pointing to the Žižka monument swathed in thin gray fog, he continued: "There is the blind general whom no tyrant ever defeated in battle. See him, sword in one hand, dagger in the other, 'Warrior of God,' defender of freedom."

I sauntered about the old part of the town on the hill, thinking of the mayor and of Dr. Kroupa and all I had heard them say. It seemed strange in the light of what I had known of Tábor that both men should speak with fervor of Socialism, for Tábor and Socialism seemed no more companionable than America's Middletown and Socialism. I had not heard the word on my earlier visit. Now it had become a slogan and a faith.

Nowhere else in Czechoslovakia does middle-class convention thrive so lustily. On meeting an acquaintance men doff their hats and add a low bow when the acquaintance happens to be a woman. A girl would feel insulted if a man invited her to dinner in a restaurant or hotel. Home is the creator of life, and the family is the sanctuary of the individual. Divorce is almost anathema. In pre-war days the town was bursting with clubs, literary, religious, fraternal, scientific, musical, social. I know of no town in America whose people are such superlative joiners. In the pre-war years Dr. Kroupa was a member of thirty local societies and president of six. Mr. Soumar, the former mayor, now a wizened old man who barely survived his years in a German concentration camp, had boasted a prouder record, having held membership in fifty local organizations. "And of how

—*Czechoslovak Consulate General*

Woodcut of Jan Hus after a painting by Holbein

Interior of the classical baroque Loreta Church, Prague

Tábor, seat of the Hussite Revolution in the fifteenth century

many," I once asked him, "are you president?" With a shrug he answered, "I never stopped to figure up."

Yet Tábor, heir to a tradition of radical thought and social revolt, was as violently arrayed against absolutism as it had been in the old days. The mayor's very emphasis of Tábor's hatred of absolutism was enlightening. Years of German subjugation had fanned the old spark into a new flame. To Tábor freedom was no verbal abstraction, and Socialism without freedom was as impossible as life without sun.

Yet Tábor was not without voices of dissent. One, particularly memorable, came from a man with a real claim to scholarship. "Expelling Germans, however much they deserve it," he said, "is not Socialism but reaction. Barring non-Slav minorities, however necessary to our internal peace, is not Socialism but reaction. Even Russia does not do it. Quite the contrary, Russia condemns it. Making Germans wear yellow armlets, however necessary for identification purposes, is taking a leaf out of the enemy's book."

"Are you opposed to it?" I asked.

"Of course not. I'm all for it. But if we allow reaction to creep into our relations with non-Slavs, are we not in danger of permitting it to seep into our relations with one another?"

"What do you mean?" I asked.

"Very simply, the possibility of dictatorship, which is nothing but reaction."

"Would Tábor stand for dictatorship?" I asked, and repeated to him the mayor's eloquent words against absolutism.

"Tábor would hate it as it always did. But Prague is not as far away in this century as it was in the fifteenth, and Prague reeks with reaction. That is the danger."

He would say no more. He was a baffled man. Instead of continuing the discussion he started asking questions about literature in Great Britain and America.

11. Teacher of Democracy

        I drove to Lány, the village in whose hillside ceme-
tery are buried Thomas Masaryk and his American wife. The
date was September 14, the anniversary of the former President's
death. The weather was sunny and warm, and a procession of
pilgrims in automobiles and busses, in horse-drawn wagons and
on foot, came to pay homage to the man who had been their
guide, their teacher, their prophet; he who had all his life striven
to mold them into a reasonable and reasoning people.

Only once before, in 1938, just a year after his death and on the
eve of Munich, were Czechs privileged to accord their respect
to the dead leader. When the Germans came they banned all
manifestations of fealty to the man who to them was anathema.
His portraits and statuary in schools and offices were smashed;
his monuments were lifted and sacked; his books, some of
which have been translated into all living languages, including Chinese and Hebrew, were seized and burned—if only
they could be found. The Germans knew that the power Masaryk
exercised over his people was as great, if not greater, in death
than in life. Any expression of reverence for him could only be a

demonstration of hostility to them. Therefore, on Czech national holidays and on the anniversary of Masaryk's death, Gestapo soldiers guarded the cemetery, forbade pilgrimages or the placing of floral tributes on the grave.

Yet Czech wit contrived to outsmart Gestapo vigilance. Under cover of darkness and sometimes in daylight, young and old crept up to the gray walls that tower above the grave and tossed over a handful of roses, a few sprigs of forget-me-nots, or a lone home-grown begonia.

Now for the first time in seven years they were free again to demonstrate their love for the dead President. A steady procession of people solemnly yet triumphantly filed past the grave. Here were college professors and Cabinet ministers; Communists and Catholics; village belles in resplendent costumes, with daisies and cornflowers in their hair, and plowmen in rumpled overalls and mud-caked boots; Boy and Girl Scouts in brown blouses and fluffy neckties and university students in Sunday dress. There was no chanting of patriotic songs or hymns. There were no eulogies and no memorial addresses. There were only silent contemplation and whispered conversation. Everyone seemed to feel that he was in the presence of something sacred and deathless.

The occasion invited a fresh appraisal of the character and achievements of the man with whose name the restoration of Czech and Slovak independence are stirringly associated. Not a few of the principles he had espoused and the policies he had enacted were pulverized into disuse by the war. Masaryk had firmly believed that an enlightened relationship between Czech and German would result in lasting friendship between the two peoples. No one in Czechoslovakia believes it any more. He had fought the Communists, yet in the election of May 26, 1946, they polled more votes than their closest rival. He had disavowed Marxism as something old-fashioned, yet in one form or another its influence is more powerful today than it ever had been during his lifetime.

Despite these and other misjudgments, he was a man who had lived in his time and ahead of his time. Never were Czechs more conscious of it than now when they were commemorating the eighth anniversary of his death. Though Masaryk had been severely critical of Marxism and Catholicism, Communists and Catholics, with but bare mention of their grievances against him, devoted nearly all the space in their daily press to eulogies of the man and his achievements in letters, in statesmanship, in progressive thought.

To a history-minded people like the Czechs, Masaryk was the incarnation of the old and the new, the traditional and the radical, the pride of yesterday and the humility of today, the dignity of rebellion and the triumph of reason. He was the moral and intellectual bridge that spanned the nineteenth and twentieth centuries. Born in 1850, when Russia was still wallowing in serfdom and America's Southern states were still saddled with slavery, he passed out of life in 1937, when Russia was pondering the third Five-Year Plan and America was fighting the battle of the New Deal. No man during his lifetime had witnessed more of mankind's transition, often in storm and blood, from one epoch to another, or had experienced more of the agonies and the triumphs that accompanied the change.

Because of his origin—a Slav and the son of a lowly coachman—and because of his education and natural gifts, he was superbly equipped to learn the meaning and import of all he had studied and observed, all he had known and experienced. He was a Slav who never forgot his Slavism and a European who ever remembered his Europeanism. In his studies and travels, in his thoughts and sentiments, he oscillated all his life from West to East and from East to West, and strove to achieve within himself a reconciliation between the turbulences of yesterday and the tranquillities of tomorrow, between Russia's revolutionary upsurge and the West's untumultuous balance.

Ardent Czech, he was also a cosmopolite. He knew Russia and England, France and America, old Austria and old Germany, not only their history and their literature, but their languages and their character. Three times he had made lengthy pilgrimages to Yasnaya Polyana, Tolstoy's old home, to engage the famed Russian in controversy. While a student in Leipzig he fell in love with Charlotte Garrigue, a Boston girl "of French blood and American vigor," and after marrying her came to regard America as his second fatherland. He had lectured in the Universities of Vienna and Prague, in Chicago University, and in the London School of Slav Studies.

He was a Socialist who spurned Marxism, a humanitarian who abhorred sentimentalism, an individualist who detested the tyrannies of capitalism, a believer who disavowed the Church, a moralist who scorned doctrinaires, a realist who never was tempted to be a cynic. Nothing so vividly demonstrates the wisdom and the earthiness of the man than the story of the manner in which he settled a conflict between two distant relatives. They had come into an inheritance of farmland and forest and could not agree on the division of the property. "Let one of you," Masaryk was supposed to have advised, "divide the inheritance in the fairest way he can into two parts." The relatives assented without a murmur. "Now," Masaryk continued, "let the other one select the part that suits him best."

Above all, Masaryk was the acme of tolerance and fairmindedness. Though he had written of Marxism as "philosophical materialism, atheistic and non-spiritual," he yet lauded it for its influence on men's minds, for compelling "everyone to concern himself with philosophical and religious questions," and for its brilliant assault on the utopian and sentimental Socialism of an earlier era. Though he had attacked the Church for its ecclesiasticism and because, as he had expressed himself, "to its followers the Church is everything, the individual nothing," he had only words of eulogy for the encyclical of Pope Leo XIII (1891) and spoke of it as "Socialism and Christian democracy." Despite his aversion for the abuses of capitalism, in conversations with Tolstoy he upheld with vigor the great gifts the capitalist machine has bestowed on the world. He was amused at Tolstoy's sewing his own boots and going on foot when he could travel by train. To him these penitent protests against the machine age were as barren of spiritual as of practical good. He chided Tolstoy for wasting time which he might profitably devote to more worthy and more creative purposes.

He searched for truth and morality wherever he could find them, in the French Revolution and the Great Reformation, in Goethe and Tolstoy, in Francis Bacon and Dostoyevsky, in Plato and Comte, in English poetry and Slav folklore. Above all, he sought truth in his own nation's past and found it particularly in Jan Hus, the man who had said, "Teach the truth, love the truth, speak the truth, uphold the truth, live the truth." "Nothing is great," Masaryk wrote, "which is not the truth."

Two incidents in his life demonstrate with special clarity his readiness to battle for truth at enormous risk to his person and his position. In 1817 two manuscripts were discovered in the bell tower of a village church. Depicting the supreme virtues of Czech culture in the seventh and ninth centuries, the manuscripts in subsequent years created a sensation among Czech intellectuals. Jubilantly they hailed the find as proof of the superiority of Czech over German civilization in ancient times. But Masaryk branded them as forgeries, the creation of irresponsible Czech chauvinists. A storm of indignation greeted his pronouncements. But he struck back with all the power of his logic and erudition and won the battle for truth. "A na-

tion," he wrote, "that is not founded on truth does not deserve to
live." "The battle of the manuscripts," as the incident is known,
has since become not only a monument to Masaryk's integrity,
but a warning to intellectuals to be wary of generalizations,
whatever their source and however alluring, unless they are
grounded in truth.

A more dramatic incident arose in 1899. A young Jew named
Hilsner was accused of murdering two Christian girls to obtain
blood for ritual purposes. Masaryk made a searching study of the
case and of the evidence on which the court had convicted Hilsner. He convinced himself that the charge was a falsehood and
plunged into the fight for Hilsner's acquittal. Hilsner was
Czechoslovakia's Dreyfus, and Masaryk was Czechoslovakia's
Emile Zola. As in France, popular sentiment was arrayed against
the Jew. But like Zola, Masaryk defied popular sentiment. One
morning as he entered the classroom the students greeted him
with hoots and shouts. Masaryk listened to the abusive uproar
without saying a word. Then he stepped over to the blackboard,
picked up a piece of chalk, and wrote the word "work." Explaining what he meant, he said, "Don't drink, don't gamble, don't
be an idler, but work. That's what the Jew does, and if you want
to best him you must do the same." Once more he won the
battle of truth and dealt Czech anti-Semitism a shattering blow.

Then came the most remarkable episode in his life. At the age
of sixty-four, shortly after the outbreak of World War I, he
fled from Austria and set out on a mission to rebuild his people's
independence. In absentia an Austrian court charged him with
high treason and condemned him to death. But he proceeded
with energy and faith on his arduous mission. He knocked at
doors in Moscow and London, in Paris and Washington. Not
always was he accorded a welcome. Again and again he was
rebuffed. In the end he won converts to his cause among the
leaders of the Allied nations. But even while he was seeking

recognition for his fantastic project he was creating on paper its concrete fulfillment. He had left Austria with empty hands. But while wandering around the capitals of the Allied nations, he was assembling—with the aid of the youthful Beneš and Colonel Štefánik, the Slovak—not only the ideas but the institutions and the tools of the republic. He accumulated an exchequer. He built on foreign soil an army of one hundred thousand and placed it at the disposal of the Allies. In Pittsburgh he signed a concordat between Czechs and Slovaks. In Paris he and his associates made public a declaration of independence. In Geneva they drafted the constitution. The foreign-born republic was transferred home, and by the time Masaryk returned to Prague on December 21, 1918, the Czech Republic was in being—not only in principle but in program, not only in law but in discipline. No other nation liberated by World War I stabilized itself so swiftly or built its new national life upon so advanced a type of democracy.

One reason the republic was so eminently successful was that Masaryk taught his people the meaning of democracy—not only in the precepts and achievements of the past, but in the dangers and responsibilities of the present and in the uncertainties and opportunities of the future. He viewed democracy as a task that could be fulfilled only by individuals who possessed knowledge and by people who were "enlightened and decent." To the development of such individuals and such a people he dedicated himself with extraordinary zeal by personal example, by promulgating a system of highly liberal education, by glorifying the need and the joy of good reading, by fostering free and serious discussion.

He did more. Having been an eyewitness and a participant in the struggle for democracy in central Europe, he was only too keenly aware that "the aristocratic ideal of indolence and violence," which a dying but fighting feudalism was desperately seeking to keep alive, would, if allowed free rein, strangle a young democracy. Feudal lords had the education and the experience, the capacity for intrigue and the ruthlessness of manner, to despoil the people of the fruits of victory. Hence his inviolate antagonism to the aristocratic tradition, to the survival of feudalism in any guise, whether in landholding, in hereditary titles, in political precept, or in special privilege. By the effective but bloodless elimination of the pillars of feudalism in Czechoslovakia during his early years as President, he saved the nation from the perturbations and violences which during the interval between the two world wars shook Hungary, Poland, Rumania, other European nations.

He strove to infuse into the concept of democracy a fresh meaning and a fresh purpose. Faith alone, he constantly declared, was of no value unless sustained by untiring effort, by work and toil, both physical and moral. He had no "theory of a leisure class," because he did not believe in leisure, either for the highborn or for the lowborn. Nor did he content himself solely with a political definition of democracy. "A genuine democracy," he said, "must be economic and social as well as political."

What is more, no man in his time, not even the late Woodrow Wilson, stressed with greater eloquence the moral basis of democracy than did Masaryk. Like a spring torrent, it overflows all his pronouncements. "Truth conquers," like "reason and conscience," was a pillar of his political thinking and his social efforts. As Beneš sums it up, Masaryk taught Czechs "to respect our liberty and that of others, to be objective and tolerant, to honor truth . . . to esteem mankind, to emulate equality and toil, to exalt moral and spiritual values and religious faith, to adjust East and West within ourselves . . . and, above all, to remember that democracy is evolutionary, still striving for perfection and strength, still in process of development, and still beset with dangers."

The Bright Passage

Because he was supremely ethical in his thinking, Masaryk counseled the perusal of the great literature of the world and particularly of poetry. He was convinced that poetry inculcated in readers "ethical and social ideals." To the best of this writer's knowledge he was the only statesman of his own or any other time who besought political leaders to steep themselves in poetry, because poetry "educates the imagination, and in politics perhaps more than in any other aspect of life we need imagination, a vision of the future, and a capacity to penetrate the souls of others."

Here, then, he was, son of a coachman, a blacksmith's apprentice, who never ceased to revere the man of toil equally with the man of intellect. Alien to him were social snobbishness, a code of the elite, or any aristocratic tradition. Democrat and Socialist, radical and constitutionalist, rationalist and humanitarian, patriot and cosmopolite, Christian and freethinker, he was a genius in reconciling contradictions and in resolving paradoxes, which so often invite bitter clash or internecine warfare. In him fused the streams of political unrest and social tumult of the two centuries which his life had spanned. In him they had achieved clarification and formed into a pattern of democratic procedure which lifted the civilization of the first republic high, and which enabled it to withstand the torment and turbulence that assaulted it from within and without. Only the treachery of friends and Allies and the superior physical might of Nazi Germany finally wrecked it.

Little wonder that, when Emil Ludwig asked George Bernard Shaw who in his judgment was qualified to be President of a United States of Europe, Shaw replied: "There is only one man—Masaryk."

But the leadership of Masaryk and his devoted pupils would have been impossible had they not profited from the rich intellectual and spiritual heritage of their ancestors; of Jan Hus, the religious reformer and social rebel; of Jan Komenský, the eminent and, for his day, highly advanced educator; of František Palacký, the historian, who reinterpreted the Czech past in terms of the rising liberalism of the nineteenth century. Even the more remote ancestors contributed, particularly the enlightened and enterprising kings like Prince Wenceslaus, George of Poděbrady, and Charles IV. Out of all that these leaders have done and bequeathed to them, the Czechs have acquired an individuality of their own. Its ingredients on the intellectual side are humanism and positivism, and on the practical side simplicity of manner, sobriety of judgment, diligence of effort, and comprehension of and competence in the manipulation of the machine age. Despite the tragedy that has accompanied it, theirs has been an altogether different history from that of Russia, Poland, Bulgaria, Yugoslavia, any other Slav peoples. That is why in this moment of crisis, their own and that of the world, they are in a position to create a new pattern of revolution, new in philosophical concept, in social outlook, in practical application.

Watching the crowds that poured in and out of the tree-shaded, flower-swept cemetery in the village of Lány, one could not help being moved by their reverence for the man they had come to honor. However much they might disagree with some of his views, they recognized in him a teacher who had helped mold their minds and their personalities.

Everyone who came brought flowers, wreaths from florists' shops, handfuls of nasturtiums from house plants, daisies and cornflowers freshly plucked from the fields. Mothers gave the flowers to children so they could lay them on the grave, already refulgent with roses and gladiolas, asters and forget-me-nots.

The grave was as simple as Tolstoy's in Yasnaya Polyana, for like Tolstoy, Masaryk had willed that no monument be erected on his tomb. He wanted people to think of him in death as they had known him in life, a simple man, a blacksmith's son who in the days of his greatest triumph lived a simple life, partook of simple fare, slept on a plain iron cot, even as he had done in the years of greatest trials and adversities.

Masaryk is one reason for the audacity and orderliness of the Czechoslovakian revolution.

Part Two: THE TWO OCTOBERS

12. Doctor of Reason

By accident rather than design Prague's official proclamation of the new post-war social order occurred in October, the same month that witnessed Soviet ascension to power in Russia twenty-eight years earlier. In the Soviet vocabulary October is a hallowed word—streets and precincts, villages and collective farms, schools and factories, even children bear the name October or a newly coined derivative of the word. In Soviet thought and parlance October is the symbol of the death of the old and the birth of the new Russia, indeed of a whole new world.

In Czechoslovakia the transition signalized by the proclamation of the nationalization decree, October 24, 1945, has not made October a symbol; it does not, as in Russia, represent the emergence of a new man and a new mankind. This is only one of many differences in the meaning of two Octobers.

Yet the actuality unfolded in the decree and the ideas and the philosophy it implies, though a result of a hard-fought battle between four political parties, are destined in the years to come to reshape and reshuffle not only the relationship of man to the community and of man to man, but the thoughts and the motivations, the hopes and the ambitions of all Czechs and Slovaks. The process, a growth rather than a compulsion, will be slower, much slower than in Russia. The direction will not always be the same. Links with the past will not be cast aside like false idols which it is a sin to recognize, as Russia originally did. But in the course of the coming years the refashioning of the human personality, however slowly, is inevitable. The absence of external fanfare and of dramatic episode such as accompanied the advent of Sovietism in Russia, the austere, almost frigid, sobriety of language and manner with which the decree was announced, cannot belittle its magnitude nor detract from its momentousness. In intent and scope it spells Revolution with a capital *R,* for its provisions make Czechoslovakia, next to Russia, the most Socialist-industrialized country in the world.

The first nation in liberated Europe to have proclaimed its economic break with the past, its program dwarfs the intent of the British Labor party, which won its election on a Socialist platform. The British plan envisages nationalization of coal, transport, power, shipping, steel and iron within a five-year period. No such gradualism or "sparring with time," as an Englishman put it, has actuated the Czech and Slovak planners. With one stroke they have brought under social ownership all commercial banks, all insurance companies, and at least three fifths of the manufacturing capacity of the country. But if the event demonstrates closer identity in economic intent with Russia's October, it testifies no less clearly to a sharp divergence from it.

Fully to appreciate the contrasts and identities between the Russian and Czech revolutions, we must inform ourselves of the philosophy which fathered the Czech October, the conditions which brought about this revolution, the nature and magnitude of the encroachment on the old social order, particularly as contrasted with Russia's October. Each of these subjects merits a separate chapter.

It is no accident that the first two presidents of the Czechoslovak Republic have been university professors. Eduard Beneš, like the late Thomas Masaryk, rose to his exalted position through the university lecture hall. Among other things, this demonstrates the abiding esteem of Czechs for education, the old folk belief so common to peasant peoples, that the learned man is the wise man, the sage whose judgments are sound, whose counsels may be trusted. A distinguishing feature of Czech history is the predilection of the people to follow and to venerate not the man of military glory but of intellectual achievement. It is this predilection that has given rise to the saying: "Knowledge and work are our salvation."

But Beneš and Masaryk were no ordinary university professors. Accomplished scholars in sociology, philosophy, and history, they viewed the tasks and problems before them not only in terms of immediate impact but of historical perspective, associating the event of today with the antecedents of yesterday and again with the trends of tomorrow. The question, "Where is the world going?" was always a determining circumstance in the formulation of their judgments, the application of their principles. Ardent Czechs, they remained unswayed by an unreasoned nationalism. Not drama but logic, not sentiment but reason were their guides. They clung to the conviction that they could and would reap their richest harvest, not by isolating but by linking their little country with the ever-pressing *progressive* forces in Europe and the world. As Beneš himself has phrased it: "After World War I Masaryk and I stressed the fact that we must proceed in a spirit of European and world politics, that we have to place our national problems within the framework of world history, that we had to learn where the world was going and act accordingly, but in conformity with truth and right, with human morality and a justly determined philosophy of history."

Ethics, like history, has ever been a conspicuous feature in the thinking of the two college professors who—not by dynastic right and privilege but by the choice of their people—succeeded each other as President of their nation. Elected and re-elected, they are the only presidents Czechoslovakia has had.

World-mindedness and awareness of historic circumstance, as well as Czech fortitude and hard-headedness, enabled Beneš to weather his years of exile (1938–45) and endure all its tumults and torments with an intellectual poise matched only by his inordinate patience. I know of no other diplomat in the Western world who so keenly understood Hitler and the Germans, Stalin and the Russians, America and England, and who foresaw so truthfully and interpreted so accurately the forthcoming sweep of events. Munich meant to Beneš world war. That was why shortly after Munich, with German pressure already strong enough to denature the quality of the republic, he hastened to exile himself from his native land, so that he might once more start work on the resurrection of the nation's independence.

The Russo-German pact of August 1939 signalized to him only one thing—war between Russia and Germany. The Russo-Finnish war further reinforced this conviction. Once Germany launched hostilities in Europe, and England and France unsheathed their swords against Hitler, he was firm in the belief that American isolationism would shatter itself on the rocks of international realities. While the Germans were steam-rolling over the Russian plains, roaring on toward Moscow, Leningrad, Kiev, Odessa, Rostov, Stalingrad, and leading statesmen and generals, with scarcely an exception, predicted the imminent collapse of the Red Army, he took voluble exception to this almost universal judgment. He summoned all the logic and erudition at his command to persuade the London Poles, who were basing their diplomacy not on the victory but the defeat of Russia, to reverse their policy and to seek an end to their ancient and fiery feud with Moscow. "I told General Sikorski," Beneš told this writer, "that the Red Army would roll the Germans back, would occupy his country and mine, would push on to Berlin, and that he and his colleagues must shape their diplomacy accordingly." Sikorski was so shocked by Beneš's prognostication that he exclaimed, "That would be terrible!" But Beneš pressed on with his argument. "Yes, yes, Sikorski, that's what's going to happen, and don't delude yourself into thinking it won't." How different would have been the position of Poland today had the London Poles heeded Beneš's sage counsel.

It is no secret that because of his views and convictions our own State Department and the British Foreign Office did not always regard Beneš without suspicion. Despite the occasional unfriendliness of the State Department and the Foreign Office, Beneš did not permit himself to be panicked by immediate catastrophe or to be swerved from his long-range plans by diplomatic pressures, however severe. He waited patiently for events to justify his prognostications and validate his judgments.

What was more natural than that he should seek an appraisal of the Czechoslovakian revolution not in terms of local and parochial but European and universal forces. Parochialism is a sin which he, like his predecessor, has valiantly striven to eschew. "I refuse," he said, "to consider the different events as separate and independent parts of the dramatic evolution of the world today. I take them all as a whole and synthetically, and I try to find in them their historical, philosophical meaning. The crisis preceding World War I, then the war itself, the Russian Revolution, the other post-war revolutions, the struggle that was waged between the two wars, the birth of Fascism and National Socialism, and the serious crisis of post-war democracy, World War II, the fall of Fascism, the present endeavors to build up the new democracies—all these are to me one big single ensemble of events, each connected with the other. Together they form the characteristics of our epoch, which began approximately with the first years of the twentieth century and are not ending by far with the present post-war time, nor even with the second half of the twentieth century." Beneš does not coddle himself into the easy consolation that world conferences and world organizations alone can still the turmoil now raging in the world and bring tranquillity to mankind by immediate agreements and resolutions, however sane and wise, however far-reaching and far-seeing. To him the struggle for world order will continue for a long time, very long, beyond the years of the present century.

On December 15, 1945, in the ancient and resplendent Spanish ballroom of the slender-lined and sun-drenched Prague Castle, from which Roman emperors and Bohemian kings once ruled a vast empire, I attended a memorable ceremony. Amid the display of old banners and costumes, ancient scepters and standards, all lush with design and effulgent with color, the University of Prague conferred on Beneš the honorary degree of doctor of laws. In the presence of the foreign diplomatic corps and the most distinguished audience that had assembled in Prague since its liberation, Beneš took the occasion to answer the ever-vexing question: "Whither are we going and whither are we to go?"

In this writer's judgment his is the fullest and most illuminating pronouncement that anyone in the Western world has uttered since the tragic days of Munich. He spoke of the epoch in which we are living as one of the stormiest in the world's history, brimming over with revolutionary eruptions. He termed this epoch a "transition, a break, a creation." Frankly he admitted that he was in no position to assure himself or anyone else that his generation, which has endured two world wars and has "experienced all these moments of distress and beauty, of military defeats and victories, of human hopelessness and jubilation," was or could be happy with its lot in life. Only the following generation could say yes or no and clear away the doubt. But he warned his audience not to treat any single event, whether Munich or the fall of Poland, Yugoslavia, Greece, France, as sundered and separate from "the big tide of history." To him each of these was only an episode, a rivulet swelling a world flood. Yet, he insisted, whatever else these events may signify, whatever the immediate setbacks and tragedies they may spew forth, in the long course of human events they cannot dam up the flow of progress. Humanity will and must triumph. "This is its fate, the law of evolution, the law of its maintenance." Always the optimist, Beneš refuses to be stampeded into pessimism and despair.

Since this is "one world," the fight for world security, for world culture, is "one and indivisible." A new law, he declared, is in process of birth, a revolutionary law, emerging from and superseding the old law by which mankind lived and throve.

What, asked Beneš, is the nature of the new or revolutionary law?

In part at least, he continued, the answer must be sought in mankind's past. "At the end of the last century, when publishing his study on suicide, Masaryk, like so many of his contemporaries, had arrived at the conclusion that the exaggerated individualism of the romantic nineteenth-century man had brought him to a crisis which created a person extremely sick and abnormal, terminating his abnormal existence with an abnormal end—suicide." Nor did the end of the nineteenth century witness a mitigation of the excessive individualism of earlier years. It pressed on, untamed and unscathed, into the present. The liberal world of that time was an expression of this collective individualism and found and still finds itself in the midst of a crisis with specific attributes of its own.

What are these attributes? What is the nature of this liberal world? "Politically, it is a society with a quarreling mankind and with numerous anarchistic political parties, subverting in their fight the nation as a whole. Economically, it is a society with an intensively cultivated capitalism and industrialism, provoking an inexorable class fight between exploiters and exploited. Socially, it is a tense struggle between the man of the past with feudal aristocratic conceptions on the one hand, and the man of the enlightened mind, seeking to assert the equality of people, on the other. Culturally and artistically, it is a society which has grown flatly aesthetic, living in a chaos of ideas and tastes, having neither literary nor artistic style. In short, it is a sick and uncertain society, looking for something new and unable to find it."

One of the last expressions of this society, "a sick expression of the nineteenth-century man, was the attempt to push his extreme individualism and subjectivism to the absurd dictatorial Titanism of Fascists and Nazis." It was a society which was swelling and bursting with all possible antis and "scarcely any pros." It denied and mocked everything positive and creative. "It was anti-liberal and anti-Socialist, anti-rational and anti-universalist, anti-pacifist and anti-Semitic. In spirit and in deed it was anti-human. It ended like the more logical of the men who led it—in suicide."

As early as 1942, Beneš continued, he had formulated for himself the three sets of problems that would beset the post-war world: the annihilation of Fascism the world over and the moral turpitudes it had spawned, and the elevation in its place "of the spiritual and moral values of democracy"; that is, of political and social and, above all, "spiritual and ethical freedom"; the creation of a "new political organization in Europe and the world—the building up of a new and more lasting peace on the basis of a restored and strengthened international democracy; lastly, the regeneration, transformation, and reconstruction of pre-war democracy into a new post-war democracy."

In most countries, Beneš emphasized, the war had been accompanied step by step with an internal revolution, a rebellion against the forms and mores that proved inadequate and catastrophic in the pre-war years. In some countries, he explained, the struggle for internal rehabilitation and readjustment had already involved them in civil wars. But all these struggles, he predicted, will "culminate in social and economic revolution." The world cannot go back and nobody has the power to push it back to its pre-war condition, if only because the democracy of the pre-war years was riddled with faults so serious that they actually aided the rise of "totalitarian dictatorships." If democracy is to chasten itself of these faults it must be reformed and regenerated, tightened and strengthened. But how?

For one thing, the political democracy of our times must evolve "into a social and economic democracy." Nor, warned Beneš, must anyone be under the delusion that the goal is easy of attainment. But it must be achieved. There is no other alternative. "It is our only cure for the sick world and the sick man bequeathed to us by the nineteenth century."

But where are the oracles of the new day and what are the cures and the remedies they propose?

In reply Beneš proceeds to expound the answer of Marxism to the question and then explains his own concept of Socialism, pointing out the divergences as well as the possible basis of reconciliation between the two. He says:

"When the individualistic society of the nineteenth century began to show more and more clearly signs of disintegration,

169

the doctrines of Marx and Engels, supplemented by Lenin, set up against its romanticism and subjectivism the idea of a new man, the realist, the objective man of the twentieth century. The advocates of this new doctrine believe in dialectical materialism and insist that society moves through the development of thesis and antithesis. So against individualism they set up an extreme collectivism. Against the idea that the individual is primary and the state secondary, they launched the idea that the state is primary and the individual secondary. Even though I am formulating these ideas quite schematically it is a fact that this is the way they were worked out in daily politics and in this way they are reacted to in spirit.

"It is also in this spirit of absolutes that people speak of and attack Communist and Socialist totalitarianism. A frequent protest, which at times is not sufficiently critical, is that we have just overthrown one totalitarianism and now we want to create another."

As for himself, Beneš declared, he shared neither this fear nor the spirit in which it is expressed. To him the present events conveyed an altogether different meaning, and he offered three reasons for his opinion:

"In the first place, this has been a world war, and solution of its problems can be only on a world basis. Every effort to bring about a different solution will be wrecked on the fundamental necessity that the three world powers, the Soviet Union, Great Britain, and the United States, must solve the problems of the war together, in unity and with all the other states.

"In the second place, these problems include, as I have already said, the destruction of the Nazi legacy in the realm of human liberty and the restoration of the spiritual and ethical values of modern democracy. This is by no means a local or temporary object—it is a world aim, independent of time. It is and always will remain one of the chief ideals of every human society. In substance the Soviet Union has also this aim and cannot ever have a different aim. You can find exponents of Communism who defend the necessity of temporary dictatorship of the proletariat. I assert that the principles of really progressive democracy make this unnecessary and that it is for such a democracy to prevent dictatorship by sensible efforts constantly to improve the social order.

"Thirdly, the Soviet Union and the Russian Communists themselves acknowledge that the transformation of a liberal democracy to higher forms—a socializing democracy—should and can come about gradually, step by step, by reasonable evolution of the economic, social, geographic, and ethnic conditions of the national societies concerned. I am of the opinion that gradual co-operation of the Soviet Union with the rest of the world will lead to a general acceptance of this view. It will be a link between the great powers. It will be a basis for the co-existence of the Soviet regime with the other regimes, for the Soviets will continue to develop toward greater and greater individual freedom within the framework of their Socialist state."

Yet, Beneš cautioned, the world must remember one irrefutable truth, namely: "We can never go back to the kind of liberal society [of excessive individualism] which Masaryk so resolutely criticized and condemned in this country. Here, in this republic, we cannot return to the year of 1938. We must accept the view that liberal society has been theoretically and practically overpowered, that we are at a transition from one social order to another, and that we are trying to find the new social forms of the future."

What are these forms? In answer Beneš cites the alternatives before mankind:

"Does this mean that according to dialectical materialism we must jump from the thesis of liberal society into the antithesis of collectivist society? Does this mean that we must obey some austere sociological objectivism and create at once the juridical forms of a new society uncompromisingly free of class distinctions and entirely Socialist? This is not the opinion of those who do not accept dialectical materialism as a philosophy of history. We hold instead that it is equally possible to believe in a different scheme of the evolution of society and that in any case actual practice is quite different from theory. For those who are real democrats, mutual respect is possible for both these views."

Further reinforcing his tolerant opposition to the theory of dialectical materialism, Beneš declared, "No modern developed society, if it does not wish to lay itself open to dangerous reverses, can act in practice according to the dialectical materialist philosophy of history. Instead it is compelled to advance itself realistically, to transform itself gradually. It does not pass from one stage into another which has no juridical forms or temporary institutions. It accepts to a considerable extent the juridical continuity of the preceding regime and transfers it to the new regime. It fights for this continuity and fights with it. It seeks a gradual, smooth transition from one phase of society into another." Even the Soviet Union had to proceed and is proceeding in this manner: "At the beginning of the great Revolution it adopted a number of uncompromising and extremely radical measures, then proceeded more slowly, and even receded somewhat from its original position. Today it expressly acknowledges the necessity for each nation and state to proceed in accordance with its own economic, social, and cultural conditions and potentialities."

But not all nations are alike because their past is unlike; therefore, the tensions and conflicts within them are unlike. Wherein lie the principal differences? "States and societies in which the masses of the people are immature culturally and politically bring

172

about the transition from one juridical system to another, mostly by a violent revolution. As a rule, mature states manage to achieve the transition peacefully and without violence. In these states so-called revolutions are achieved by means of evolution, sometimes rapid, sometimes slow."

Czechoslovakia, according to Beneš, definitely belongs to the category of a mature state. Yet despite conditions that favor a peaceful transition from one epoch to another, Czechoslovakia can attain its goal only if the people are unified, by means of a program that not only maintains but furthers this unity and by action which "proceeds quietly, without violence, with all the principal groups of the nation participating, and always in the spirit of world evolution."

To Beneš it is clear that on the continent of Europe the liberalism of the pre-war days is dead or dying and that the excessive individualism of the nineteenth century from which it stemmed is beyond anyone's power to re-establish or resurrect. It would therefore be suicidal for a little nation like his own to resume its national life at the point where the Germans had made an end of it. Too much has since happened, too much substance has been squandered, too much blood has been shed, too many sanctities have been shattered, too many illusions have been blown away, too many contradictions have been whipped up, too many hates have been unleashed, to wrest security and peace, good morals and good living, from the principles and practices that obtained in 1938. Though its planners and perpetrators thought only of perpetuating the old world that they knew, Munich is the grave in which the old world is buried and the very agreement by which it is remembered is its eternal tombstone.

Beneš's emphasis on world evolution is as significant as his tolerant repudiation of dialectical materialism. The Marxian-

minded Russian and the Marxian-minded Czech will welcome
the one, will more than frown on the other. But Beneš and those
who think as he does, and these include the overwhelming mass
of the Czech population, do not believe that conformity or
identity in philosophical approach is indispensable to a successful solution of the crisis of the moment. The Communists may
make as much as they choose of their philosophy without hin-
drance from any governmental agency. Those who disagree
with them may no less stanchly abide by their conviction. The
important thing for all to observe and take to heart is that,
while there may be more than one conception of the laws of
historical progress, there can be no more than one policy to
meet the challenge of the times. The immature countries, or
those with a feudal or semi-feudal heritage, whose peoples have
had a limited acquaintance with democratic procedure or a
limited experience in the creation and operation of a modern
mechanized industry, and who have much historical dross to
shake off before they can attain a unified clarity of purpose, may
not be in a position to make the transition from the old to the new
epoch in history without internecine conflict or civil war. But a
mature country, and Czechoslovakia is that, can achieve unity
of purpose and policy with no such disastrous eruption. The
pacing of the advance may be slower in the West than in the
East, but by virtue of the immutability of the law of evolution
both are destined to attain a more or less similar end. Only, one
"must not fear to go ahead and act boldly."

13. *The Roots of the Revolution*

Students of the post-war revolutionary upsurge in Europe, with its emphasis on nationalization of private enterprise, must reckon with the deadly moral and economic blows which Nazi Germany dealt the institution in the countries it conquered or occupied. By luring or badgering native financiers and industrialists into collaboration, the Nazis discredited them in the eyes of their own people, above all with those groups in the resistance movements, out of which have sprung dominating factions of the new governments.

By looting state treasuries, banks, industries, Nazi Germany plunged country after country into bankruptcy. Czechoslovakia was a major victim of Nazi economic plundering. Its holdings in the International Bank of Basel, Switzerland, some thirty million dollars, were by right of conquest and with the speedy consent of the British Government appropriated by the German invader. No Communist or any other revolutionary propaganda, no Comintern strategy and intrigue, however cunningly conceived, could have sapped the moral and material lifeblood of capitalism as did Hitler. Though he had mustered enormous support in his own country and in foreign lands by posing as the St. George who would slay the Bolshevik dragon and rid capitalism forever of its grisly nightmares, he, far more than all the Communist and other revolutionary parties, has shaken and loosened the very roots of capitalism in Europe. The fact is that though pre-war Europe was rife with social conflict it was not the caldron of revolutionary ferment that post-war Europe is.

All the more disastrous was Nazi plundering in Czechoslovakia because banks and cartels controlled an overwhelming share of the nation's industry. The Baťa family was the outstanding exception. Like Henry Ford, Thomas Baťa frowned on "money lenders" and shut his doors to banks and bankers. But the Živnostenská bank alone controlled seventy of the largest companies in the sugar, chemical, coal, iron, metal, textile, ceramic, alcohol, malting, food, cellulose, paper, building-materials, and other industries. Rarely was a large-scale enterprise in the hands of an individual family. About one hundred cartels, with many of which the afore-mentioned bank was closely associated, dominated the most vital manufacturing establishments of the country.

With banks stripped of gold and foreign assets and weighted down with worthless German paper certificates, the industries that depended on them were likewise sucked dry of substance. The banks might have staved off insolvency and rehabilitated their industrial empire with foreign, particularly American, loans or by inviting foreign capital into partnership. In either event the nation would have had to face more foreign direction in its internal policy and more foreign pressure in external affairs than it had known in the pre-Munich days or was in a mood to tolerate. "Foreign money," remarked a Prague editor, "would then rule our roost."

In such an ardently patriotic country as Czechoslovakia, had any Cabinet Minister or political leader presumed to whisper

176

such a proposal, his prestige and position would have endured no longer than the time it would require for his words to become known to the people. Three hundred years of servitude under Austria; Munich, which was an outright manipulation by foreign powers; six years of German occupation have seared the Czech mind with an implacable distrust of any and all foreign encroachments on their independence. A general strike by labor would have been one of the first fruits of the effort to mortgage a substantial part of the nation's economic institutions to foreign investors.

Above all, it would have stirred a crisis in Prague's relations with Moscow. Always explosively sensitive to actual or potential foreign intrusion into the economy and politics of a border state, Moscow would have assumed rightly or wrongly that Prague was conniving with foreign capital to build an enemy outpost against the Soviets. It is well enough for an American observer in Prague to brand nationalization as "some more of this Bolshevik nonsense." But Czechs must ponder their own condition and accommodate themselves to their own scheme of salvation. People who regard the Czech nationalization as "nonsense" fail to grasp or identify themselves with a condition of life and a process of thought contrary to their own; this incapacity has been not the least prodigal sin of American diplomacy, especially of the more ancient career men.

Once nationalization became the rock on which to erect the new social order, its fulfillment was facilitated by an array of economic and ideological circumstances peculiar to Czechoslovakia. Germans and Austrians had held a powerful position in the country's financial and industrial life. For example, the Vítkovice steel plant, the largest in the land, was the property of two Austrian families who directed its destinies from Vienna; fifty-five per cent of its clerical staff and ninety per cent of its executive authority were in German hands. More than ninety per cent of the paper, kaolin and porcelain industries were under German domination. In the Catholic *People's Democracy* I once read the following enlightening item: "The German specialties [in Czechoslovakia] include in particular the manufacture of ball bearings, typewriters, sewing machines, cameras, cinema equipment, optical instruments, special lathes, electric lighters, spark plugs, lighting installation for motorcars and motorcycles, spray pumps for Diesel engines, arms of all types, precision instruments, metal toys, pharmaceutical products, and a varied assortment of chemicals." The textile and glass industries, which in pre-war days constituted the chief source of export items, were likewise overwhelmingly in German hands. Glass was one of the sickest industries in the country, but because of its importance in foreign trade it was the beneficiary of no little government patronage.

Since the new Czech law confiscates the properties of Nazis and their collaborators, and since the Germans were overwhelmingly both, the state took over their holdings. "Are we," said Beneš, "to divide these among Czech capitalists and industrialists, according to some arbitrarily chosen principle and criterion, or is it not better to give them to the state and the nation as partial reparation for the enormous war damage caused us by Germany?" Here, then, was an assemblage of business enterprises—banks, steel and iron, textile and glass, lands and forests, dispossessed of former ownership and ripe for picking by the state.

Nor was the first republic without experience in public and state ownership. In the management and proprietorship of large enterprises, in its laws and public benefactions, in its social and economic ministrations to the people, pre-war Czechoslovakia was one of the most statist nations in Europe. The state was the proprietor of 1,062,500 acres of forest. It rigidly controlled all forests. Only the state forester could authorize the

Vladislav Hall in Hradčany Castle, Prague, where presidents are inaugurated

Dr. Eduard Beneš, President of the Czechoslovak Republic

cutting of trees, and then with the obligation that a like number be replanted within two years. The land reform of the first republic made the state heir to a number of highly mechanized feudal estates, the property of Austrian nobles, which for economic reasons and for experimental purposes it operated as state enterprises. Salt and potato-brewed alcohol were state monopolies. Tobacco was a state enterprise; the Jachymov radium mines, the near-by radium spas were state properties. Many hotels and health resorts and sanitariums were under government ownership. Railways, telegraph and telephone, like the post office, and several hundred bus lines were operated by the state. In the timber trade, the brewing industry, the production of armaments, including Škoda, the state was a majority stockholder. The fisheries were a state monopoly; the commercial air lines were a state project. The broadcasting stations were state-owned. Employment agencies were the sole concern of the state. In 1937 there were 414 such agencies, and they placed over a million applicants for work. The state was in business and in competition with private enterprise on a gigantic scale, quite unknown in pre-war England, France, or America.

So were and are the municipalities and the co-operatives. The city of Prague, for example, owns and manages not only the street railways, the power plants, the waterworks, the slaughter house, but is one of the largest landlords in the capital. In pre-war years it also operated a number of banks, including the Prague Municipal Savings Bank, with deposits of eighty million dollars, and a highly prosperous Municipal Insurance Company. In the countryside public ownership was even more pronounced, as the reader will recall from the description of the village of Strážnice. In 1935 one third of the savings in the country were on deposit in the co-operative banks.

Czechoslovakia was unusual among parliamentary countries, not only in Europe but in the world, because it knew few

labor strikes. I was astounded when the manager of the Vítkovice steel mill, the largest in the country, told me that the
plant had not been harassed by a strike since 1923. In Třinec,
which is only second to Vítkovice in the output of steel, there
had been no strike since 1919! This was neither accident nor
miracle. State sponsorship of a highly progressive labor code and
a highly ramified system of social and individual benefactions
is the chief reason for the comparative absence of labor upheavals between the two world wars.

The Factory Council is no creation of the present government.
Its influence and functions have been expanded, its role has
been spiritedly dramatized, but it was a creation of the first republic. It was obligatory in all workshops with thirty or more
employees. As defined by law, its task was "to protect and support the economic, social, and cultural interests of the employees." Together with the Labor Arbitration Boards the Factory
Councils channeled industrial disputes into compromise and
agreement.

The nation's social legislation was a solid bulwark of internal
peace. The code was far-reaching and well integrated, contain-
ing enlightened though not always adequate safeguards for
children, youth, women; for work hours, vacations, here and
there employment security; for injury and death, dependency
and maternity benefits, modest dowries for brides. The state
embarked on extensive public works—building dams, highways,
apartment houses, railroads, and other projects as a means of
combating unemployment.

With such a far-reaching social program the Czech worker
and office employee, whether privately or publicly engaged,
was guaranteed substantial protection against the everyday hazards and mishaps of working and living. Never intended to provide luxury, not always ample, often quite niggardly, this protection was a vital part of the worker's life, his thinking, his

attitude toward the state and society. He could feel that he was not all alone in the world, dependent on charity, or on his own resources and wits, to breast the tide of adversity or misfortune. Since in the official pronouncements of the present government and of all political parties, the Catholic as much as the Communist, nationalization promises to lift his welfare, his security, his education, his opportunity for advancement, to an ever-mounting level, once the machinery of production attains full speed, he is, with or without benefit of Marxism, its stanchest supporter.

This history of co-operative ownership, of state and municipal proprietorship, of social ministrations and personal benefactions, did much to prepare Czechoslovakia for nationalization. Even for the business community its coming could not be the shock that it would have been in countries in which individual initiative and individual effort have been the custom and the law of the land.

Nor are business folk wanting who, despite losses to themselves, are welcoming the nationalization decree. Here, for example, is Engineer Jerie, president of the Northern Coal Mines, formerly the largest and richest coal-mining corporation in the country. During the afternoon I spent with him in his extraordinarily artistic and livable home in the Beskydy Mountains he talked at length of himself, his trials with the Nazis, who had sent him to a concentration camp because he refused to work for them, and of the economic plight of his nation. "We're bankrupt, completely bankrupt," he said. "We must nationalize. We cannot depend too much on foreign help. Foreign investors would be interested not in our country and our people but in their dividends, which would have to be paid them in foreign exchange, just as we were doing under the first republic. They would drain us of our balances in foreign lands. But if we nationalize we can use foreign exchange for the further development of our own resources and for the improvement of the lot of our people. We must be masters in our own house and use our profits for our own good."

Subsequently, in the company of a representative of the American Embassy, I listened for several hours to former textile manufacturers and bank executives, who repeated almost word for word Mr. Jerie's arguments in favor of nationalization. Let no one underestimate the power of the nationalist idea or the sentiment of patriotism among Czechs of all classes, regardless of wealth.

The similarities and the contrasts between the Russian and Czech October can be understood only when measured by or set against the similarities and the contrasts in the conditions that molded the life and the thoughts of both nations. What would Russia have been like had she, prior to 1917, attained the level of living and culture of pre-Munich Czechoslovakia? What would Czechoslovakia be like today had she been no more advanced educationally, industrially, or politically than was Russia in 1917? It is futile to make decisive comparisons when so much fortuitous speculation is involved. Yet the conclusion is inescapable that neither nation would have been what it is today.

There is no question but that the Russian October has blown a fresh energy into the Socialist idea which has been floating around Europe for over a century. In one form or another it is exercising a drive or a spell over all war-ravaged nations, particularly those which Germany has bankrupted and has emptied of the good life they had once known.

Moreover, it has always been this writer's contention that, despite its flamboyant Marxian cloak, the Russian Revolution has been essentially not an international but a national event, stemming from sources and forces latent and innate in Russian history, culture, geography, the character and the manner of the Russian people.

The Czech revolution, which in its economic aspects is of the same pattern as the Russian, but nowhere nearly as all-inclusive, must likewise be viewed as essentially of an indigenous Czech nature. Beneš's interpretation of the inevitability of the revolution and the direction it must pursue makes that abundantly manifest. Only if it were pushed out of its own mold in disregard of the nation's history, in subversion of the character of Czech humanity, would it stir up disaffections and collisions, the end and consequences of which no man, Czech or foreigner, is in a position to forecast.

14. The New Economic Order

Soviet Russia started out with a complete negation of the principles and the practice of private enterprise. Czechoslovakia has neither abrogated the principle nor outlawed the practice.

Originally Russia branded owners or holders of so-called functional property as outcasts and pariahs, stripped them of citizenship, banned their children from the universities, subjected them to unending social contumely, and in other ways caused them to suffer protracted periods of arduous and heartbreaking expiation of their "sins." In Czechoslovakia not a shadow of social contumely, not a glimmer of social discrimination has been visited on anyone because of ownership of property, however massive or extensive, and regardless of whether or not any or all of it was liable to nationalization. The principle of equality of citizenship and all that it implies in opportunity for education, public office, or service in nationalized enterprise has never been trespassed. The only exception is former collaborators with the enemy.

In Russia the method of expropriation was revolutionary

and coercive. In Czechoslovakia nationalization was achieved legally and constitutionally. Differences in philosophical approach, in historical background, in immediate heritage, as outlined in preceding chapters, have made for differences in immediate objective and in mode of procedure.

In the field of manufacturing and finance the Czech decree abolishes private ownership in the upper brackets, some in the middle, but leaves it virtually untouched in the lower categories. The final and basic test of whether a firm or plant shall be nationalized is the number of employees during a specific period of time. No manufacturing or productive enterprise with more than five hundred employees is exempted, and few with one hundred and fifty or less are included, in the decree. Small industry, which is the specialty of artisans and craftsmen, particularly numerous and thriving in villages and small towns, remains untouched by the new social order. In Russia during the first Five-Year Plan only those artisans who did their own work or maintained no more than two apprentices were left to their own devices; the pressure, direct and indirect, and always powerful, was to draw them, too, into co-operative or state-supervised associations. In consequence the woodwork and pottery, the leather goods and hardware, the cakes and the candies and other products of home industries, which were always a bright feature of Russian market places, all but disappeared during the first Five-Year Plan. Nor had they become abundant in the immediate pre-war years. In Czechoslovakia, on the contrary, the makers of such products are beginning to flourish again, and neither the farmer nor the housekeeper suffers from a serious shortage of any of the commodities in which they specialize.

The Czech attitude toward the printed word, which Russia has always regarded as an exclusive state or party monopoly, is particularly illuminating. Not a single publishing house has been nationalized, yet not a daily newspaper and only one periodical, *Kritický Měsíčník,* have been left to individual ownership. But the state has not taken over the press. Regarded as an instrument of enlightenment and education that is supposed to be wielded with earnest awareness of social and national responsibility, the daily press is now in the hands not of individuals but of organizations—political parties, cultural and professional bodies, such as the intelligentsia, the universities, the war veterans, the Army, the trade unions, the Sokol physical-culture society, the youth organizations, scientific and benevolent associations. The churches, of course, continue as formerly to publish their own religious and philosophical journals.

Books are still the sole concern of the book publisher. He alone is responsible for the manuscripts he accepts and the books he prints. Yet it is well to remember that, as under the first republic, most of the largest publishing houses are either co-operative associations or partnerships between private capital and political parties. There are few completely independent book publishers, and on these the nationalization decree does not encroach.

Thus the Socialism that Czechoslovakia is sponsoring is centered chiefly in finance, insurance, and industry. Outside of these fields there is insignificant nationalization. There is none in retail trade and, save for some products that come from nationalized industries, not much in the wholesale business.

Land is untouched by the decree, and the peasant is in full control of his farm. Nearly four million acres of arable land, three million more of forest, which were formerly the possession of Germans, have been taken over by the state. Some of the newly acquired arable acres are so denuded of fertility and are so inconveniently located, on high hills or mountains, that they have been converted into grass or pasture. But more than three and a half million acres of tillable land have been allotted as individual homesteads to Czech families who were land-poor or had no land at all.

The Czech peasantry has always been inclined toward co-operation, and the government is pledged to aid the co-operatives and extend and expand their activities. How far co-operation will proceed in the field of tillage, once mechanized implements are introduced, remains to be seen. But not even the Communists are advocating the type of collectivization which Russia initiated at such extraordinary cost in livestock slaughtered by the peasants, who killed one animal out of two in protest. Nor do Czech Communists desire the social upheaval of the Russian Revolution, accompanied as it was by the "liquidation of the kulaks," and the resultant expulsion from their homes and exile to remote places of at least a million of the sturdiest peasant families. The small farm, which is typical of Czechoslovakia, does not lend itself to easy mechanization. But whatever mode of joint farming may be fostered, it will of necessity be with the consent and support of the peasantry. The last thing the Communists would care to risk is an upsurge of rebellion in the countryside, where they polled more than half of their vote. Loss of the confidence of the rural population would blight their chances of growth and seriously demoralize their ranks.

Real estate, except when a part of the nationalized enterprise, has been unaffected by the decree. Rents, as in the first republic, remain under rigid government control. But there is no indication that homeowners or those who make homes available to others at a profit to themselves are in jeopardy of losing their properties. Not even the manufacturer whose business has been nationalized or the financier whose bank has been taken over by the state has lost his home. His personal possessions are his, not only home, furniture, jewelry, library, art collection, automobile, but summer cottage, hunting lodge, savings, and everything else that has survived German confiscation and German looting. Savings are certain to be drained of the "water" with which the Germans have inundated Czech currency. The higher the amount of savings, especially those accumulated during the years of German occupation or through trade in the black markets, the greater will be the tapping of "water" and the more severe the consequent shrinkage of savings funds. Such procedure the government has found necessary to save the country from a runaway inflation which, if uncurtailed, would wreak havoc with all accumulations, might even wipe them out, particularly in the higher brackets.

In Russia, it should be remembered, the bourgeoisie lost even their personal possessions.

Nor is the opportunity to open a business of one's own blocked by the new law. I know several manufacturers who, shortly after their plants were nationalized, applied for and obtained licenses to start anew. Yet it is not likely that such men, however gifted, will of their own volition advance a new business to the limits of its potentialities. They will not dare tempt fate, not in the field of production. They will not trust the future course of national economy or a future interpretation of some legal provision which may render their new business subject to nationalization. A new Baťa, a new Zlín, a new Škoda, or a new Vítkovice is legally and practically as much an impossibility as the return of the above enterprises to their former owners. In this writer's judgment the day of private big business in Czechoslovakia is over. The future development of large-scale enterprise, as in Russia, can come only through state sponsorship and state initiative.

But small and medium-sized business has been assured the good will of the state. It has been promised not only financial aid but protection against the hearty appetites and the devouring powers of trusts, cartels, and other combines. It is guaranteed the same rights as state-owned properties. Its taxes are proportionately the same. The wages it pays labor are no higher. The labor laws it is obliged to observe are no different. "Minnows will not be swallowed by whales," as one Czech economist has said.

None other than Klement Gottwald, leader of the Communist party, has declared: "The Constitution must give protection to small and medium-sized enterprises, and the legitimately acquired property of farmers, traders, shopkeepers, and all other persons and corporations must be especially safeguarded." If these commitments of the Prime Minister are scrupulously fulfilled, particularly if the Ministry of Internal Trade, which is headed by a Communist, refrains from interpreting or applying the existing law to the disadvantage of the non-nationalized enterprises, there is nothing on the scene to thwart their flourishing. Yet were obstructive action attempted, it would meet with the fierce resistance of the opposition, particularly of the Catholics and the Czech National Socialists. Communist or any other impulse toward arbitrary procedure cannot, under the prevailing political system, run away with itself. The checks it is certain to encounter can only be overcome by a majority of votes in Parliament.

Communists themselves realize the contributions the small manufacturer can make to the comforts of everyday life. "He will season our economy with new inventions of the little things that people always want to buy," said a Communist economist to this writer. "He will create new wants, new tastes, and enrich the everyday life of the worker and of others. He will be all the more inventive because he will face the competition of the nationalized industries." I cannot conceive of any Russian Communist—committed as he is to the political precept of the complete abolition of "exploitation"—expressing so favorable an opinion of *any* private enterprise—not at present, anyway.

The Czech shopkeeper is one of the most polite and efficient in the world. As in so many European countries, shopkeeping is a hereditary occupation. It has tradition and pride, not only personal but ancestral, and the Communists are not intending to disturb or disrupt its ministrations to the public. Neither are the Czechs starting out, as the Russians originally did, with new and untried theories and practices of production and management and human motivation. All political parties are committed to the principle that authority in nationalized enterprises shall be vested in men whose sole qualifications are skill and competence. Not that political favoritism has been entirely avoided. There have been serious transgressions which have again and again hampered the speedy or effective rehabilitation of factories. There have been unruly National Councils and Factory Committees which have trespassed their authority and have by pressure of their own squeezed out appointees of the Ministry of Industry or made them so unhappy that they left of their own accord. Yet if the Two-Year Plan is to become a reality and the nation is to achieve its goal—output ten per cent over what it was in 1937—such practices must cease, regardless of whether irrational and high-handed action is initiated from above or below, by misguided authority from Prague or by the mischievous designs of a local body. All parties—the Communists in particular, if only because the plan is largely their inspiration—must, for purely business reasons, adhere to the principle, not of partisanship, but of competence in the choice of managers and directors.

Distrust of the intelligentsia, particularly of technical experts, which at one time poisoned the atmosphere of Russian factories and laboratories, is no problem. The ruling parties are eloquently assuring experts not only of respectful and dignified treatment but eventually of higher reward for superior talent and exceptional achievement than private ownership had accorded them. As in the case of managers and directors, there have been derelictions, yet not sufficiently grave or widespread to cause serious trouble. As a rule, ordinary workers have evinced no "proletarian" suspicion of the trained expert or the educated man, whom they have always highly esteemed.

With businesslike sobriety the government defines in law the functions and responsibilities of labor under the new scheme of ownership. The trade union is to negotiate contracts between labor and management, but membership in the union, as in Russia, is to be voluntary. Workers are to be eloquently propagandized and urged to join but are not to be penalized if they do not respond to the appeals. There is to be no closed shop, and nobody is to be refused work because of indisposition or unwillingness to become a union member. The right to work is, under no circumstances, to be denied to anyone. Shop stewards and Factory Councils are obligated to defend the interests of the non-union man with no less vigor than of the union member.

Every shop, office, and institution, whether under government or private ownership, whether theater, factory, school, ministry —every place where men and women work for salaries or wages —is to have a Council. The membership and functions of the Council are explicitly set forth and regulated by law. In places where the number of workers is from twenty to sixty, the Council consists of three members; from sixty to one hundred, of four members; from one hundred up, one additional representative is added for each two hundred workers. Election by acclamation or by a show of hands, which was the practice immediately after liberation, is banned. Only the direct and secret ballot is valid and legal. Elections are to be held once a year, and *lists* of candidates must be submitted by the trade unions. The use of lists instead of individual names is a concession to the rivalries of the political parties, the theory being that the trade unions will not favor any party but will be guided by the standing and the interests of all political parties. Though membership in the Council is an "honorary function," in the event of necessity the management is obligated to release a member from his regular work and pay him his usual wages or salary.

Primarily the Council is concerned with "the economic, social, and cultural interests of workers." But its functions do not end with these. It participates in management, though theoretically only in an advisory or consultative capacity. It may make whatever proposals it deems advisable to the management, and the latter is under obligation earnestly to ponder them and to report its answer within a month from the date they are presented. But the Council has neither power nor authority to enforce its recommendations. If dissatisfied with the report of the management, it may file a complaint or appeal to higher authority, such as the Central Arbitration Board or even the Minister of Labor. Abuse or misuse of power by either labor or management is punishable by a fine of one hundred thousand crowns or six months imprisonment.

To facilitate the relationship between labor and management and to give labor the feeling of participation in the enterprise, management is enjoined from withholding trade secrets from the Council, and the Council is under oath not to divulge these to any outside source. Likewise, the Council has a right to demand inspection of records relating to "work and wages," income and profits, or any other information that may be within the possession of the management. At all times the Council must help build the morale of workers, stir their interest in invention, in scientific research, in any measure calculated to advance production to ever-mounting levels. It has a voice in the hiring and firing of labor. It promotes social welfare. It engages in cultural activity. It arranges lectures, concerts, dances. It supervises the publication of the factory press. It opens nurseries for the children of working mothers. It co-operates with the trade unions and fulfills their mandates as well as the directions it may receive from rank-and-file workers. For the pursuit of its social and cultural work it receives a subsidy from management, never less than ten per cent of the profits. The functions and powers of the Factory Councils are still in an experimental stage. Their final status will be defined as much by the services they render to the individual worker as the contribution they make to production.

In Russia nationalization meant automatic confiscation. There was no appeal and no redress. The Czech law declares itself firmly for the principle of compensation but bars payments to all who were the nation's enemies during the years when its independence was subverted and wrecked. In the list of such enemies the law includes the German Reich; the kingdom of Hungary; German and Hungarian political parties; German and Hungarian citizens, except those who may demonstrate their loyalty to the Czechoslovak Government, their integrity toward the Czech and Slovak nations, and either their active participation in resistance or their suffering under the Fascist terror. Nor is compensation to be made to Czechs and Slovaks who proved disloyal to the first republic, or who joined Fascist organizations, collaborated with Germans or Hungarians, and fostered and countenanced Germanization or Magyarization of their peoples. Thus there is no racial discrimination in the denial of compensation to owners of nationalized properties; Czechs and Slovaks do not escape penalization for their collaboration with the enemy.

The amount of compensation is computed on the basis of the value of properties at official (as distinct from inflated or black-market) prices on the day of the enactment of the nationalization decree. Taxes and liabilities are deducted, and payment is made in securities, in cash, or in other values "within six months after the amount has been determined." To expedite payment a

"Fund of Nationalized Economy," henceforth referred to as the Fund and enjoying independent administrative power and subject only to the Supreme Auditing Office, is established. Its income is derived from the surplus profits of nationalized enterprises.

This is the principle of compensation. Its realization is something else. It is not likely that after taxes and other special duties, including capital levies, are deducted any significant number of dispossessed owners will be wealthy enough to constitute a leisure class.

The striking contrast between the Czech and the Russian Octobers is evident not only in the method of their coming but in the manner of their being. In Russia the end was achieved through a secretly conceived and audaciously executed military coup. It conformed to the Marxian formula of dictatorship of the proletariat and the supremacy of the Communist party. It was intended as a complete deathblow to all capitalism, and not only in Russia. It was nurtured in the Marxian doctrine of "historic necessity" and ruthless dispossession of the bourgeoisie. It was garbed in the cloak of internationalism. The opposition it stirred inside and outside the country was formidable, and the new regime soon found itself embroiled in one of the cruelest and most sanguinary civil wars any nation ever has fought. When the battle was over the dictatorship was still beset with hosts of internal conflicts, with plots and counterplots, with feud and terror. Only later did the Soviet Revolution settle into the mold of a national revolution, or what Stalin termed "Socialism in one country." The fight over this issue, known as the battle with the opposition, was long and violent and finally terminated in the blood purge of 1936-37.

Nothing like so radical a departure from established practice was contemplated by Czechoslovakia's leaders. Instead of dictatorship there is the Government of the National Front, embracing four Czech and four Slovak political parties. The decree is a result not of conspiracy and military coup but of negotiation and compromise between the representatives of these parties inside the government. Instead of the will of one party, there is agreement of all parties achieved by compromise. Hence the absence of internal violence and internal revolt.

Because there is no dictatorship of one party, there has been no attempt to array class against class, or to push the revolution into the social life of the country. There has been no encroachment on the rights of the church, any church. There has been no battle against religion. There has been no official pronouncement, not even in the Communist press, in disparagement of religious faith. Because of Slovakia's clerical Fascism during its Hitler-given "independence" (which the more enlightened Slovak clergy never ceased to combat), the church schools in that country have been secularized. But there have been no attacks on any faith, not a hint or a glimpse of Russia's one-time anti-God crusade. Likewise, the intelligentsia has neither been alienated nor forsworn as it almost was at one time in Russia. There has been no battle of brain against brawn.

The family remains a sanctum sanctorum. There have been no experiments in free divorce, free abortions, such as Russia knew until the summer of 1935, nor are any contemplated. There has been no break-up of families, with daughters rising against mothers and sons against fathers. The dead are, as ever, remembered tenderly and reverently.

Nor has there been a repudiation of the past, a denunciation of historic heroes, historic glories, historic beliefs, historic traditions, such as shook Russia in the early years of the Revolution. It was not until the outbreak of World War II that Russia made intellectual and spiritual peace with the past and embraced it again as a long-lost and much-beloved parent. I know of no other country in which the past, out of which has sprung the inspiration for the present, is so continually and so fervently exalted as in Czechoslovakia. Let the reader recall the chapter on Tábor and on the meaning of the Hussite movement in all Czech political and social thought.

"We are pioneers in a new way of economic life," the former Prime Minister declared shortly after the enactment of the nationalization decree. It *is* pioneering on a gigantic scale, experiment of vast dimensions, conceived with audacity, but executed with none of the blithe recklessness which proved so catastrophic to Russia and which the Kremlin has since disavowed and abandoned. Here is no blind imitation of Russia and no refractory insistence that the old system has neither merit nor virtue. Here is an attempt at a reasoned balance between the collective ownership of the Russian Soviet and the individual stimulations of Czechoslovakia's historic democracy. Here is cognizance of Russia's failures and acceptance of capitalism's triumphs, not in mode of ownership but in method of achievement and individual emulation.

Here is no blind plunge into the future, neither in philosophic postulate nor in technique of fulfillment. Here is neither extravagant rhetoric nor lofty promise of the millennium in the immediate or faraway future. Here is neither passion nor melodrama. Though political wrangling is incessant, there is great caution and great calm.

Errors and disruptions are neither rare nor insignificant. The practice of mass meetings during working hours, which all political parties condemn, though less frequent than in the first year of liberation, is still a source of vexation to the planner and the executive. Discipline and work morale still lack the force of an inner urge or an external compulsion. The Two-Year Plan promises to rectify these failings. Meanwhile, within the ranks of the responsible leadership there is singular lack of hysteria, there is only spectacular awareness of responsibility.

15. Christian (Catholic) Socialism

Shortly after the return of the Government in Exile to Prague, two members of the newly constituted Cabinet, a Communist and a Catholic, were driving by the Parliament Building. Pointing to the building, the Communist said:

"I suppose, Monsignor, your party will be occupying the seats on the right of the House?"

"Not at all," replied the Catholic.

"Why not, Monsignor?"

"Because we Czech Catholics do not belong to the right. Nor do we belong to the left. We belong to the right of the left."

Foreign diplomats and correspondents often speak of the Czech Catholics as rightists or as the party of the right. These are false appellations.

The Czech Catholics are rightists only in relation to the extreme leftists—the Communists. In the economic precepts they follow, in the social reforms they espouse, they are farther to the left—that is, more Socialist—than the British Labor party or the Social Democrats of any other nation in Europe. As Josef Doležal, editor of the leading Catholic daily in Prague, wrote on

197

September 28, 1945: "We are going further than the Socialist parties of the West, further than the British Labor party and the French Socialist party."

There are individual exceptions: Catholics, to whom the suggestion of revolution, even when as peaceful and orderly as in their own land, spells collapse of the nation's economy and the death of its liberties. The revolt of the recalcitrant wing of the party came to a climax during the elections of May 1946, when under the guidance of a brilliant and determined woman, Helena Koželuhová, it strove to put itself into ascendancy, with a view to displacing the old leadership and scrapping its program. This faction would have nothing to do with Socialism or social reformism, and to attract the voter who shared its philosophy, it proclaimed the Catholic party as the only one that was non-Socialist. It sought to keep Czech Catholicism identified with the individualistic liberalism of the nineteenth century, which the National Front had repudiated. Its program was a coalescence of what a Catholic editor termed "the planks of the British Conservative and Liberal parties." It would have neither the nationalized economy nor the far-reaching social program of the Coalition Government. It attracted into its ranks an influential body of former members of the Agrarian and National Democratic parties, both banned because of their pre-war hostility to progressive legislation and because of their close collaboration with Nazi Germany during the years of occupation. Politically homeless, these men were seeking to bore their way into control of the Catholic party and use it as an instrument for the promulgation of a platform of their own. Only two men in the hierarchy were favorably inclined toward the rebellious group, which, had it succeeded in its aim, would have split Czech Catholics into two warring sections with nothing in common but their faith. An unbridgeable political schism would have yawned between them.

198

But the opposition this movement encountered was so formidable that it ended in defeat. It never did govern the spirit or the policies of the Catholic party, which as a body constitutes what is no doubt the most radical group in the Church and one of the most radical in the world. This in itself gives Czechoslovakia, a predominantly Catholic nation, a political complexion quite at variance with that of other Catholic countries.

As I journeyed around the country I heard only high praise for the behavior of the Catholic clergy during the years of the German occupation. Except for an inconsequential priest here and there, they stood up resolutely and irreconcilably against Nazis and Nazism. I have heard of not a single more or less eminent functionary in the hierarchy who evinced the least disposition to compromise with the enemy or who cherished anything but fierce disdain for Nazi theories and Nazi practices. To the Catholic clergy of Czechoslovakia, Nazi racialism was not only a denial of the basic tenets of their faith, but the cruelest disgrace of our century. Not a few surviving Jews owe their lives to the timely and always dangerous intercession of Catholic priests, many of whom, including several distinguished abbots, lost their lives because of their militant antagonism to Fascism. Eight Czech Catholic priests were executed, fifty-eight died in concentration camps, 111 survived persecution and incarceration.

Pregnant with meaning is the very title, *People's Democracy,* of the leading daily newspaper of the Czech Catholic party. For the name corresponds to the phrase by which Communists and Socialists all over Europe designate the new democracy they are championing in distinction to the pre-war "bourgeois democracy." The issue of November 4, 1945, contained these illuminating words: "After six years of war Socialism is on a victorious march, and its purpose is to bring material welfare to all." In explaining the type of Socialism he has in mind, the author writes: "We know two streams of Socialism, materialist and

199

Christian. . . . No doubt materialist Socialism is lacking neither in plans nor in fighting spirit. But time, evolution, the biological realities of human life will confirm the truth of the view that the spirit and moral law of man are no less decisive than matter."

Czech Catholics no more accept Marxian materialism with its negation of spirituality and religion than Czech Communists and Social Democrats—that is, those who are versed in Marxism —accept mysticism with its negation of materialism. The theoretical and philosophical gulf between Czech Catholicism and Czech Marxian Socialism remains unbridged and unbridgeable. Yet again and again one encounters language in the Catholic press, or one hears and reads speeches of Catholic deputies in Parliament, which neither Communists nor Social Democrats would dispute or would hesitate to applaud.

"The state," wrote the Catholic organ, *People's Democracy,* "must regulate private enterprise not only in subordinating it to the social interests of the nation, but to its own plans of production and distribution. . . . Such phenomena as temporary booms and economic crises can either be completely avoided or dealt with by the state-appointed experts, through the release of credits and other measures." Nor does the writer share the fear common among non-Socialists that state control would thwart or paralyze individual initiative. "Although," he continues, "it is still possible to find the old-fashioned type of private owner who is out for personal gain, we already observe the emergence of those who have grasped the meaning of the new trends and are building and creating for the sheer love of their work and for the general advancement of the scheme of things."

One may laud or decry such utterances, but here they are in clear and unmistakable language in the leading daily journal of the Czech Catholic party. Suspicious as it is of the Communist party, distrustful as it may be of its ultimate aims, and uncompromising as it is in its antagonism to Marxian materialism,

Czech Catholicism has yet co-operated with it in a spirit and a measure that is unparalleled in Europe or the world. It did so during the war, when the Czech Government was in London, and it has done so since the day of liberation. It engaged in long and vigorous controversy with the Communists over the nature and magnitude of nationalization. It favored from the very beginning state ownership of banks, insurance companies, key industries. So large a proportion of these had been under German ownership that, for the Catholics, nationalization here meant the Czechization of enemy property. But the Catholics fought and will continue to fight any encroachment on small and medium-sized industry. The Catholic party is so jealous of its own position that it will not countenance an all-powerful state, which complete nationalization would make inevitable and which might encroach on its religious life or on its political liberties. Their "Christian worry," as an eminent priest expressed himself, is the rise of such a state. They believe in "plurality of ownership," with not only the state but the municipalities, the co-operatives and private individuals doing the business of the nation. Under such a system, they hold, competition would be more keen and more fruitful of benefits to the people; individual and community incentive would be continually fostered; the state would be prevented from using economic power to further political ends, and the balance between contesting forces would make for a healthy democracy and promote greater economic progress.

Despite sharp disagreement with Marxian opponents, the Catholic party finally accepted a program of law and action which preserves the principle of "plurality of ownership." Without its support, Prague's sweeping nationalization decree never could have become the law of the land.

The Catholic party favors not only nationalization but planned economy. Without it, a Catholic economist explained to the writer, Czechoslovakia, which possesses as much industry as a great power but squeezed into a small territory, would plunge into mismanagement and chaos and would be especially unable to solve the problem of unemployment which nationalization is supposed to remove. The party, therefore, accepts the Socialist theory that only through planned economy can basic economic evils be remedied or uprooted. Provided the state does not become "the mastermind" of the country, the Catholic party does not perceive in planned economy a weapon for the repression of the individual. It has been particularly solicitous in reassuring small manufacturers whose plants have not been nationalized that they need cherish no fears of too much government interference in their business or too much government curtailment of liberty of action under a system of planned economy. "The responsibility and risk of the private owner," said *People's Democracy,* "will be . . . lessened and he will no longer be menaced by the capital of large trusts and private owners who formerly, and out of purely selfish motives, got rid of the competition of their own eager rivals. The nationalization of trusts and industries will guarantee to small and medium-sized enterprises the opportunity of free competition with those who command larger capital."

Nor does the Czech Catholic party voice the objections one often hears from property-minded people, that allowing workers a voice in management will degrade production and ruin industry. It refuses to acknowledge that workers as a class have no managerial talent, or that their inexperience is too great a risk for any nationalized industry to face. It does not advocate indiscriminate or exclusive workers' control. (Nor do the Communists.) Yet it not only approves, it advocates workers' participation in management. Let the official pronouncement as printed in the *People's Democracy* speak for itself: "The most far-reaching change in individual initiative is that it is no longer the preserve of the private owner but is also to become the province of the worker. Much has to be done in training workers to make use of this right of initiative. The system of Factory Councils has laid the legal foundation for this purpose. Now special attention should be given to the Councils so they will have a sufficient scope for promoting the task. Experiments in rewarding initiative have in certain instances produced remarkable results and deserve further encouragement."

From these pronouncements on nationalization and private ownership, on the relation of the state to the individual businessman, on workers' participation in management, and on planned economy, it is clear that the Czech Catholic party is officially on record as no longer upholding the inviolability and sanctity of private enterprise. It disbelieves in confiscation, but so do other parties, including the Communist. It is far more sensitive to constitutionalism than are the Communists or Social Democrats. It does not accept a public parade or demonstration as a substitute for the ballot or as a real expression of "the will of the people." It champions civil liberties and is jealous of any attempts to subvert or dismiss them. Yet it does not associate the right of private enterprise with political freedom. It rejects the theory that state ownership as a principle spells death to human incentive and to economic progress. The word Socialism rouses in it neither anxieties nor misgivings. Though the Catholic party never speaks of Socialism without the qualifying "Christian" as a prefix, it uses this word and others which have a distinctive Socialist connotation, freely and unequivocally, with no effort to disguise or underestimate their epochal significance. While it postulates its social creed not on material but on spiritual values, it, too, is staking the future of the country on the success of nationalization and on other purely Socialist innovations.

Let the reader ponder the religious accent and the social radicalism of the speech of Dr. Josef Novák, an eminent member of the Czech Catholic party, before the Provisional Parliament on January 23, 1946. Dr. Novák began with the declaration that the nationalization decree is more than an economic project, if only because it is destined to refashion and re-create all social life. "It seems," he said, "that even our working people are not quite conscious of the magnitude of this step. By these decrees we are emulating the great ideals of Pope Leo XIII and Pope Pius XI: The liberation of the proletariat from serfdom. The nationalization of industry is not just an invasion of other men's possessions by a group of orthodox Socialists. Without it we cannot rebuild a national state in the true meaning of the term. Nationalization does not contravene moral sentiment; it is just and right according to all human standards. . . . Nationalization is one of the greatest social revolutions of all times. Its benefits will be enjoyed by all future generations, and we shall rid ourselves of unemployment, which caused such enormous losses to our working people and to the state. Let us then strive for success and set an example to those who may wish to follow us."

This is the language of a Socialist, a Catholic Socialist, who rests his case not on the teachings of Karl Marx and Friedrich Engels, of Lenin and Stalin, as he himself emphasized, but on the pronouncements of Pope Leo XIII, who in his *Rerum Novarum* said: "The Church has never neglected to adapt itself to the genius of nations," and of Pope Pius XI, who in 1933 declared: "The Church accommodates itself to all forms of governments and civil institutions, provided the right of God and Christian conscience are left intact."

In conversations with Catholics I have rarely heard the authority of Pope Pius XI cited as does Novák in justification of their support of Czech Socialism. But Pope Leo XIII is almost a household word with them. As a Catholic editor once remarked to me: "The Communists have their *Communist Manifesto* of Karl

Marx and Friedrich Engels, but we Catholics have our encyclical of Leo XIII."

Not that the Vatican and the Czechoslovakian state have always maintained the most cordial relationships. The fact that Masaryk, the first President of the republic, was born a Catholic and renounced the faith in favor of Protestantism could not but be displeasing to the Vatican. While it is not true, as has often been alleged in the foreign press, that Beneš is an agnostic or atheist, it is a fact that, though born a Catholic and without ever having renounced the faith, he is not practicing it. Since Beneš's boyhood days Jan Hus has been his great hero. Like Palacký and Masaryk and a host of other Czech intellectuals, Beneš has perceived in Hus the incarnation of Czech patriotism and the quintessence of Czech progressive thought. But to the Vatican, Hus is only a heretic. Though Hus never renounced Rome, the Council of Constance condemned him for heresy. Since no Pope has ever rescinded or reconsidered the condemnation and since Hus to this day is the fountainhead of Czech nationalism and Czech humanism—the inspirer of the ethical concept of the state and of society—the relationships between Prague and Rome have often been marked by discord, sometimes by hostility. For example, when the first republic proclaimed July 6, the date of Hus's execution, a national memorial day, and hoisted the ancient Hussite banner over the castle, Monsignor Marmaggi, the papal representative in Prague, protested and departed from Czechoslovakia.

There is the wish and the hope among certain distinguished Czech Catholics that for legal as well as spiritual reasons the Vatican will someday reopen the trial of Constance which branded Hus as a heretic. That throughout the centuries since the burning of Hus the Vatican has shown no inclination to re-examine the Constance verdict has not dampened the faith that someday in the future the Holy See will initiate action that will restore Hus as Joan of Arc has been restored and sainted.

The most celebrated Catholic figure in Czech politics and the father of Czech Catholic Socialism is Monsignor Jan Šrámek. Now seventy-six years old, a white-haired man with a broad, kindly face and shrewd, brooding eyes, averse to rash or voluble speech, almost diffident in the presence of strangers, he is as close to Beneš in political thought as he had been to Masaryk. Like Beneš, he is of peasant origin and has held high office in the Prague Government since the very founding of the first republic. In 1905 he was appointed assistant professor of sociology in the theological seminary at Brno. Here, together with other progressive-minded priests, he founded the Christian Socialist party of Czech Catholics and has since stanchly upheld every forward-looking movement of his people—trade unions, social insurance, liberal education. An energetic and determined nationalist, he joined Masaryk and other enlightened and democratic Czechs in the battle for Czech independence and simultaneously sought to disrupt and dispel the influence of Austrian Catholicism over the Czech clergy. . . . Neither Church authority nor internal and international political pressure has ever swerved him from his devotion to his nation and to the progressive traditions which he, like Masaryk and Beneš, had made their own. In 1935, when after the resignation of Masaryk from the presidency, the Agrarian party, together with other factions, including the Sudeten Germans, sought to break with the Masaryk tradition and to elevate to the presidency not Beneš but one of his opponents, it was Šrámek who, by swinging the Catholic vote in support of Beneš, decided the election and insured the continuation of the progressive tradition.

During the bitter days of Munich no leader was more firmly arrayed against foreign interference than was Monsignor Šrámek. He opposed the forced invitation of the Runciman mission which the British had sent to mediate the conflict between the Czechs and the Sudeten Germans. Stubbornly he fought against *any* outside proposals that involved the sacrifice of the country's sovereignty. No man was more heartbroken over the forced Munich surrender. Shortly afterward, Hermann Göring demanded Beneš's resignation from the presidency. On October 5, 1938, the Cabinet and army leaders gathered to discuss Göring's demand. Beneš signed his resignation, and Šrámek, sullen and gloomy, was the only one of those present who demonstratively walked over to Beneš, shook his hand, and said: "We shall re-elect you President." The Agrarians were infuriated, accused Šrámek of disloyalty and sabotage. But the white-haired, hard-headed monsignor stood by his declaration and the spirit it embodied. After Beneš's departure he was approached with a proposal to join the newly formed collaborationist government. His answer was a resolute "No." Of all the leaders who remained in Prague, he, more than anyone, reflected the mood of the man in the street, who in his heart raged against the capitulation and loathed the very thought of subservience to a German master.

Šrámek's life was in danger. With the aid of Czech trainmen who had secreted him and Monsignor František Hála, his closest disciple, in the brakeman's box of a coal train that was bound for Poland, he fled from his homeland into exile. Shortly afterward he traveled to Paris to solicit the recognition of the newly formed Czechoslovak National Committee. Beneš, too, went to Paris, but the French Prime Minister refused to see him. Beneš returned to London and Šrámek remained to negotiate. The French Government, desirous of keeping Italy neutral in the event of war and of placating Mussolini, who fumed at the mere mention of Beneš's name, proposed that he, Šrámek, supersede Beneš as chairman of the committee. Stanchly Šrámek rejected the proposal. "I came into exile," he said, "not to supersede Beneš but to say that the nation is with him." The French argued and pleaded. But Šrámek remained unshaken. Finally the French Government recognized the committee with the understanding that it choose its own chairman. Promptly it elected Beneš as chairman and Šrámek as vice-chairman. After the fall of France, Šrámek fled to London on a British destroyer. When the committee was recognized as the Czechoslovak Government in Exile, Beneš became President and Šrámek was chosen Prime Minister.

While in London, Šrámek was confronted once more with a serious challenge, this time from British statesmen, which he met with his customary firmness. The Government in Exile, together with Czech leaders in Moscow, had come to the conclusion that without an alliance with Russia they could not hope for national security. In the words of Monsignor Hála, now second-in-command of the Czech Catholic party: "The friendship with England and America and France was insufficient to secure the future of our republic unless we made an alliance with the one great Slav nation [Russia]. . . . Many British statesmen were against the signing of any treaty [with Russia], but the Prime Minister [Šrámek] declared that *we were even prepared to part for a time with England rather than not sign the treaty* of friendship with the Soviet Union."[1]

Now, despite his old age, Šrámek is deputy Prime Minister, the indisputable leader of his party, and one of the most popular figures in the country. Modest, affable, shrewd, reticent, scholarly (he has lectured at Oxford in Latin), he is as highly esteemed by non-Catholics as by his co-religionists. On several occasions I saw him in Parliament sitting on the platform beside the more youthful Klement Gottwald, leader of the Communist party, the two whispering and nodding to each other, breaking into laughter and displaying a close and comradely personal relationship. Though controversy between the Communist and Catholic press is neither rare nor mild, no Communist writer indulges in philippics or reproof against Šrámek. He is one of

[1]Address in Znojmo, February 28, 1946.

the most exalted personages in the nation, and respect and affection for him transcend party rivalry and ideological controversy.

Yet Šrámek's immeasurable influence on the political thinking of Czech Catholics is not solely the result of his magnetic personality or his gifts for leadership. Czech history and Czech psychology supplied a fertile soil for the propagation of his ideas and teachings. The Czech clergy came from the people, overwhelmingly from the peasantry. With no native aristocracy to dominate or sway their thinking, with their aversion to the alien culture of Austria, particularly its antipathy and contempt for Czech civilization, they could no more resist the stimulations of their own history than could non-Catholic Czechs. Besides, they shared with their flocks the daily travail that was upon them. They smarted as much as did the peasant, the shopkeeper, the factory worker, the university professor, from the burden of repressions and inferiorities that old Austria and the Germans in their midst had visited on the Czech population. To them, too, language, culture, folkways were a weapon of redemption which could best be wielded with whatever help they could secure from Slav brothers in other lands.

The Slav consciousness of the Czech Catholics, of the clergy even more than of the laity, has been a distinguishing feature of their mentality. This consciousness flows from two sources, history and geography. In response to the request from Prince Rotislav of Moravia for missionaries who could speak Slavic, the Byzantine court appointed the brothers Cyril and Methodius in 863. Slavs themselves, they readily adapted themselves to the speech and the customs of the people. The memory of these men has remained deep and hallowed, and the feeling for Byzantium, despite its break with Rome, is equally warm. It has inspired the hope and fostered the desire, popular among all Czech Catholics, to bridge the gulf which the schism had wrought. Nowhere else

in the world is there so much hopeful talk of an eventual reconciliation between the Eastern and the Western churches. The
feud between Moscow and Rome has not discouraged the pursuit of this hope or the faith in its ultimate triumph.

Nor could the Czechs, even when they were under Austria,
resist the attraction of their brother Slavs, particularly in Russia.
Surrounded by Germans, repressed by Germans, despoiled by
Germans, they were and are among the most ardent advocates
of Slav unity. There were difficulties, of course. Poland was of
the same religion as they but was guided by an aristocratic tradition. The Serbs were of a different religion, in part Mohammedan
but largely Greek Orthodox, and were only slowly emerging
from the torpor of long subjection to Turkey. Russia exercised a
powerful spell over them, especially nineteenth-century Russia
with its great music, its great literature, its progressive awakening. Pride of race stimulated pride of nation. Educated Czechs
found a haven in Russia. In city after city they almost held a
monopoly on the teaching of classical languages in Russian
gymnasiums.

The deep-rooted Slav consciousness is in no small measure
motivating the present friendly attitude of the Czech Catholics
to the Soviet Union. Let the reader recall the answer given by
the village priest whom I asked why he was honoring Josef
Stalin by displaying his photograph side by side with those of
Beneš and Monsignor Šrámek. To him Stalin, the apostle of
materialism, is an irreconcilable opponent. But Stalin, the commander in chief of the Russian Army, is the symbol of Slav
power arrayed against a possible resurgence of German military
arrogance.

Obzory, the foremost Catholic weekly journal in Czechoslovakia, once scolded Czech publishers for neglecting to render
into Czech Russian medical and technical textbooks and political
and social studies.[2]

[2]*Obzory,* October 27, 1945.

Klement Gottwald, leader
of the Communist party

Msgr. František Hála, Minister of Post, Telegraph, and
Telephone

—Czechopress Photo, Prague

Msgr. Jan Šrámek, leader of the Czech Catholic party

In its issue of November 7, 1945, the same journal featured on its cover a well-known portrait of Lenin, illuminated by the Hammer and Sickle banner. The inside of the cover was richly illustrated with photographs of Stalin, posters and proclamations of the October Revolution, the anniversary of which occurs on November 7.

There was further official and more pregnant cognizance of the Soviet advent to power in St. James's, one of the oldest and most beautiful churches in Prague. Dr. Josef Fiala, a monk of the Minor Order and one of the officiating priests of the church, invited foreign correspondents to the special Mass he was celebrating in honor of this anniversary. A red flag over the church doors bore not the hammer and sickle but the number "7" over "11" embroidered in yellow—the day and the month of the Soviet rise to power. The church was so overcrowded that though I had arrived early I managed only with difficulty to make my way inside. The church choir, one of the most famous in Prague, rendered a special program of ancient Slavonic church music, and Dr. Fiala, in his sermon, stressed the importance of "the great social reality" which the Soviet Union symbolized.

Subsequently, when I met Dr. Fiala in his cell in the monastery which is attached to St. James's, I asked if he had received the permission of the archbishop to accord official recognition to the October Revolution. "Our Prague archbishop," he said, "is dead. But I did receive written permission from the office of the archbishop."

Still quite young, only thirty-two, he is, in his political thinking, even more left than Monsignor Šrámek. Of medium size, with broad shoulders, coal-black, slightly graying hair, and brilliant dark eyes, he is not a Czech but a Slovak, the son of a blacksmith from the village of Spišská Nová Ves, Slovakia. He studied philosophy and theology in Rome. Handsome, eloquent, gifted with a singularly melodious voice, he draws immen̦se crowds. Non-Catholic Czechs often attend Mass when they know he is celebrating it, out of pure enjoyment of his extraordinarily musical voice.

When I asked him what he thought of the nationalization decree his reply was brief and telling. "To us Catholics," he said, "the decree is not a question of conflict between capital and labor but of national survival." This is precisely what Social Democrat and Communist have been saying.

In explaining his friendliness to Russia he said, "Think what the Germans did to our Church. They closed our theological seminary and converted it into a Gestapo office. Monsignor Beran, rector of the seminary, they dragged off to a concentration camp. The theological students they deported for forced labor to Germany. In Nová Říše, Moravia, the abbot and ten monks of St. Norbert's Monastery paid with their lives for their loyalty to their people and the Church. Our Merciful Brothers maintained in Prague a hospital for incurable diseases. The Germans closed the hospital and the monastery of the brothers, and the rector died in Dachau. They banned our press and forbade *duchovní cvičení*—going into retreat." Pointing to two heavy volumes with black covers, he said, "Look at those books." Both were in German, one *Mein Kampf,* and the other Alfred Rosenberg's *Myth of the Twentieth Century.*

"I have read these books," said the monk with rising emotion. "They speak of Christianity as 'Poison from Palestine.' Had Germany won the war, the Nazis would have exterminated the Church. Plainly enough they say that's what they would have done." Again he pointed emphatically at the two black volumes. "As black as sin, the ugliest sin, both of them."

Because he was anti-Fascist and helped Jews get out of the country by converting them and making it possible for them to obtain visas to South America, and because of his defiant opposition to the Nazi occupants, he had to flee from Prague. He

212

sought refuge in Slovakia and there organized a Catholic Council to fight Fascism, German and Slovakian. He became a partisan and fought with the Red Army. "Let the world say all that it chooses about Russia and the Russians, all I can say is that they were careful not to subject our churches to military attack, and they haven't interfered with the opening of our church institutions. Our schools, our churches are functioning again. We are as free to pursue our faith as we were in the pre-Munich days."

He, too, had a framed photograph of Stalin. "A Red officer gave it to me and I have framed it," he said.

Nor does the Czech Catholic party manifest the least sympathy with General Franco or approval of his regime in Spain. Quite the contrary. In a long review of the Czech translation of Ernest Hemingway's *For Whom the Bell Tolls,* there is this illuminating passage in *Obzory:* "It is ten years since Franco, together with Fascists and Falangists, tolled the funeral bell over the beautiful peninsula, the bell which pre-tolled the fate of the fallen in World War II. . . . Hemingway is one of those who understood that the crisis which brought mankind to World War II and which even today disturbs the atmosphere of the forthcoming peace found its initial expression in the battle of the Spanish people for freedom, both political and moral."[3]

There are Czech Catholics who, like other Czechs, are distrustful of the Communists and even more of Russia. They are fearful lest someday both conspire to engulf their little country, not only into the Soviet orbit but into the Soviet political structure. Leopold Prečan, the eighty-year-old archbishop of Moravia, issued a pastoral letter on the eve of the last elections in which, without mentioning the Communists by name, he set forth his grievances against them and their teachings and made it emphatically clear that "under pain of mortal sin" Catholics

[3]*Obzory,* August 17, 1946.

must vote for the party that "will defend the unswerving religious rights of religious freedom and of Holy Church." It is still a question, on the answer to which Catholic leaders do not agree, whether the letter won or lost votes for the Catholic party. Despite its injunctions, the Communists polled an unexpectedly heavy vote in Moravia, pushing the Catholic party into second place. When I saw the archbishop in August 1946 in his summer home on a high hill outside of Olomouc, he spoke serenely and optimistically of the future of Czechoslovakia and of the Church. "We must find the golden mean in our country," he said, "and we are finding it. The good Lord will show us the right way to a fruitful life."

Holding aloof from the Rome-Moscow feud, the Catholic party, which is now accepting non-Catholics into membership (which it did not do during the first republic) and is on most cordial terms with Protestants, is steering its course along a Socialist path without benefit of Marxism or materialism, and with no interference from the state in its purely religious allegiance to Rome. Prague's relations with the Vatican are more than cordial.

In its secular quest the Catholic party is guiding itself by its rich Czech heritage, the lessons and challenges of Czech history, its own experiences with the outside world, including Russia, and particularly by Christian morality.

"Above all," Mr. Klímek, national secretary of the party, said to this writer, "we are faithful Catholics. 'Love thy God,' is as much our inspiration as 'Love thy neighbor as thyself.' We are socially minded and carry religion into every phase of our lives— politics, economics, education—and we're not afraid of the word Socialism, only it is Christian Socialism we emulate." In reply to the question of a possible rupture with the Communists, he said: "We have all suffered too much and it is natural for all of us to deem it our duty to work together for the good of our country. We and the Communists are like two persons walking along the opposite banks of the same river, but heading in the same direction. No, we're not having a bad life here."

It is this writer's conviction that only in the event that laymen like Mrs. Helena Koželuhová and her supporters attain leadership of the Catholic party would it face a serious and turbulent crisis, which would endanger its present program and would inevitably lead to a split in its ranks and possibly to a rupture with the Social Democrats and the Communists. But so long as priests remain at the helm, the party is destined to pursue, in an ever-deepening sense of the phrase, the policy of Christian Socialism.

16. Czech Communism

The venerable Professor Zdeněk Nejedlý, who spent his years of exile teaching in Moscow University, is one of the more voluble and more effervescent spokesmen of the Communist party. His speeches in the early months after liberation abounded in glowing tributes to Sovietism and in undisguised hints that Russia rather than the West, including of course the English-speaking countries, must be the guide and inspirer of the new Czechoslovakia.

Yet in February 1946, when he was still Minister of Education, he appeared before the Cultural Committee of Parliament and argued *against* the separation of Church and State. He did more; he upheld the *congrua*—state payment of salaries to the clergy—and called for an increase of these salaries!

Whatever else this may mean, it stamps the Czech Communists as being neither Marxian pundits nor Leninist doctrinaires, for on the issue of Church and State they are in dramatic discord with Marx, who spoke of religion as "the opium of the people," and with Lenin, who wrote that "the state should have no concern for religion, and religious organizations should not be concerned with the state." The new Czechoslo-

216

vakia, Nejedlý testified, must be "a truly national state. It is therefore important that the clergy be included in its organizations and that the churches do not isolate themselves and do not break away from the nation. Everyone must participate in the rebuilding of the new Czechoslovakia."

I asked Rudolf Slánský, general secretary of the Czech Communist party, who, like Nejedlý, had spent his years of exile in Russia, whether he endorsed the policy Nejedlý was advocating. "Of course," was his instant reply. "We judge a person not by his religion but by his manhood and patriotism. Priests suffered in concentration camps, fought with the partisans, died for their country. Why shouldn't we favor them? We increased the salaries of state employees and officials and of course we included the clergy." Here is no attempt to force life into the framework of theory but to expand and even denature theory so as to fit it into the framework of life.

When I asked another eminent Communist leader for an explanation of his party's quite radical departure from Leninist teaching on the subject of Church and religion, his answer was: "Why fight religion? When we have attained the conditions of society in which religion is superfluous, it will die by itself." The explanation may have a logic of its own but misfits the dynamics of Marxism, which leaves nothing to chance, trusts nothing to fate, propels everything forward by its own coercive energies.

During my stay in the country I could not help making constant comparisons between the Communist party in Russia and in Czechoslovakia. The war has made both passionately and reverently patriotic, yet while the Russian party drapes the mantle of Marxism over its patriotism, the Czech party parades around in the garb of dazzling patriotism, with scarcely a glint of Marxist coloring. Moscow's *Pravda* has never removed from its masthead the universal Marxist slogan, "Workers of the World, Unite." Since liberation no Czech Communist publica-

217

tion has followed the practice. In all official and unofficial pronouncements there is, explicit and implicit, the exhortation: "All Czechs, unite." There are no Pioneers, the Communist equivalent of the Scout movement. There are only the Boy and Girl Scouts. There is no Komsomol, Communist Youth Society. There is only the Union of Czech Youth.

I felt almost dazed when on walking into the lobby of the Communist headquarters in Prague I saw a display not of Marxist but of patriotic Czech slogans and symbols, of which the most conspicuous and most impressive was the double row of large portraits, twenty in all, of outstanding leaders and intellectuals in Czech history. Above the portraits, carved in letters of wood which were painted red, was the inscription: "Proudly we emulate the progressive traditions of our people," and underneath each was a quotation from the man's utterances. Underneath the portrait of Jan Hus I read: "Love one another, keep united, do not permit any circumstances to cleave you apart." Underneath the portrait of Jan Žižka, the blind general who led the Hussite armies to war, was one of his famous pastorals to his soldiers: "Dear Brothers in God! In the Lord's name I beg you stoutly to stand up against the evils which the Germans perpetrated on us. Emulate our ancestors, who fought not only for God but for themselves"; Josef Dobrovský, noted for his messianic Slav complex: "From Slavs must come the new enlightenment of the world"; from Jan Kollár, the poet: "Whenever you say Slav you mean man"; from František Palacký, the historian: "My life and my breath I shall dedicate to my country." Not one of the quotations but was an exaltation of the Czech nation or an expression of triumph of Czech achievement. The only purely Marxist symbol was a bust of Lenin in a corner and above it a citation from Gottwald: "The teachings of Marx and Lenin are our unerring compass." Among the portraits was not a single exponent of Marxism or of the materialist philosophy of history.

There is barely any talk of class struggle in Czech Communist utterances, written or spoken. There is not the remotest suggestion of the advisability or inevitability of class or Communist dictatorship, nor any insistence that violent revolution is necessary. Let the reader recall Gottwald's declaration that "dictatorship of the proletariat and the Soviets are not the only road to Socialism."

During the months the Prague Cabinet was in daily and heated wrangling over the nature and extent of the nationalization decree there were in the Communist press sharp and impetuous denunciations of those who might be blocking its passage, but the language in which these were expressed was singularly void of allusions to "class enemies," "capitalist exploiters," or similar stereotypes. Now having won the battle of nationalization, there are no individual capitalists with great economic power on whom to visit violent denunciation.

Nor do the Czech Communists, officially or unofficially, at least in public, deem it necessary, as do Russian Bolsheviks, constantly to invoke official Communist authority as personified in Marx and Engels, Lenin and Stalin, for their principles or policies. They speak for themselves, the working people, the nation, the republic, and their language is as Czech as roast goose and dumpling, with scarcely a phrase that a Czech worker or Czech peasant, however limited his education, would fail to comprehend. In their drive for higher production they have boosted into usage such Russian words as Stakhanovism, brigade, competition, several others. But except for the words brigade and competition, the borrowed expressions have acquired neither vogue nor popularity. Whether it is because a Czech miner has broken all Stakhanovite records of production, including that of Stakhanov himself, is immaterial. The fact is that the Communist vocabulary has remained exceptionally chaste of the philosophical and Bolshevik terminology which heavily interlards all Russian writing and all Russian oratory. "If we kept citing authority," said a university professor, himself a member of the Communist party, "in justification of our policies, our people would say we cannot think for ourselves and would mistrust us and laugh at us, and don't imagine that wouldn't hurt us." The fact is that literary Czech Communists glory in their language, with its rich colloquialism, as much as did Jan Hus, who exhorted his colleagues in the pulpit and in the university to make it the vehicle of communication with the people. Not that they are mild or objective in their treatment of political opponents or refrain from explosive rhetoric in the charges they hurl against them. Their journalism, though rarely their oratory, bristles with caustic and virulent phrases, particularly the compositions of those who spent their years of exile not in London but in Moscow. With them passion and partisanship often enough take the place of fact and argument. Yet even they are cautious to avoid the language of doctrine and precept, of revolutionary fervor or metaphysical theorem— the supercritical Czech population would not and could not "swallow" it. Yet, it would be an error to assume that their opponents evince in debate either restraint or courtesy or are free from the sin of distortion and exaggeration.

Czechs have always been responsive to new ideas, whether in literature or art, in architecture or philosophy, in politics or science. During the first republic scarcely a Soviet author of consequence but was readily rendered into Czech. Lenin and Stalin were highly publicized. Marx and Engels were published and republished. At present more and more of the political writings and speeches of Russian leaders are being translated, especially by Communist and trade-union publishers. The study of Marxism is being sedulously cultivated and propagated. Yet no special knowledge of Marxism, Stalinism, or Leninism is a prerequisite to membership in the party. Anyone who is a good Czech—without the stigma of collaboration with Germans or enemies of the republic—is warmly embraced. His social origin is of no matter; his past or present career is of no consequence. A large segment of the membership is Catholic. No small number of these are "birth-certificate" Catholics rather than people who practice the faith. But it is neither Marx nor Engels, neither Lenin nor Stalin, nor any other doctrinal authority, who is luring most of them into the ranks. They know little of such authority—as yet. Dialectical materialism is not a phrase which drips off their tongues as readily or as blithely as it issues from the lips of the Russian party member. For most of them it is no more than a phrase. It will become more than that but not without strenuous effort by party functionaries.

Let the following incident speak for itself. One evening I was driving from Zlín to Prague with an executive of the Bața industries, and on our way we stopped to visit my companion's father, a peasant in one of the smallest villages in the country. A tall, sturdy Czech with a face seamed and brown from exposure to sun and wind, the father proudly showed me through his barns and stables which were modern, with electric lights and with water tapped from a spring on a high hill and flowing in pipes into drinking cups in the mangers. He was equally proud of his electric motor, his straw-cutting machine, other modern implements. On a farm of only twenty-seven acres he managed to keep a team of horses, a yoke of oxen, three milch cows, four heifer calves, a flock of hens, and to fatten from six to eight hogs a year. I asked him how and by what miracle he succeeded in whipping so much bounty out of so small a land-holding. "Oh," he said nonchalantly, "by hard work, I suppose. My two sons and I work all the time, and the wife helps a lot."

He had slaughtered a pig that day and insisted that we stay for a meal. As we were eating the two sons entered, full-grown sturdy youths, each sporting on the lapel of his coat the badge of hammer and sickle, which is the insignia of the party member. I asked them why they joined the Communist party, and these were the most significant words in the reply of one of them:

"We're a small nation. Alone we can never defend ourselves against the German enemy. But with Russian help we need not fear German attacks." The motive was pre-eminently Czech and nationalist, which only emphasizes the overwhelming nationalist appeal in Czech Communism. The other son added: "The Communist party has been good to us farmers."

These farm youths are no exception. The might of the Red Army—a Slav army—the sensation of triumph its victories have stirred, the sentiment of security it inspires have roused the response of large masses of Czech youths in the factory and on the farm. Since membership in the Communist party, more than in any other, imparts a feeling of close kinship to Russia and the Red Army, it acts as a magnet that draws into Communist ranks many a Czech, and not only youths, though these predominate.

Romance and faith, adventure and self-interest, also cupidity and careerism, far more than Marxian doctrine, are the stimulations and motivations that have swelled the membership of the Communist party to more than a million. Though now members are required to attend a series of lectures on the meaning of Marxism, and no new cards are issued to those who have failed to fulfill the requirement, no one is subjected, as in Russia, to a searching examination of his knowledge of Marxism or to a minute probing into his personal life. The party remains not a class but a mass or people's party and, except on the upper level, is so far but mildly tinged with Marxist doctrine. Bankers, manufacturers, lawyers, pastors,

priests, shopkeepers, all are welcomed into the fold. The party
has made a deliberate, strenuous, and not unsuccessful effort to
woo into its ranks the managerial, technical, literary, and academic intelligentsia. It neither enjoins nor warns members
against possible ideological or any other pitfalls from free association with non-Communists. It does not intrude into the personal
life of *any* member. Among the new members there have been
plenty of first-class rascals, especially in some of the National
Committees, who have exploited the Communist label or the
party card for personal aggrandizement and for nefarious
adventure. While seeking to weed out the undesirables, the
party is brushing out of the way social or real intellectual
barriers to membership. Despite partisanship in debate, it is in
this writer's judgment the most non-sectarian Communist
party in the world.

Nor is there any evidence that the Czech party is attempting
to invoke and popularize the leadership principle, for which
Russia has set the pattern and which Communist parties in
other lands have with greater or lesser zeal sought to emulate.
Klement Gottwald, the new Prime Minister, is commonly recognized as the party's most popular and most brilliant leader.
A modest man of fifty-one, with defective eyesight, a large
finely shaped head, a stoop in his shoulders, a cool manner
and deliberate mode of speech, he brings to mind the university
professor or the scholar who pores over tomes and treatises
in a library stall, rather than the political leader. No one within
or without the party speaks of him with heightened emotion
or special reverence. No panegyrics are bestowed on his person.
Neither his wisdom nor his judgments are accepted as sacrosanct. However highly he may be respected, he is neither worshiped nor exalted. No one attempts to invest him with omnis-
cience or infallibility. He commands nowhere nearly the popular
acclaim and adulation that President Beneš spontaneously

arouses among all groups of people whenever he makes a public appearance.

Likewise there is no attempt to glorify the party to the exclusion of the state or the nation. The party is an instrument, not a sanctuary. It is no end in itself but a means to an end. It is part of the state and the republic, but superior to neither. "Our slogan," said Klement Gottwald in the course of his address before the Communist Congress in February 1946, "is more work for the republic." The party is sure of itself, lauds itself, sets itself up as the truest exponent and the most faithful servant, not of the proletariat but of the people. There is more substance than rhetoric in the exclamation of Zdeněk Fierlinger, leader of the Social Democratic party, that Czechoslovakia no longer has any proletariat.

I asked Klement Gottwald how he accounted for the striking differences in the vocabulary and attitudes of the Czech and the Russian or even the American Communist parties. "I don't even read the words 'class struggle' in your daily or periodical press," I said.

"First," he replied, "you must remember that there is dogmatic and creative Marxism, and we Czech Communists are no dogmatists. Secondly, in our country, at this stage of our development, class and national interests coincide." The accent again on national issues, not to the exclusion of, but in synchronization with, class interests. "As for class struggle," Gottwald continued, "what do you suppose the nationalization decree means? We had to fight for it, and it was not easy to advance it as far as we have. Removing control of big industry and finance from private ownership is class struggle. Of course if reaction were to lift its head and subvert or sabotage the decree we should be neither silent nor idle."

But such class struggle, though in a lesser measure, happens to be also the program of the other parties. Neither the Catholics

nor the Czech Socialists have disputed the principle of nationalization. Without the vigorous insistence of the Communists
and Social Democrats in the Cabinet, the decree would not
have encompassed so much of the nation's industry, though
all parties were agreed on the nationalization of commercial
banks, insurance companies, and key industries. The line of
demarcation is not the idea of nationalization but the degree
of its implementation and the scope of its application. On this
issue there was and will be a clear-cut division between Communists and Social Democrats and the other two parties.

The fact is that the Communists, like their opponents, are
wary of open class war. They are too Czech to countenance it
and are striving to avoid it, even to the point of discouraging
strikes. There have been none of any consequence since the
day of liberation, and when they did occur in a few small plants,
the Communists were loud in condemning them and threatening
action against those who may instigate the recurrence of labor
stoppage. As a Communist secretary in a Moravian village said
to me: "We are a small nation. We cannot afford to lose people
or property, such as a class war would make inevitable. We must
work out our revolution in our own way, unless the reactionaries
launch a war against us." Therefore, Communists and their
opponents haggle and battle, compromise and yield, until unity
is attained and action agreed upon.

"What is the difference between you Communists," I asked
a Communist leader, "and the other parties who likewise
support nationalization?"

"We want to move faster than they," was the answer.

Most decidedly they do. They have abandoned neither the
hope nor the policy of the ultimate nationalization of other
segments of economic life which have been left to private
ownership. Still they are pursuing the method of revolution
by evolution instead of evolution by revolution. They are

copying neither the language nor the methods of the Russian Bolsheviks. They are seeking to build up and uplift not the class they theoretically represent but the nation and the republic of which they are a part. Their ultimate goal is no less the achievement of a classless society than of the Russian Communists. But their method is not the liquidation by special laws or special penalties of any one class but the amalgamation of all classes. There is nothing in their methods that can be spoken of as the "democratic dictatorship," by which Andrei Vishinsky, Russia's Vice-Minister of Foreign Affairs, in addressing an assembly of jurists in Paris, recently designated Russian Sovietism. If, as the leaders say, they are not abandoning Marx or Marxism, they are investing both with a flexibility which to the orthodox Marxist must spell flagrant and inexcusable heresy. I cannot escape the conviction that together with the nationalization of industry the Czech Communists are nationalizing Marxism.

How the Czech Communists would have acted had there been a real proletariat in the country with an impassioned class-consciousness, with as flaming a hatred of the bourgeoisie as the Russian factory worker shared or which it was possible to inculcate and fan in him, is anybody's guess. But Czechoslovakia being what it is, a land with but a feeble Marxian tradition among the intelligentsia; with the worker overwhelmingly non-proletarian or at least non-Marxian in his psychology; with Czech patriotism animating all groups alike; with no hereditary aristocracy and no powerful plutocracy to combat; with the Catholic as much as the Protestant clergy recruited from the people and never lifting itself into a caste of its own; with no illiteracy in town and village; with the heritage of democracy dating from the days of Hus and reinvested with modern meaning by his disciples, deeply ingrained in all; with a cultivated peasantry performing miracles of production on the small farms they individually possess; with the innate Czech dislike of peroration and distrust of dogma; with his gift of satire for pomposity and piety, whether in language or manner; with all these and many other specifically Czech traits and circumstances in history and in everyday life, the Czech Communists are turning their own furrow, with their own plow, and with their own hardheaded Czech cautiousness. One may or may not agree with their ideas and policies, but their sober language, their businesslike manner, their coolheaded, if at times one-sided and bumptious, appraisal of passing events on the home front are perhaps the chief reasons for the comparative tranquillity that prevails on the Czech political scene and for the capacity of other parties to come to terms with them on questions of domestic and foreign policy, however troublesome and explosive.

The Communist impulse toward dictatorial tactics, like the truancy of a wayward pupil, has more than once threatened to upset the order of the day. Following the elections in May 1946, in the city of Plzeň, members of the National Council of the three other parties, with a comfortable majority on their side, refused to re-elect the Communist mayor. Plzeň Communists took exception to this democratic procedure. To force their own decision on the National Council they called a strike, thereby not only violating the program of the National Front but disrupting the work in the factories. The arbitrary action was of no avail. Communist leaders in Prague interceded and put a halt to the adventure. A similar incident occurred in the city of Olomouc, where Communists were likewise determined to force the election of their mayor. Again the effort failed. Prague Communist leaders abjure such irregularities which, had they been initiated by other parties, would have evoked from Communists everywhere the thunderous cry of "reaction," "Fascism," "treason."

The Bright Passage

To the Czech Communists, as to Communists everywhere, Russia is beyond reproof. Not a word of doubt or aspersion ever marks their utterances on the Soviet Union. But then, for reasons which I shall explain in a subsequent chapter, serious criticism of either Russia, England, or America rarely creeps into the non-Communist press. The radio, which is government-owned and is under the direction of the Communist-headed Ministry of Information, is partial and partisan in the transmission of Russian news and Russian views. On any issue within the sphere of international relations, the Czech Communists invariably lend their full-hearted support to the position Russia assumes or defends. In any conflict between Russia and the English-speaking nations, Russia is always right. Tilts with political opponents over Russia are infrequent, but when they do occur they are sharp and impassioned.

There are foreign observers in Prague, and Czechs too, who maintain that the Communists are only opportunists who are biding their time. When the right moment presents itself, with or without the aid of the Red Army, they will "show their real colors" and spring on the country "a Moscow-made dictatorship." But this is easier said than done. One should not venture to predict with positiveness the future action of the Czech Communists. Though the overwhelming mass of the party membership are unschooled in the intricacies of "dialectic materialism," the leaders, especially those who spent their years of exile in Russia, are manifestly well versed in them. What new facet of the dialectic will flash forth someday in the future to twist out of focus or completely to obliterate the prevailing social panorama of the country is beyond the powers of this writer to envisage.

Yet one need be neither scholar nor prophet to appraise the known facts in terms of Czech historic reality. If the Czech Communists were plotting a dictatorship they would be striving to disunite and disorganize the country, overwhelm it with chaos and conflict, and create *the revolutionary situation* which makes dictatorship possible or probable. Instead, they are among the nation's most indefatigable champions of order and discipline. Fear of the cruel consequences of civil war, dread, perhaps, of the acquisition of the atomic bomb by internal enemies through foreign aid may be thwarting and halting circumstances. Whatever the motives that guide their actions, the incontrovertible fact is that, despite their habit of staging political "manifestations" during working hours, no other party seeks as energetically to infuse workers not only with the thought but with the emotion of an all-out effort for the good of the republic. Their loudest slogan during the elections was: "The republic and more work." On week ends, Communist leaders, like those of other parties, scatter over the country and address mass meetings of workers and other citizens. Invariably the burden of their message is work and sacrifice, discipline and faith. They are making no extravagant promises. They are indulging in no florid portrayals of a paradise to come. They eschew drama or melodrama in their appeals. "High wages and salaries," said Antonín Zápotocký at the conference of the trade unions, "are useless without sufficient food and other necessities." Their pronouncements to workers brim over with sober pleas and reasoned invocations for ever-increasing output in mines, factories, and farms.

Again and again they have pledged themselves to refrain from political manipulation in the appointment of managers, directors, and other executives in the nationalized industries. Thunderous applause greeted Slánský in Parliament when he said, "Party interests must not interfere . . . with the appointment of managers in industry. . . . Technical and administrative experts deserve to be well paid, and we shall not hesitate to pay them more than capitalists did, provided they show superior technical and managerial abilities."

Not that they have scrupulously abided by their commitments. Again and again their political opponents have charged them with constant and flagrant violations of their pledge. Because so much of the managerial and technical intelligentsia is in their ranks, they have not refrained from manipulations which have lifted their "man" into an executive position. That they have overreached themselves in their insistence on utter loyalty, as they interpret the word, to the program of the National Front is indisputable. That if they press on with such a policy industry will suffer serious setbacks is likewise beyond doubt. Yet they, too, must think of the electorate which in a future election will not hesitate to penalize them for errors that may prove catastrophic. Since they are passionately and strenuously production-minded, staking their own future and the welfare of the people first and foremost on ever-increasing output in shop and factory, they are under compulsion to fulfill their oft-repeated call for the subordination of politics to the fulfillment of the ambitious program which the Two-Year Plan envisages. Should they fail to do so, catastrophe not only to the economic life of the country but to their position as the leading party would be as inevitable as the coming of dawn or darkness.

It is obvious that, the more production there is in the country, the more sound it will become economically; the more food, shoes, clothes, other comforts people are in a position to acquire, the more tranquil they become, the firmer their faith, and the greater their stake in the existing political regime and in the prevailing method of achieving change and innovation. The more prosperous the country the farther it moves from "the revolutionary situation," out of which dictatorship may spring.

In the election of May 1946, neither political dictatorship nor Marxian ideology was an issue. The Communists campaigned on a purely nationalist platform and enunciated purely nationalist slogans. They won the May election by about a million votes over their closest opponent because of the clarity of their aims, the lack of hesitancy and ambiguity in their proposals, the superior energy they displayed, the more tightly drawn organization of their party, the faith of the electorate in the resoluteness and audacity with which they will prosecute the program of national revival on which all parties had agreed.

To this writer nothing that the Communists have attempted is more significant than the agricultural policy they have been pursuing and the Two-Year Plan they have been sponsoring. Julius Dŭriš, Communist Minister of Agriculture, has displayed a singular comprehension of peasant mentality and peasant needs. He has committed his share of errors, but the magnitude of the task before him makes some errors inevitable. He has taken great pains to disabuse the farmers of the preconception they may have harbored that his party would force upon them policies which were not of immediate benefit to them or which they would have reason to oppose. Eloquently he has held before them the picture of the individually owned farm lifted to new heights of efficiency and productivity. He has abjured all forcible measures that would upset their habits of thought or work or would wrench them loose from their customary way of life. Since four fifths of the farmers fall within the class of small landowners, his policies, which of course the Cabinet has had to approve, have been directed to aiding them more than the affluent group.

When in November 1945 prices for agricultural produce were fixed, the increase in the price of meats and dairy foods was proportionately higher than of grains because the former are a greater source of income to the small farmer than to the larger landowner. Wheat had always commanded a higher price than rye, which gave the farmer in the rich valleys a decided advantage over the man in the hilly and mountainous country that could not grow wheat but that was adapted to rye. The new law equalized the prices of wheat and rye. Prices were also graded according to the acreage a farmer cultivated. The man who tilled up to twenty hectares—forty-eight acres—received a higher price for his produce than the farmer who cultivated up to thirty hectares—seventy-three acres; and the man with thirty got more than the man with fifty or more hectares. The half billion crowns which the government accumulated from this disparity in prices it reinvested for the improvement of the cultural and social life of the village.

"How are you spending this money?" I asked Julius Ďuriš, the Minister of Agriculture.

"We are sending from thirty to forty books to the libraries of six thousand villages. We have bought one hundred and fifty electric ranges for rural nurseries, maternity homes, town halls. We have four theatrical companies that travel around giving performances in communities that had never known a theater. We have portable motion-picture equipment for villages in which there is neither a motion-picture house nor as yet electric light. We subsidize the building of Homes of Culture or Town Halls. We help villages put in new water pumps and other communal improvements, and we have already set aside two large castles as homes for the aged."

"Your opponents," I said, "call this buying votes."

"Not at all," he laughed. "It's something altogether different— it's keeping election promises. It's my *job* to help the farmer every way I can."

When the new land reform was under discussion there was a proposal to limit landholdings to thirty hectares. The Communists disapproved the measure on the ground that it would rouse needless suspicion and ill will in the village. They were not obsessed by fears of kulaks who might sabotage government reform. Like all the other parties, they opposed the continuation of big estates which the first republic had tolerated, but they would not subject the richer farmer to restrictions other than the slightly reduced prices he was to receive for his produce.

The scheme of mechanization of agriculture which Minister Ďuriš is sponsoring is void of any suggestion of compulsion. He is establishing two types of so-called tractor stations, one co-operatively owned, the other state-managed, with emphasis on the first. Farmers who for some reason cannot organize one with their own resources are assured that the state will bring them the advantage of the tractor and other mechanized implements. Four fifths of the farmers are certain to have the first type of tractor station, which they themselves will operate to suit their own needs or their own tastes. Nowhere is there any duplication of the Russian system, for the Czech Communists are not inclined to repeat Russia's catastrophic errors and remember only too vividly Stalin's counsel that they must work out their revolution in their own way and avoid the mistakes the Russian Communists have made. Conditions in Czechoslovakia call for an agricultural policy that meets the nation's own problems and that responds not only to the psychology but to the cultural background of the farming population.

It is therefore no accident that the highly individualized Czech peasantry, habituated to voluntary co-operation but hostile to repressive state control, swelled the vote which the Communists received in the May elections. More than half of this vote came from the peasantry. For a Communist party to draw such immense political support from the farming community demonstrates something new in Communist tactics and in Communist "dialectic." Were the industrial population and the National Councils in the towns to demonstrate as high a grade of prudence and application as does the Czech countryside, the Two-Year Plan, which is to lift national output ten per cent above 1937, would be a foregone conclusion. The voices of pessimism that one hears in city circles, among the intelligentsia as much as among other groups, would then die down to a whisper or be lost in the tumult of optimism that would sweep the land.

Even foreign observers who distrust Communists and regret the popular following they have won are constrained to admit that their positiveness, their optimism, their certainty of themselves and of the program they have drafted are a challenge that the other parties must meet if they wish to contest the Communist power and leadership in forthcoming elections.

If the experiment of revolution by evolution continues undisturbed, Czechoslovakia, far more than Soviet Russia or any country in the world, will answer the most hotly debated question: Whether private enterprise or Socialism can best cope with the problem of production. Years ago, before Trotzky became a Trotzkyite, he wrote: "We are acquainted with the fundamental laws of history; victory belongs to the system which provides society with the higher economic plane. The historic dispute will be decided—and of course not at once—by the comparative co-efficiencies of labor productivity." But these co-efficients, Trotzky emphasized, "must include quality; otherwise they become a . . . delusion." No Socialist or other advocate of nationalization can take exception to these words. Stalinites and Trotzkyites, Christian Socialists and atheist Socialists, Social Democrats and Bolsheviks, French and Italian, British and American Socialists, whatever the ideological gulfs that divide them and however bitter their hostility to one another, have one thing in common—faith in the superiority of the Socialist over the capitalist *mode of production*. Over this issue more than any other the dispute over Socialism versus capitalism has been raging with mounting fury for over a century. As long as the Socialist idea remains no more than a paper document, or a blueprint, however brilliantly corroborated by graphs and figures, however eloquently expounded in words, the dispute remains unsettled. Since the advent of Sovietism in Russia the controversy has been growing increasingly acrimonious. Today, with Socialist sentiment deriving fresh and robust sustenance from the ruins of a war-wrecked world, it has reached a new pitch of intensity.

The Czechoslovakia of today, more than any other nation, is the laboratory which is subjecting the idea to the supreme and most searching test.

Though Russia has been collectivist for a whole generation, it is well to remember that the Soviets inherited from the czars a backward nation, backward in education, in discipline, in technological development, in the skills necessary for the proper exploration and exploitation of the nation's resources, backward in everything except passion for sacrifice and resolution to win the battle of collectivism. Withal it was riven with internal strife and was haunted by the dread of war. The major portion of its energies it has had to devote to fighting the opposition, to educating the people and developing administrative and mechanical skills, to preparing for war and to promoting machine civilization all over the land, even to the remotest outposts in the Arctic. Russia is still fighting the battle not of surpassing but of catching up with capitalism in efficiency of administration and production.

Czechoslovakia is burdened with few of these disabilities and frustrations. Its people are highly literate and skilled. The German occupation has left a sorrowful heritage of laxity and demoralization, the correction of which demands more than verbal pleas. The one-time individual integrity, not in the village but in the town, has been seriously impaired. Not a few of the ills which afflict industry, politics, and office administration are the bitter fruit of what one Protestant minister has termed "the collapse of character." This is not a specifically Czech ailment—all post-war Europe is afflicted with it—but it is particularly dangerous to a nation which has made so radical a shift in the control of its major industries. Yet one must not underestimate the positive energies and creative capacities of the people, however much these may have been damaged in the years of the Great Black-out. On the completion of the first year of nationalization, industrial leaders could already announce certain astounding achievements. Productivity of labor had risen from fifty to eighty per cent of the pre-war level; the output of locomotives, which had averaged five a month in 1937, the highest pre-war year, had trebled; the manufacture of freight cars had leaped from 97 a month to 1,144 in August 1946, where the Two-Year Plan calls for a monthly average of only 1,250 during 1948; the output of motorcycles and electric motors had risen to the highest of the pre-war figures, and all industry had achieved seventy per cent of the pre-war norm. Meanwhile, the famous Škoda works had won the bid for the construction in Buenos Aires of one of the largest and most modern breweries in the world.

The recuperative powers of post-war Czechoslovakia are neither accident nor miracle. The Czechs have grown up with the machine age of the nineteenth and twentieth centuries. They have demonstrated a brilliant talent for organization. They are among the most skilled engineers and workers in Europe. The country is highly industrialized. The German occupation has left it technologically behind America, but post-war reconversion and the Two-Year Plan are intended to lift it to a high plane of modern achievement. Here is a nation which, despite immediate lapses and failings, is ideally suited to the working out of the experiment in Socialist production and to settling once for all, not in rhetoric and epithet but in graphs and figures, in goods and welfare, the old, old argument.

236

Yet it is the prevailing attitude of the Communist party as much as any circumstance on the Czech scene that makes the experiment immediately feasible. By abjuring dictatorship, by basing itself not on a class but on a national platform, it is removing the sources of internal strife and social turbulence which have hampered to an astonishing degree the normal working out of the Socialist idea in Russia in the field of production.

Speaking before the Executive Committee of the Communist party, Klement Gottwald said: "The historical test for each economic system is its ability to produce better goods at cheaper cost and to guarantee a better life while saving labor. This is what we have to prove during our Two-Year Plan." Two years may be too short a period to prove or disprove Gottwald's thesis. Yet given internal tranquillity and freed from the baneful interference by one or more of the big powers, Czechoslovakia will, in the not-too-distant future—not more than five years, in this writer's judgment—supply the scientifically tested answer to whether or not Socialist economy is superior to capitalist, not only in social welfare but in the domain of production.

17. The Four Freedoms

On September 4, 1946, I attended the reopening of the Voskovec-Werich Theater in Prague. Founded twenty years earlier by two brilliant and iconoclastic law students, this theater grew up during the last decade of the first republic and made spectacular theatrical and social history. Superb clowns and irreverent wits, the two youths built up a large repertoire of plays and sketches which they themselves had written and produced, and in which—now with good-natured levity, now with biting irony, now with savage satire—they lampooned the social foibles and the political pieties of the moment. They originated the choicest anecdotes in the country. They gave breath, sometimes fire, to the urge, never dormant in Czechs, of self-scrutiny and self-criticism. They won for themselves a national reputation and created a new theatrical tradition, as mirthful as it was merciless in its assault on native and sometimes foreign "Babbitry."

With the fall of the first republic after Munich and the ascension of the former Agrarian party into decisive authority, this theater fell victim, as did the progressive press and all other progressive institutions, to the ultra-reactionary policy this party espoused but was powerless during the first republic to enforce. Its reopening, like the displays of choice fruits and vegetables in shops and market stalls, was one more signal of a return to one-time normalcy, made all the more felicitous by the presence of George Voskovec, who, like Werich, had spent his years of exile in America and had just returned to Prague.

The play of the occasion was the well-known Hart-Kaufman comedy, *The Man Who Came to Dinner*. Jan Werich himself had rendered it into Czech and played the leading part. The theater was crowded to the doors, and the audience rocked with mirth throughout the performance. On the same day the press carried the story of Moscow's ban of the Hart-Kaufman play, which, together with Pinero's *Dangerous Age* and Somerset Maugham's *The Circle* and *Penelope,* the Russian Communist party had branded as fostering "a bourgeois reactionary ideology and morality."

Yet the reviews of the performance in the Prague Communist press, while characterizing the comedy as trivial—a judgment in which the Catholic press and in language more forceful concurred—nowhere hinted at its unfitness for the Czech public. Neither openly nor publicly did anyone voice the desirability of emulating the Russian example and retiring it from the stage. The play continued to draw packed houses. It was the outstanding theatrical hit during the season of 1946.

Not only plays but books which have been banned in Russia or which for one reason or another have not been translated into Russian circulate freely in Czechoslovakia. This applies to Russian as well as to non-Russian authors. Illuminating is the Czech attitude toward two Soviet writers who in the years of the first republic had won for themselves a wide following and who have recently fallen into disfavor in Moscow. One is Akhmatova, the poetess, who because of the excellent translation of her lyrics into Czech has been a particular favorite in the Czech literary world; the other is Zoshchenko, the humorist, who is well known to the general public. In spite of the Russian interdiction which spoke of Zoshchenko as a writer of "foul banality and political non-partisanship," and of Akhmatova as the preacher of "pessimism and defeatism," their works have not been withdrawn from sale or circulation. It is not likely that Communist publishing houses will favor either with new editions. But non-Communist publishing houses will continue to supply all the copies the reading public may demand. There is no law to stop them, nor is there any political urgency to sustain the Russian interdiction.

While the Czech Communist party has taken no official action on the Moscow literary purge, Vaclav Řezač, the novelist and a member of the Communist party, printed a letter in *Práce* (*Labor*), the trade-union and Communist-dominated daily, which is singularly enlightening. "The case of Akhmatova and others," he writes, "is an internal Soviet affair." Conditions in the U.S.S.R. create special reasons for such action, he added. Then, quoting Thomas Masaryk's statement that "the state is held together by the ideas which have given it birth," he points out that the basis of Soviet culture differs radically from that of Czechoslovakia. As for Czech writers, Řezač proceeds further, they have pledged themselves to work for the fulfillment of the government program. They can and will do nothing else. . . . Yet their duties as citizens need not conflict with their mission as artists. He ends his communication with the significant declaration: "When I write a book I shall permit no one to guide or order me around, and for such performance no one anywhere at any time can subject me to ostracism." Whatever else this letter may mean, it sets forth the view that Russian problems and Russian needs and Russian culture in their present stage of development call for special measures that are not applicable to Czechoslovakia, which in art, as in politics and economics, must search out its own values and fulfill its own aims.

Let the reader ponder the words President Beneš addressed to the Czech writers' conference in June 1946. I am quoting from his long speech only the most trenchant passages: "The object of all our efforts, material and spiritual, cannot be in the interest of one party, one class, one nation, one state, but must be for all mankind. . . . No art can exist without freedom, nor can it fulfill its tasks in the absence of freedom of expression. . . . Literature and art are the bastions of human rights. . . . The writer, like any other citizen, may be a follower of a political party but must never forget his mission in public life. He must stand above all parties. . . ."

Then, defining the meaning of the revolutionary tendencies of today, Beneš proceeds: "I reject the mere political conception of democracy. The democracy of our days is highly revolutionary. Yet I deprecate blind praise of the state. . . . The war and the political struggle which preceded and has followed it has wrought great confusion in the meaning of such terms as democracy, freedom, humanism, revolution, unity, reaction, political party, other similar expressions. . . . I call upon you to clarify the meaning and the content of the slogans of today. . . . Our artists and writers are fighting for a new world, a new way of life, which in our present revolutionary period means fighting for a new moral, economic, and social regime. The writer will serve the nation by studying these problems, criticizing them. He must tell the truth . . . and when necessary he must fear neither to encourage nor to condemn. . . . He must fulfill his duty as an awakener of the national consciousness. . . . Only a free man can discuss the problems of life as related to the individual and the nation. . . . No nation can become mature and cultivated without freedom for writers and philosophers."

Doctrine-minded Czech Communists neither can nor do unreservedly accept Beneš's interpretation of the function of the artist in our times even in a country that is economically as advanced and politically as mature as Czechoslovakia. They uphold the idea of purposefulness in art. They discourage and anathematize what they term triviality in the theater and in literature, however diverting and entertaining. They foster tendentiousness, though neither as passionately nor as reverently as Russian Communists.

Rudé Právo, for example, draws a clear-cut line between American and English film producers and those in the Soviet Union. "The Soviet film is seeking to portray real life and help man find his place in society, warning him of life's emptiness. Anglo-American production fulfills this purpose only as an exception. The spectator is offered what the producers want to give him and what serves their own interests. The offerings distort the consciousness of the spectator. How many people have already had their character twisted by this doubtful illusion of happiness? . . . The film always belongs to two worlds, and it is up to us to see to it that it belongs only to the one in which people are alive and filled with beauty and go forward pursuing . . . not a silly illusion but a full and vigorous life." The writer promises his readers that there will be an end to such pictures as *The Eternal Eve, The Four Feathers, The Count of Monte Cristo.* "Then no one will give us a worn-out farthing for a coin with a true metal ring."[1]

Since liberation Czechoslovakia has, perhaps, seen more Russian films than any nation outside of Russia. The films which realized their themes in terms of drama were accorded a hearty and enthusiastic welcome. Such documentaries as *The Battle of*

[1]*Rudé Právo,* October 15, 1946.

Gamekeeper's cottage of ancient Bechyně Castle

Castle in Troja, near Prague. One of many old castles in Czechoslovakia

Slovak peasants of High Tatra

Stalingrad and, even more, *The Battle of Berlin,* one of the most beautiful pictures that has ever come out of Russia, were acclaimed as masterpieces. But the films which dealt with purely Russian themes and were bald social or political sermons left Czech audiences cold and bored. After seventeen months of tumultuous tussle with Hollywood, the Ministry of Information, which is headed by a Communist, has finally come to an agreement with American producers for the purchase of eighty full-length American pictures and eighty shorts at a much higher expenditure in dollars than pre-war Czechoslovakia ever spent on American films. The Ministry, which is obliged to offer the public films which it would enjoy and therefore patronize, was compelled to make this move. Too few Russian films achieved such a purpose.

What is true of motion pictures is true of literature and the theater. Writers may create tendentious novels and plays, publishers may bring out the novels, producers may put on the plays. But unless these are vested with the appeal of art or entertainment or both, the Czech public will have none of them. The Fifth of May Theater in Prague, sponsored by the trade unions, specialized in plays that were political sermons, and while it lost money it won no friends. It was a dismal theatrical failure.

In literature as in theater, in motion pictures as in music, the new Czechoslovakia, despite all the wangling of Communists and non-Communists, has sacrificed none of the artistic values for which it was noted, in the pre-Munich days. With the changed economy of the country, new experiences, new struggles, new ambitions, new catastrophes, new triumphs will no doubt foster new values. But only if they transcend political verbiage and political syllogism or clothe ideas with human symbols that stir the imagination or captivate the mind will they find acceptance by so exceptionally mature and super-critical a people as the Czechs.

In setting forth his views on the new Constitution which the newly elected Parliament is to draft, Klement Gottwald, the Communist Prime Minister, said: "The new Constitution must guarantee full equality to women, personal and civil liberties, freedom of religion, and freedom of the press, of speech, freedom of assembly and association, freedom of scientific research, of artistic expression, as well as all other personal and political freedoms guaranteed by the existing 1920 Constitution."

In the light of the Four Freedoms which the late Franklin Roosevelt enunciated, what do these declarations, which are certain to be incorporated into the new Constitution, mean, not only in principle but in everyday practice?

Freedom of speech is encumbered with new qualifications yet is relieved of certain limitations which the first republic had imposed. The official censorship which the republic maintained is still valid but is never applied. While some of the old professional chiefs of departments in the Ministry of Interior had advocated its invocation, the Communists within the Ministry insisted on its abrogation. There is no official censorship in the country.

The greatest change is in the control of the press. Political parties and other collective bodies, such as intellectual, military, scientific, cultural, youth, and other organizations, of which there is a plethora in the country, command sole control of daily and periodical journals. There is no ban on money-making from a publishing venture, but there is the interdiction, to which all political parties have agreed, some quite reluctantly, against anonymous or private ownership.

The argument is that the press, like the schools, is an educational institution and should therefore not be operated by private capital. An individual owner, profit-minded or politically ambitious, the argument continues, may be more powerfully swayed by personal aspiration than by public welfare. In support of this contention, Czechs who accept it cite the case of the Sudeten Germans, or their own small groups of tumultuous prewar Fascists, who by virtue of unrestricted ownership of the press fostered dissension, incited conflict, which led to the collapse of the republic. A private owner of a newspaper or magazine, it is averred, may again be in the hire of a foreign power or a native enemy, particularly the dispossessed owners of big industry, who will stint neither energy nor gold to discredit the revolution and to wreck the nationalization program. "You must never forget what we have gone through since 1938," said an editor of a daily journal. "We must guard vigilantly and ruthlessly against a repetition of the catastrophe."

Communists and Social Democrats are the most ardent champions of collective ownership and collective responsibility for the press. Once in the course of a discussion of the subject with a Social Democrat he flourished before me a copy of the July 6, 1946, issue of *Time,* which is gaining an ever-increasing audience in the country, and pointed with emphasis to the following paragraph: "In pre-war France it was said that 'every journalist is for sale,' and the saying was embarrassingly close to the truth. The papers for which they wrote—rowdy, defamatory, opinionated, and corrupt—hastened France's collapse." "Czechs are no angels," he went on. "We had plenty of writers who were willing to sell themselves for money. We'd have them again if the opportunity presented itself, and we cannot afford to take chances with private owners who, if they wished, could obtain all the gold in the world—yes, in your America and England too—to destroy our Socialist program and our republic. Besides, it is not anything new in our country."

Most of the daily newspapers and quite a few periodicals, even when privately or co-operatively owned, were always organs of political parties, not in the American but in a purely Czech

245

sense, their editorial policy being dominated and dictated by party leaders. The ČTK, the Czech News Agency, like the radio, was always government-owned.

Under present conditions no editor of talent or with a message of his own which does not conflict with the basic program of the new government need despair of an opportunity to publish a journal that will bear the unmistakable imprint of his personality or his genius. Ferdinand Peroutka, the most celebrated publicist in the country, with a vigorous strain of skepticism in his mentality, is again publishing a weekly named *Dnešek* (*Today*). Emil Burian, composer and theatrical producer, with a flair for highly individualistic thought in art, leftist but nonconformist in politics, is the editor of what he terms an "independent weekly," named *Kulturný Politika* (*Culture and Politics*), which is decidedly the spokesman of his own views on life and art.

Neither Peroutka nor Burian experienced serious difficulty in forming co-operative societies that have assumed collective responsibility for the journals they individually edit with scarcely any reserve in their criticism of the passing social and political scene. Whatever else the elimination of private ownership of the press has achieved or may in the future achieve, it has not, despite a shortage of paper, artificially held back the growth of daily and other journals or prevented any distinguished or undistinguished publicists from finding an outlet for their writings. The sole exceptions are the men who willfully or zealously participated in the promulgation of Nazi or Fascist ideas during the years of the German-ruled Protektorat. They are barred from practicing their profession.

Already ten daily and seventeen weekly journals are in the field in Prague alone, and the end is not yet. If only because of the livelier journalistic competition it would inspire, individual ownership, released from the clasp of party policy, Communist and non-Communist, might more promptly and more blithely lift or dissipate the somberness that shrouds so much Czech journalism, particularly in the daily papers. It needs vigor and brightness even as a parched plant needs moisture. Yet one reason for the literary slump in Czech journalism is the dearth of talented writers, a consequence of the slaughter of the intelligentsia, of the paralysis of higher education and creative effort during the German occupation. There is no lack of controversy in the press. Charges and countercharges fly back and forth with the ease, often with the violence, of a football in a game of soccer. But it lacks the tang and the glow of the superior journalism of earlier days. One must hope that the young generation now learning the profession will emulate the example and the inspiration of the great Karel Havliček, the late Karel Čapek, who after Munich died of a broken heart, of Julius Fučik, who was executed by the Germans, or of the pre-war Ferdinand Peroutka and Jaroslav Stranský. The tradition is here rich and brilliant, and the need for its mastery is beyond compute.

Because there is no official censorship, not once has any publication appeared in the "white dress" (blank columns) which I often saw, especially in the Communist press, in the pre-Munich days. Neither the Ministry of Information nor any other governmental agency has ever issued instructions as to which subjects may or may not be discussed, though when under the pressure of some foreign protest the Ministry of Foreign Affairs or Information will issue special requests or suggestions to editors.

The press has news sources of sufficient variety and integrity to make objective, impartial journalism possible. The government-owned news agency has rarely been accused of slanting stories to favor Communist or any other partisanship. The Associated Press and the United Press of America sell news sometimes directly by teletype to individual publications. The British and American Information Services freely distribute their bulletins. Broadcasts from Great Britain, France, Russia, the American army stations in Europe, and from other places, however far away, add to the fund of information at the disposal of editors and public and provide enlightenment and edification to nearly every home in the land. Political rivalry is so keen, often so tempestuous, that not a few of the more partisan-minded editors choose whatever stories will best advance their own cause or reflect on the cause or the character of their closest adversary.

Nor are Czech readers limited to their own press. Newspapers and not a few magazines from Holland, England, France, Russia, America, and other nations circulate freely in bookshops and on newsstands; and in the British and American reading rooms, maintained respectively by the British and American embassies and open to the public, the leading literary and scientific journals in the English language are always available. The post office has already authorized direct subscriptions from Switzerland, Sweden, Norway and Denmark and is negotiating for an extension of the privilege to other countries.

Marxism, which is beyond and above all criticism in Russia, is a subject of continuous debate in the Czech press. It is still a question whether the Czech National Socialist party, the second largest in the country, is more vigorous in its opposition to Marxism than is the Catholic party.

Founded in 1897, the Czech National Socialist party is a unique political phenomenon on the European scene. It is Socialist but anti-Marxist. It spurns the materialism and internationalism of the Communists and Social Democrats. At the time when Marxists scoffed at nationalism as an instrument of the bourgeoisie, it fought for the revival and glorification of their nation. The National Socialists saw no future for their people in the German world in which they were living nor in international Socialism. Under old Austria they preached the gospel of the enrichment of

Czech culture in the Czech language, not only in the town but in every village and every hamlet. They believed in Pan-Slavism as the sole antidote to the Pan-Germanism which threatened to engulf the Czech nation. Yet they championed the Socialist idea of economics as the sole means of ridding their people of the class conflicts and the economic perturbations which individual ownership of finance and key industries made inevitable. With the publication of Stalin's work on the rights of minorities and on the national self-determination of subject peoples, they discovered a new weapon in their battles against their own internationally minded Marxists. Their slogans were: "More bread for our people," and "More freedom for our nation." Being an Austrian, Hitler, since the very beginning of his campaign for German leadership, perceived the appeal of "national socialism" and plagiarized the name from the Czech party for his own purposes.

Its present platform and ideology may be gathered from a speech which Petr Zenkl, the official leader of the party, delivered on August 26, 1946, in which, among other things, he said: "The National Socialist party never deviated from its popular democratic, truly Socialist program and shall never abandon it. In terms of sociology our party is the one which in reality represents all work people. Its merit is that it has educated the middle class into National Socialism and humanitarianism and thereby has succeeded in preventing it from falling a prey to Fascism, which has been the case in other lands. . . . We must be on guard against reactionary forces . . . the peaceful and fruitful work of the people must not be rooted in the idea of class war. . . . Marxian Socialism does not harmonize with the idea of political democracy, and that is why we repudiate it and emulate instead our own progressive Socialism."

Catholics, who predicate their Socialism on Christian doctrine and Christian morality, are rarely more acrid or more expert in their attacks on Marxism than are the National Socialists, nor are they more alert in combating any move or proposal of the Communists which looms to them as dictatorial. Communists, of course, strike back with no less vigor, often with far more fervor. The ideological feuds between Communists and their opponents, in the press and on the platform, enliven, at least for the outsider, not only the political but the literary scene of the country.

Yet no party and no publication engages in violent controversy over Russia. Marxism is one thing, Marxist Russia is quite another. Russia is an ally and a symbol of Slav military power. The alliance with Russia means no less to the National Socialist and the Catholic than to the Social Democrat and the Communist. Russian sensitiveness to criticism is proverbial, and the non-Communist parties refrain from passing basic judgments on Russian internal policy, Russian leaders, Russian international diplomacy. Yet I have read again and again in the non-Communist press unfavorable allusions to certain situations in Russia of which it disapproves: the literary purge, for example, or reprints from foreign publications of reports and judgments severely critical of Russia.

The publication that ventures too openly into hostile criticism of the Soviets is certain to invoke Communist indignation and wrath. Perhaps the most dramatic incident illustrating this situation is the case of the Catholic magazine, *Obzory*. Dr. Bohdan Chudoba, one of its editors, published a sharp criticism of Stalin's "dialectic and historic materialism." *Obzory* also made unsavory comments on the conduct of Russian and American soldiers during their stay in Czechoslovakia. It also attacked the attitude of certain Czechs toward Germans and took issue with the Ministry of Information on certain of its policies.

The Ministry attempted to suppress *Obzory* on technical grounds. It was charged with violating the ordinance of October 26, 1945, dealing with the paper shortage and calling for the suspension of the periodical press for two weeks. All parties had supported this ordinance, yet *Obzory* failed to carry out the agreement. The Ministry of Information seized upon this incident to air its pent-up grievances against the magazine. It accused *Obzory* of "attacking our Allies, especially the Red Army," of defending collaborators and Germans, of "dishonoring the Czech Army," of "systematically damaging the National Front." Since *Obzory* is a party publication, the Ministry did not have the power to suppress the magazine without the approval of the Cabinet. It is significant that the Cabinet refused to act. *Obzory* continued uninterrupted publication.

Shortly afterward Dr. Bohdan Chudoba was arrested because of a denunciation that he was in the intelligence service of the Vatican. The legal grounds for such arrests are rooted in the antiquated judicial system which the first Czech republic inherited from the old Austrian Empire. Under this system the police must act upon a denunciation of a serious nature, but if after the lapse of eight days the denunciation proves to be baseless or if the police fail to interrogate the arrested person he must be freed.

It was on the basis of this law that Dr. Chudoba was arrested. At the end of eight days he was released.

So long as the antiquated law remains on the statute books and the country has no habeas corpus act—a further testimony to the defectiveness of the old Austrian judicial system—denunciation to the police, if of a serious nature, must, as under the first republic, result in arrest, regardless whether the Minister of the Interior is a Communist or not.

Despite the revolutionary upsurge in the early months of liberation and save in the instance of active collaborators with the Nazis, very few writers have been under arrest and nothing has ever come of the denunciations and charges against a single one of them. Yet the non-Communist press has missed no opportunity to flay the Ministry of Interior for these arrests and to insist on absolute immunity from police intrusion on freedom of expression.

Unlike the press, book publishing has undergone no change of status in ownership. Some is under private and some under co-operative or party ownership, as in the pre-Munich days. For a small country, book publishing, always a thriving enterprise, has, despite the paper shortage, boomed into unprecedented proportions, with four hundred separate houses in the field! But only forty of these are of major importance. None of the well-established publishers need submit manuscripts to a censorship, for their reputation and their experience are a guarantee of their good taste, their prudence, their sound literary judgments. But the multitude of small publishers scattered all over the country are on demand obliged to submit manuscripts to the publication section of the Ministry of Information, which was formed not by the government but on the initiative of publishers and writers to prevent the printing of sensational or salacious books or of anything in derogation of the program of the National Front. The committee that passes on these manuscripts is non-partisan, with a good sprinkling of experienced pedagogues who weed out offerings which in their judgment would be particularly harmful to children.

Yet even established publishers feel the restraints that their own good taste and the political contingencies of the moment dictate. No publisher would offer the public an anti-Russian book. For that matter, while the Communist press has been severe in its attacks on American and British foreign policy, no publisher would bring out an anti-British or anti-American or anti-French book. Nor would anyone publish a book on anti-Semitism, on racialism, that is in disparagement of Negroes or any race, or on any subject reminiscent of Fascism, any more than on pornography, which the established publishers have always eschewed.

Freedom of speech, therefore, despite the absence of an official censorship, and while fully realized in literature, philosophy, science, is yet in the political realm and solely there, beset with the restraints, chiefly self-imposed, which the events of the moment make necessary and inevitable.

Freedom of religion is as unhampered as in the freest country in the world. Nowhere is there the least curb on religious expression in any form. Missionaries may come and go as they please. Barred during the war, the American Mormons are back again preaching the gospel according to the book of Mormon. The Salvation Army, an American importation, the Y.W.C.A., and the Y.M.C.A., likewise of American origin, have resumed operation, though not yet as extensively as of old. Monasteries and churches which had been left vacant in German territories have been taken over by Czechs, sometimes with the aid of American churches or American congregations. However atheistically minded Communists or Social Democrats may be, they refrain from airing their religious views in public, and religion among Czechs is neither a political nor a philosophical issue.

Because of the nationalization program no citizen may engage in private business as freely as formerly, though the restrictions are chiefly in the field of finance and manufacturing. Economic freedom has thereby been drastically curtailed. But this very curtailment is intended to give new life and new validity to "freedom from want." The sole purpose and the main driving impetus of the nationalization decree is to build a fortress of economic security for everyone which neither booms can shake nor slumps can shatter. Former owners who no longer operate their own business properties may be indignant or heartbroken. They may feel that the world has toppled over their heads and is certain to bury all Czechoslovakia in ruin. But their cries of terrible and imminent doom, as the results of the elections of May 1946 testify, evoke no response in the population, least of all in the peasantry, in the factory worker, in the white-collar folk. To them the new economic dispensation is the Gibraltar of their security and the sole guarantee of "freedom from want."

"Freedom from fear" has a special and particularly hallowed appeal to a small nation. Three centuries under Austria, reinforced by six and a half years of Nazi occupation, have made Czechs only too poignantly aware of the meaning of fear. Until such time as the world lives in an atmosphere of universal good will, predicated on universal disarmament, which will bar one nation from gnashing its teeth or shaking its fist at another, the small nation everywhere must carry the burden of fear in its heart.

But if as a nation Czechs may still be consumed with the fear of external danger, there is nothing on the internal horizon to engender it in them individually.

Fear was the daily burden and the daily torment of young and old during the Protektorat days. A man left his home for a walk or for his office; a woman went out to do her shopping; a boy romped off to a park for a meeting with his girl, and they failed to return. Sometimes they came back after a few days' detention. Sometimes they were gone half a year or longer. Sometimes they never reappeared. In answer to the question on an application blank concerning what he was doing during the years of the Protektorat, one Czech wrote: "I lived in fear."

That is why the Czechs are particularly sensitive to any government action or to the maneuver by a political party which may conjure forth the memory and the agony of the fear they had known under the German occupation. Besides, though they are a law-minded people, the Czechs, in their literature and folk sayings, have poked no end of fun at the abuses and asininities of the police.

Karel Havlíček (1821–56), the greatest publicist in the history of the nation, once exclaimed: "Oh that I were a policeman!

What fun! He seizes whomever he pleases and dumps him in the jug!" The Czechs still quote with pleasure his mordant poem:

> *Hear me, O people,*
> *In sorrowful warning*
> *I give you this song:*
>
> *Against the police*
> *God Himself*
> *Is helpless!*

Popular contempt and mockery ror a police state was intensified during the years of the Protektorat. Fear and torment did not dry up Czech wit, as is testified by the collection of stories under the title *The Voice of the People,* which the youthful Jaroslav Vojtech has brought together in a volume of 198 pages, and which for a long time to come will provide hearty laughs at the expense of the police state the Germans fastened on the Czech population. Because of their traditional detestation of such a state it is this writer's conviction that Czechs themselves, despite political pressures from within, could never bring it into being of their own volition, and that if it ever again clamps its might on them it will be as under a new Protektorat, chiefly through and by the efforts of an outside power.

Czechs who hate the nationalization decree and foreigners who echo their sentiments have charged that the existing police system is virtually converting the country into a police state. On what evidence they base the accusation is beyond the knowledge of this writer.

That the SNB—Council of National Security—which is the new name of the police, replacing the old "Guardians of National Security," has perpetrated abuses, especially in the early months of liberation, is well known. That some members of the SNB, which the Czech populace has already favored with the nickname of "Sunnyboys," have, especially in the Sudetenland, joined the charlatans and black marketeers who have flocked there in the wake of the German eviction is common knowledge and common talk. In the press and in Parliament the abuses of the SNB have evoked violent denunciation. They have made not only unlawful arrests, they have beaten people and subjected them to indignities. A new police force, the SNB has drawn into its ranks former partisans and inmates from concentration camps, some of whom have grown callous to human suffering and have let cruel whim or impulse dominate their behavior.

On Friday, October 4, 1946, on the eve of the Jewish Day of Atonement, five members of the security police posted themselves in the vestibule of the Prague synagogue and demanded identification papers from all visitors. Since this was the most solemn Jewish holiday of the year, there were loud protests on the part of incoming worshipers, accompanied by shouts of "Gestapo." Threatened by a riot, the intruders withdrew from the scene. Yet as soon as the chief of the security police learned of the incident, perpetrated by a subordinate who was given instructions to uncover illegal entrants into the country, he summoned the offender and, pending further investigation, suspended him from office. At nine-thirty the next morning, accompanied by his first assistant, he called on the president of the Prague Jewish community and apologized for the odious incident.

The Ministry of Interior faces a formidable task in weeding out and bringing to trial and disciplining the offenders within its ranks. That it is succeeding in the purge is testified by the decreasing volume of complaints against the abuse of police power.

National Councils in certain communities are still arrogating to themselves prerogatives in conflict and even in defiance of the Prague authorities. They are guilty of mischief against individuals they happen to dislike or whose property, when not subject to nationalization, they insist on operating communally or, still worse, for their own private benefit. Instances of lawlessness which pass under the revolutionary slogan, "the will of the people," are not wanting.

A Communist police inspector told this writer: "The National Council of the town of Usti became a den of pirates. And the worst scoundrels of the lot were the Communist members. They are all under arrest now and awaiting trial."

It would have been a miracle had the lusts and passions engendered in the years of the Protektorat remained in abeyance. This is especially true of those who had suffered most and fought the hardest against the enemy and of young people who have not had the corrective of a disciplined education. Excessive zeal, self-indulgence, greed for the other fellow's fleshpot have again and again dulled rectitude and given way to rascality and depravity. But the incident of the moment, however flagrant and brutal, does not necessarily indicate a basic trend. Nor does it belie the fact that there is an underlying stability, achieved by the balance of political power, which, like an indestructible dam, halts the backwash of political distemper or police abuse.

The Ministry of Interior, which controls the police, has no laws by which it may try or penalize anyone, however sordid or sinister his offense. The SNB is a uniformed and non-secret police force. The citizen need not fear that neighbors or strangers will inform on him, though as previously explained, the antiquated laws, now as in the first republic, may lead to arrests and detentions of innocent people for a period of eight days. Unlike a police state, there is no juridical body anywhere that can try a political offender in secret and sentence him to exile, imprisonment, or death on its own authority. Only a trial in an open court with witnesses and an attorney for the defense may bring punishment, light or stern. The judiciary is independent of political parties or of the executive and legislative organs of the country. The attempt of the Communist party to set aside the verdict of the People's Court on the five members of the Protektorat Government, none of whom was sentenced to death, failed of materialization. There were plenty of non-Communists who were as resentful of the verdict as the Communists, but they would not establish a precedent which might jeopardize the independence of the judiciary and endanger the protection of the individual.

So long as the Ministry of the Interior is prescribed by law from passing judgment on offenders, whether criminal or political, and so long as there is an independent judiciary, neither the spirit nor the performance of a police state can lift its head in the country.

The very expression "police state" rouses derisive comment among Czechs. As the government becomes better organized; as personnel gains in skill and competence in the administration of the law; as the law becomes more clearly defined so that incidents of confusion as to what is old and new law no longer occur; as the newly settled borderlands are cleansed of racketeers and fortune hunters, it is certain that the police abuses which now and then encroach on personal liberty will disappear.

The new Constitution which is in the process of being drafted, the commitments of all political parties, the desire of the people, the Hussite-humanist tradition of their schools and universities, and the inordinate influence of the academic, managerial, technical, and literary intelligentsia are more than a promise that there will be not less but greater freedom than under the first republic.

18. The New Society

"Our men," said a Czech woman, "like Czech buns and Czech dumplings too much for our women to take up careers." Though spoken in jest, there is much substance in these words. Home-minded and family-minded as she is, the Czech woman is not likely to be stirred into a radical departure from her customary way of living, though she is certain to become increasingly responsive to the new social gospel.

Unlike Russian women, who during the nineteenth century pushed out of the fog of feudal isolation into the limelight of social action and revolutionary leadership, the Czech woman has no tradition of public service to rival or match that of man. Nor did feminism in the American and British sense hold any lure for her, and for the simple reason that in her own Czech world she did not feel herself repressed by men. One has only to read a novel like Božena Němcová's *Grandmother* to appreciate the sense of dignified equality which women asserted in family and social life even one hundred years ago, when the book was first published. The passion for education which the Hussite movement had stirred communicated itself not only to men but to women. Mastery of Christ's Law, emulation and glorification of the Word of God, as recorded in original sources, were no less an obligation of women than of men. Women learned to read and write. They, too, perused the Bible, Hus's correspondence, the lives of the saints. The tradition of education did not die out with the loss of the nation's independence, and when the first republic was born, schools and colleges were as open to women as to men. The Constitution guaranteed women complete equality in all fields of effort, including politics. Only in industry, though not universally even there, did women hold an inferior position. They were among the lowest paid workers, not only because they were less skilled than men but because of the inheritance of the old Austrian tradition that woman's labor did not merit equal compensation as man's.

In the first republic only seven women were elected to Parliament. It is not that they lacked interest in public affairs, but their duties as wives and mothers were so taxing, their devotion to home and children so unflagging, that they had little time for the realization of other ambitions they may have cherished. There were exceptions, of course, and the Socialist dispensation is certain to draw more women into public careers. In the newly elected Parliament twenty-three women have won seats. But not even Communist women speak of the day when, with nurseries available for all children, with housekeeping mechanized, women will be as much a part of the outside world as men. The grandiose language of ultimate emancipation which one often hears in Russia is no part of the vocabulary or the ideology of Czech women. Lenin's precept that every housewife must learn to govern the state has evoked no special enthusiasm among them. When the Red Army came to the country Czechs were astounded at the presence of so many girls as traffic policemen, chauffeurs, snipers, and in anti-aircraft batteries. Catholic sentiment, peasant usage, middle-class tradition, three centuries of subservience to

Austria which tightened family bonds, and even Czech humanism have made the family a sanctuary as hallowed to the Communist as to the non-Communist. The sweep of new ideas is
destined to stimulate in young girls a new conception of their
place in society, and an increasing number of them are certain
to become career-minded; a far greater number will yield to the
appeal of a lively participation in communal life. Women of exceptional talent may rise to eminent leadership or become sturdy
crusaders. Yet *buchty* (Czech buns) and *knedliky* (Czech dumplings), symbols of family pleasures and womanly duties, will
continue to exercise the old spell over men and women, regardless of political affiliation.

"Would you and women like yourself," I asked a career-
minded young woman who spent her years of exile in England
and who is a member of the Communist party, "care to live in an
apartment house in which there would be a community dining
room, a community nursery, a community laundry, so you could
pursue your careers unhindered by domestic ties?"

"Definitely not," was the firm reply. "During my years in
England I worked in a Czech children's home. Twenty-five
Czech women worked there, some married, others unmarried.
Yet evenings we loved to get together in the kitchen, cook something extra we might have picked up, and talk of the time when
we should have homes of our own with bright and spacious
kitchens in which we could prepare our favorite dishes. Though
we had a parlor and other social rooms, it was the kitchen that
lured us. There we had our greatest fun."

Revolutions may come and go, invasions may be followed by
liberation, exile by repatriation, but the home always remains,
the one permanent source of security and solace, the one unfailing and indestructible refuge from all terror and turmoil. While
divorce is not difficult or expensive, birth control is outlawed and

so are abortions, and not even Communists are favoring the free practice of either.

In his *State and Revolution,* Lenin depicts at some length the classless society that Communism is eventually to achieve. According to Lenin, once this society is enthroned there will be no repressions by or for anyone, no compulsions anywhere. Conditions of living will be so comfortable that the slogan, "from each according to his ability, to each according to his need," in material abundance, in cultural elevation, in aesthetic enjoyment, will become the order of the day and the privilege of everybody who works. In short, the classless society as envisaged by Lenin, and before him by Marx and Engels, will be the society of the good man, the free men, the cultivated man; the society of the abundant life, without benefit of "jail or confiscation," to use Emerson's phrase. Even the state, for lack of functions, will "wither away." Here is a blueprint of the kingdom of heaven on earth.

Czech Communist leaders who know their Marxism and Leninism no doubt have before them the vision of the ultimate fruit of the Socialism in which they believe. Yet in their pronouncements they are silent on the subject. In his speech at the eighteenth Russian Party Congress in 1938, Stalin held out no hope of a speedy achievement of the classless society, or the "withering away" of the state. Since then, even Russian Communists, in their everyday thoughts and preoccupations, rarely allude to it. It is an ideal to stir the imagination, a Holy Grail to excite the emotions, but beyond the attainment of mortal men in the world of today or the immediate tomorrow.

The fact is that the average Czech is one of the least ideologically minded persons on earth. He cares less for doctrine and abstraction than for facts and achievements. A hardheaded, concrete-minded realist, he is as eminently practical as the average American. Formulas and precepts, unless clothed in terms of possible fulfillment, leave him unimpressed. He is too rational to be inspired by a mere vision, too unromantic to hitch his wagon to a star. Unlike the Russian, the Pole, the Yugoslav, he has no flair for the spectacular performance or the grandiose gesture. He is a little man whom history and experience have schooled to look before he leaps, yet have endowed him with the strength and the audacity to measure his tread not only with the arithmetic of today but with the mathematics of tomorrow. Caution has not prevented him from being bold in concept, dauntless in execution. Else there would have been no independent Czechoslovakia, no Czech nation at all. Karl Marx grossly misjudged the quality of Czechs and the power of Hus and Hussitism on their mentality when in an article in the New York *Tribune* of April 22, 1852, he scoffed at "Slav fanatics" in Prague, a "half-German city," who, after the "sobering" lesson that Austria had taught them in 1848, would never again venture to shake off the Germandom in the midst of which they were living.

The average Czech, who is now enduring privations which he rarely knew in the pre-Munich days, is preoccupied with the immediate future, with the rewards he may reap today and tomorrow. What are these rewards? First and foremost, personal security is no longer to be at the mercy of booms and slumps. The accumulation of personal wealth, while not barred, is sharply curtailed. A Prague trader found himself the object of a searching investigation when it was learned that within the short period of five months he had amassed a small fortune of twelve million crowns, which is the equivalent of $240,000. Yet he had engaged in no black-market transactions. He had done nothing in violation of any law proclaimed since liberation. Superior business gifts, even in the highly nationalized economy, still yield exceptional rewards. But such men are a law unto themselves. Like the oak on the Czech roadside, they remain upright even when the whirlwind smites down other trees.

Immunity from the misfortunes of economic collapse is intended not for them but for the multitude. The workers, whether in factory, schoolroom, office, on the land, and eventually even the trader and manufacturer are to be shielded from the onslaughts of economic crisis. Booms and slumps are to be supplanted by a well-regulated flow of the national economy. Regardless of political persuasion, Czech leaders are confident that though theirs is a small country, depending for its livelihood on foreign markets and foreign raw materials, it can, under the new system, weather with safety a world economic crash, as the former republic, which carried on more than two thirds of its trade with the Western world, never could. They are convinced that the Russian market will provide opportunities which pre-Munich Czechoslovakia never had exploited. This market, they feel assured, is immune from economic slumps. They also feel certain that, if markets in the West which they are now cultivating find it impossible in time of crisis to purchase from them the customary amount of merchandise, they can uncover new markets in the backward countries that are now striving to modernize and industrialize themselves. They are emphasizing, as the first republic never did, the manufacture of machinery and other steel products, not only because of the anticipated competition with Germany in the field of light industries, but because of the Russian market and the ever-growing demand for such products in the Middle East, the Balkans, India, China, and other nations that are rapidly discovering the boon of the machine. They are scattering their foreign trade all over the world. They are bartering machinery for raw materials. When in a position to do so they will extend credit to sound business risks. They will trade manufactures for food. They will do everything they conceivably can to keep employment at full capacity.

"During the crisis after World War I," said a Czech economist, "Estonia offered us a million dollars' worth of geese and other poultry in exchange for machinery. But the Agrarian party, not wanting Estonian competition, turned down the proposal. That never could happen under our planned Socialist economy. We could keep up the local price of geese, or lower the price of manufactures, so as not to hurt the farmer. Our workers would eat goose, and we'd keep them employed." This very employment, universal and continuous, is expected to increase and sustain the home market, because native purchasing power will not diminish.

The individual is to fit himself for whichever career best suits his energies and talents, and he is to be assured the opportunity to make use of these to the best possible advantage to himself and the community. The state shall not presume to dictate his career or profession. But because of the planned economy it will be in a position to guide him in his choice, so he will not prepare himself for a career or profession for which there may be little need or none at all. This will save him from the confusion or distress he may otherwise face when on completing his training or education he may be forced to readjust his plans for the future.

Education, always high, will be lifted to a still higher level, "with a view to giving all young people as wide a general education as possible and to providing higher education for talented children, irrespective of the social position of their parents." Any boy or girl qualified to pursue a college education will not lack the opportunity, though colleges and universities are to be kept free of students who may seek to attend them because of the easy life they may provide or as an escape from productive labor of one kind or another. The "eternal student," of whom Chekhov wrote in his *Cherry Orchard,* and who was not entirely unknown in Czechoslovakia, is to become as extinct as the feudal landlord or the private investor in big industry.

Eventually everyone is to have a middle-school education. Meanwhile, though the national treasury is low and must meet constant calls for funds for industrial and other purposes, there are to be more middle schools in the country; elementary schools are being elevated to junior high schools. Teachers in elementary schools are to have college instead of only secondary-school training. There are already more colleges than in the pre-war years.

The only new feature in the curriculum is political education. While the nature of such education has not yet been fully worked out, it is to be neither partisan nor purposeless. It is to awaken a new political consciousness in students so they will know what their own country is seeking to achieve and what the systems of society are in other lands. Whatever the ultimate formula of political education in the schools, it shall base itself on a principle acceptable to all parties. The parties themselves emphasize specialized political education under their own supervision. Not having a Komsomol, or Communist youth organization, the Communist party is accepting members at the age of sixteen; the Catholics even younger, at the age of fourteen.

One principle the new education will emphasize is that manual labor is no less honorable than mental work; the gulf between the man who works with his hands and the man who works with his brains shall be narrowed.

"The new Constitution," said Klement Gottwald in his address to Parliament, "will express the principle that every citizen has the right to work, for a fair reward for his work, the right to education, recreation, and to maintenance if he is incapable of working."[1]

The individual is not only to be guaranteed employment but full protection against all hazards and mishaps. The old insur-

[1] "Statement of Policy of Gottwald's Government in the Constituent Assembly," July 8, 1946.

ance legislation, however advanced for its time, is wanting in adequate safeguards against disaster, whether caused by man or nature. There is to be a complete change in the old system, with a view to providing full and universal health and accident insurance, as well as pensions not only for the salaried man, the wage earner, the small farmer, the farm laborer, but in time, as the national treasury grows richer, for all farmers and all business-men.

Unlike Russia, Czechoslovakia does not contemplate the abolition of private charities, though "the general social welfare" of those who rely on outside support will be put on a new footing, "unified and made into a public service with the widest cooperation of voluntary bodies."[2]

Mothers and children, according to Gottwald, are to receive "special attention." So shall women who work. Under the first republic there were 1,000 nurseries in the country. There are already 2,560, still quite poorly equipped and operated. But more and better ones are to be built when additional funds are available. The housewife is likewise promised that her position will be improved "socially and economically" in the rural community through the introduction of mechanized agriculture, the extension of utilities, modern plumbing and waterworks, and electrification, where it is still unknown. Nothing, however, has been suggested or is contemplated that would encroach on the privacy and the self-contained economy and social life the family has always known.

The more exuberant optimists, particularly the Communists, are convinced that the new economic security will further the social destiny of the family. Assured of employment, uninterrupted earning power, and state aid in time of mishap or adversity, young people, especially white-collar folk, will no longer be under compulsion to postpone marriage to as late an age as now.

[2]Ibid.

The expulsion of more than two million Germans has opened new space for additional population, of which the nation is in great need. The Two-Year Plan and other plans that are to follow will provide not only increasing amounts of home-grown foods, but more work in factory, in office, in executive chamber, in school and college classroom, and everywhere else. There is to be a lifting of the creative impulse in man and fresh opportunities to exercise it. There are only ten and a half million people in the country, and when its creative energies are fully developed it can provide an ample living for at least twice that number. The nation is as yet too poor to subsidize motherhood and marriage on a lavish scale. As it grows richer it will acquire the means to do so through individual allowances and social services. Because they are the only Slavs with whom the small family has become almost a cult, it is unlikely that, cautious and calculating as they are, Czechs can be coaxed into departure from established usage. Yet if prevailing obstacles to early marriages are removed, the birth rate is certain to rise. All this, of course, is theory, the fulfillment of which is predicated on a successful realization of economic blueprints.

In return for the rights and privileges which citizens shall enjoy they will be under obligation to fulfill indispensable duties. Save for the ill, the aged, students, soldiers, minors, everyone will have to work. This is not to apply to housewives who may be averse to forsaking home for a career. Work is to be "the primary source of permanent prosperity of the nation and the republic." As much as possible, citizens shall also participate in social activities outside their immediate jobs or professions. If farmers lack labor to plant or harvest the crop, non-farmers shall offer them aid. If a community project is at hand and there is lack of labor to perform it, the private citizen is to lend a helping hand. Once while driving on an unpaved street of a village I saw piles of cobbles and crushed stone in front of the houses. Inquiry disclosed that the community had distributed these so that the individual householder, under the guidance of a competent overseer, could pave the street in front of his house with his own labor. This is only an example of the social functions, which were not entirely unknown in the first republic, that the individual may be called upon to perform for the benefit of himself and the community. Brigades of volunteer workers are now a part of the social scene of the country.

As already emphasized in previous pages, the Czech farmer, though so often obliged to till his land with cows and old-fashioned implements, achieves astounding results and manages to cheat nature of a chance to pour its malevolence upon him. But he has not exhausted his possibilities. What could a farmer so gifted with patience, foresight, and diligence not achieve were he provided with the up-to-date laborsaving implements and the mechanical power which the American or Russian farmer has at his command?

"The network of local and regional co-operatives," reads the government statement of July 8, 1946, "for the joint use of machinery must be extended and their equipment enlarged and supplemented by all types of binders, threshing machines, sowing and planting machines, milking apparatus, electric power, etc." The annual output of tractors specially designed for Czech needs is to rise in 1948 to nine thousand units, against only six hundred in 1937. The tractor is to supersede not only the cow, but, wherever feasible, the ox and the horse.

The political administration of the community is to be simplified so as to permit the exercise of greater local power over its own affairs. Under the first republic the head of a province was not an elected governor but a *hejtman* appointed by the Ministry of Interior. While the local community had its own administration—an elected mayor and a council—the *hejtman,* with but rare exceptions, was the functionary to which it looked for guidance. As he was sundered from personal association with the people of a village or town, he was disposed to follow the old routine of doing no more than necessary and encouraging as little. Only in the event that there might be an exceptionally public-spirited mayor or an unusually energetic local council was the community impelled to break with the old routine and to launch into fresh and radical social innovations.

With the revolution have come the National Councils in each community. Organized underground or elected in the early days of liberation in the public square and by acclamation, these councils have been a source of ceaseless, often vituperative discussion in the press and in government circles. Despite the abuses which they have perpetrated, they have nevertheless released local creative energies. Here, for example, is the village of Liebenice in Bohemia. It is a small village of only thirty-five farming families, neither poor nor particularly prosperous. It has always been so conservative-minded that it was averse to saddling itself with a public debt for such improvements as a waterworks. Now the old conservatism is yielding to a new social spirit which stems from no particular ideological source, but from the purely psychological changes that the people have undergone during the occupation and since liberation. While Communists are particularly energetic in fostering this spirit, Catholics are likewise imbued with it. Public indebtedness no longer looms as a burden that might depress individual welfare but is welcomed as a boon for the advancement of communal and individual well-being. The public square in which geese strut and cackle all day is to be converted into a community park. The village is to build a new schoolhouse, new waterworks, and a Town Hall, which shall minister not only to social diversion but to enlightenment.

The village now has two inns that are, as everywhere in Czechoslovakia, social clubs more than hostelries. On festive occasions the two amateur orchestras, made up of the butcher, the carpenter, the barber, farmers, other local residents, play for dances in both inns. But aside from newspapers and magazines, neither inn provides purely cultural diversion or elevation. The sports society, no longer divided along political lines as in pre-war years, is the promoter of musicals, dances, theatricals, excursions, festivals, athletic games, and carnivals. But it needs quarters in which fully to realize its ever-expanding activities. Hence the project for a Town Hall, which shall be a meeting place of all parties and all ideologies, all tastes and all aspirations. Not only Liebenice but villages all over the country are astir with new ideas of communal enterprise, some with five-year plans, even with ten-year plans—nothing tumultuous, nothing specially radical or overambitious, but much that is definitely new and intended to enrich the social life of the village.

One evening a young agricultural expert called to see me. I knew him in the pre-war years when he was a stanch member of the Agrarian party. None could be more out of sympathy with the Communist idea. Yet he told me that he had been seriously at work on a project to organize young people in the villages for the cultivation of the acreages which, because of the shortage of labor, farmers were in no position to till, and devote the income from the sale of the crops to communal purposes, such as building a Town Hall, a mechanized laundry, a summer nursery, or some other immediately necessary communal enterprise. I could think of no Czech among my acquaintants who, because of his past experience, might be less disposed to such projects as he described. Yet here he was speaking a new language and thinking in new social terms. "You see," he said when I reminded him of his pre-war outlook on the world, "our villages have to be modernized and the life of the people enriched, for with the new opportunities in industry, youth will leave, and then what will happen to our farmers? Besides, we are living in a changing world, and new ideas have to be acted upon."

The concept of factory life is already undergoing a transformation. The Russian example of bringing culture to the industrial community is being energetically emulated. The trade unions maintain a special section dedicated to this purpose. Workers' schools, workers' clubs are rapidly coming to life. One hundred and fifty-two factories already command their own motion-picture theaters; 71 have formed theatrical companies, 52 have their own musical organization, 488 their own libraries. This is only a beginning. The aim is to make the factory not only an instrument of production but a cultural community that shall provide as many good things in life as available talent and ready funds, of which there is still a serious paucity, will allow.

There is therefore nothing particularly spectacular or visionary about the new society which liberated Czechoslovakia is contemplating. Collective effort is limiting but is not choking individual enterprise—not even in the economic sphere, far less in other pursuits, least of all in art and science. The nation is seeking to achieve a balance between social function and individual fulfillment without forcibly wrenching the community or the individual from established usage. It is rearing a new structure but on an old foundation.

Part Three: DANGERS & HOPES

19. Russia

In the course of my travels in Czechoslovakia I spent a week end at the Červený Hrádek (Red Castle), Sudetenland, in the ancient castle of Prince Max Hohenlohe. The prince was no Czech citizen. A descendant of an ancient family from Luxembourg, he, like his forebears, had never relinquished his original allegiance. His was one of the estates which, for historical more than for political reasons, the first republic had left largely in possession of its owner.

Throughout the years of the republic and during the German occupation the Hohenlohe family remained masters of the ancient and opulent domain, with its forests and hunting preserves, its streams and fields, and one of Europe's most thriving fruit farms. Perched on a high hill, in a setting of luxurious lawns and flowers, with mountain and forest for a background, the immense and ornate castle remains a priceless museum of feudal sovereignty and feudal prodigality.

The Hohenlohes were no longer in the castle. They fled, presumably to their estate in Spain, and in such haste that they left behind not only costly furnishings and art works but precious personal documents. Two of these—a neatly framed map of pre-war Czechoslovakia and the castle guest book, are of such historical value that the Czechs keep them locked in the local archives. František Vanya, the administrator of the castle and a local schoolmaster, invited Mr. Godfrey Lias of the London *Times* and myself to examine these documents in the cell-like study on the ground floor in which they were discovered.

The map was printed in two colors, orange and white, the orange sketching the German-inhabited areas. Across two thirds of these areas were drawn heavy pencil lines, and our host explained that these were charted in secret session in the very room in which we were sitting, on August 18, 1938. The pencil lines projected a scheme for the partition of the country more than a full month ahead of the actual consummation of the act in Munich.

No less revealing was the guest book. Under date of August 18, 1938, it bore the signatures of Runciman of Doxford, Hilda (Viscountess) Runciman, Geoffrey Peto, and Ashton Gwatkin, who accompanied Runciman on his mission of so-called good will to Czechoslovakia; also of Konrad Henlein, who on May 10, 1945, shortly after capture by the American Army, shot himself, and of Karl H. Frank, virtual dictator of the Protektorat, who after trial by a People's Court was hanged in Prague on May 26, 1946.

The documents, the Czechs contend, reveal the extraordinary and absurd situation in which free and independent pre-Munich Czechoslovakia had found itself. On its own territory, in the castle of a foreign citizen, an unwelcome foreign diplomat and Hitler's wiliest plotter in the Sudetenland had secretly conferred on preliminary measures to seal the fate of the country. No Czech had been consulted. No Czech had the least intimation what was transpiring inside the cloistered studio of the Hohenlohe castle.

The signatures in the guest book and the pencil lines on the map, both since reproduced and publicized in the Czech press, are ghostlike reminders to every Czech of the evil flung upon them by outsiders in a moment of their gravest peril, an evil which, because of the smallness of the nation, they were helpless to avert. As the schoolmaster who had fetched the document from the secret archives had expressed himself: "We were an independent country. We played an important role in the League of Nations. Beneš was a popular figure in Geneva. And what did it get us? These"—pointing at the map and the guest book—"and Munich and six years of enslavement."

British and American diplomats and writers who secretly or openly voice displeasure or rancor at Czechoslovakia's close bonds with the Soviet Union must ever remember that it was not the East but the West that betrayed the little Slav republic in 1938. It was not the East but the West that had torn to shreds the commitments made to Prague and transmuted into mockery the very word independence when applied to a small nation lacking the might to defend its freedom. What more natural than that Czechs should shudder at the very thought of a possible repetition of that gruesome experience. As never before, every Czech yearns for some *positive* assurance transcending mere verbal good faith or written pledge that never again will enemies collaborating with supposed friends pronounce a death sentence on their independence.

Munich, preceded by the Runciman mission and followed by dismemberment, then by occupation, stirred Czech leaders, who are exceptionally historically minded, into a reappraisal of their position in Europe and of their future. They were keenly conscious of the smallness of their country, of its limited military might, of the seven-to-one superiority of German man power. They were uneasily aware of the past unfriendliness of near-by Poland, of the hostility of vanquished Hungary, and remembered the readiness with which both had rallied to Hitler in 1938 and helped him ravage their lands. They therefore felt compelled to search for outside affiliations which in their judgment were more firm and trustworthy than those on which they had rested their security in the years of the first republic. Never again could they trust France, which in 1938 had arbitrarily scrapped its military alliance with them. Never again would they depend on the good will and assurances of the nation whose Lord Runciman and Neville Chamberlain were, as they expressed it, "the real gravediggers of Czech independence."

America is rich and powerful but is too remote from Europe. Munich had evoked in America compassion and warmth, even tears, but America could not be expected to consider an assault on Prague by a future Germany as an attack on Washington. To whom, then, could they turn for the much-longed-for guarantee of protection? There was only Russia, which during the war had demonstrated extraordinary military power. To Russia, so Czech leaders reasoned, in the light of Germany's age-old *Drang nach Osten,* an attack on Prague would be tantamount to an attack on Moscow. Russian self-interest was therefore bound up with their own security. Russia was near by and mighty. Russia was Slav. Under a new dispensation and by means of a new technique Russia was seeking to unite the Slav race everywhere in Europe for defense against a possible fresh outburst of Teutonic rage against Slavdom. The choice, therefore, was as natural historically as it was inevitable militarily.

To Czech leaders it was not a choice between Russia and the West, rather was it a choice between Russia and aloneness, between Russia and insecurity and possible doom. As Beneš has phrased it: "We are not between East and West. We are between Germany and Russia." With Russia committed to its defense, Czechoslovakia need not be continually harassed by the nightmare of another Munich or another occupation. If Russia betrays her she is doomed anyway, but Czech leaders are not counting on such betrayal.

Hence the treaty with Russia of July 18, 1941, slightly less than a month after the German invasion of the Soviet Union, pledging mutual assistance against the common foe. This was supplanted by the more detailed and all-embracing treaty of December 12, 1943, calling for a military alliance between the two nations and for close post-war collaboration in peaceful pursuits. Let the reader ponder the words of Ferdinand Peroutka, Prague's brilliant editor of the liberal *Svobodné Noviny,* who in an editorial under the suggestive title of "Our Chief Need," in the issue of October 7, 1945, warns his people to be clear-minded and stout-hearted about their alliance with Russia. All the more noteworthy are his words because the writer is an opponent of Marxism. In the event, writes Peroutka, that Russia and the Western powers fall apart, Czechs cannot and must not count on England and France to aid them in a possible struggle with a revived Germany. "All of us," he continues, "must realize that the alliance with Russia is the concern not solely of the Communist party but of every Czech party, and must remain the basic foundation of the state, regardless of who is at the helm. . . . Not only Communists but every one of us must be the guarantee of the alliance with Russia."

The program which was drafted and proclaimed by the newly constituted Cabinet on April 2, 1945, in the Slovakian town of Košice, when Prague was still beleaguered by the enemy, speaks of "the closest possible co-operation in arms with the Red Army." The "organization, equipment, and training of the new Czechoslovak defense forces shall be the same as the organization, equipment, and training of the Red Army." The pronouncement calls for a foreign policy that shall unswervingly be dedicated to the maintenance of "the closest possible alliance" with the "triumphant Slavonic power," not only in military but in "political, economic, educational, and cultural relationships." To no other nation is Czechoslovakia so closely bound as to the Soviet Union, for only on the Soviet Union is it staking its chances and hopes of survival, not only as an independent state, but as Slavs and as human beings.

Despite this close attachment Czechoslovakia has manifested no disposition to sunder itself from other nations. Consistently and methodically it has been re-establishing shattered links with other countries. It has negotiated trade or diplomatic treaties, or both, with old friends and even with some old enemies.

There was no "iron curtain" over the country during the first republic, and despite Winston Churchill's ill-willed charge in the House of Commons on August 16, 1946, there has been none under the new government. Nor is it the intention even of the Communists, if one may judge them by their words and deeds, to forge one or to permit anyone from the outside to thrust one over them. In the classic land of the little man, with neither prince nor pauper, the policy now, as in the pre-Munich days, is to build a civilization which, like the nest of a bird, insures security, comfort, exclusiveness, yet is not shut off from the light and balm of the outside world. From the official and unofficial pronouncements of all parties it is clear that, while the passion persists to give a purely Czech coloration to all that infiltrates from the outside, there is no thought and no intention to bar the infiltration or to hamper free intercourse with the outside world.

Yet in foreign commitments and allegiances it must pursue a far more guarded policy than under the first republic, when during Munich its protectors forced it into capitulation to the enemy. The fact is that in the world of today, especially in Europe, a small nation cannot hope to enunciate and pursue a foreign policy with as full a measure of independence as it did in the pre-war years. Holland is perhaps the most illuminating example. A Western nation which until the outbreak of World War II disdained to confer recognition on the Soviet Union, Holland pursued a stanch and inflexible policy of neutrality. It was vigorous in its repudiation of any suggestion of alliance with anybody, yet now Holland has cast aside even the pretext of wanting neutrality. The war has taught Holland how helpless a small nation is when a powerful neighbor chooses to take advantage of its helplessness. What is more, Holland realizes how feeble is its influence in the councils of the big powers. It was in The Hague that a highly placed official said to me: "We are suffering from a new disease with which all small nations are afflicted; the name of the disease is 'consciousness of unimportance.'"

The most any small nation in Europe can aspire to achieve is independence of action in internal affairs; in social, economic, and cultural relations with other countries; and in diplomatic associations which do not encroach on a major policy of the big power with which it is allied.

Czechoslovakia is no exception. Its alliance with Russia has not hampered it in concluding trade treaties with nations all over the world or in maintaining friendly social and cultural bonds with them. Despite the conflict between Russia and the Vatican, Czechoslovakia has its representative at the Holy See. It is the only Slav nation so far which maintains formal diplomatic relations with the Vatican. So, too, while Russia and Turkey are sparring over the Dardanelles and other issues, Prague maintains her traditional friendly relations with Ankara. Though Russia refused to join the International Bank, Czechoslovakia hastened to become a member at the first opportunity. Russia stayed away from the International Trade Conference in London in October 1946. Czechoslovakia attended. At this writing, Russia contents itself with observers at UNESCO. Czechoslovakia is a full member.

The new historic conditions under which all European small nations find themselves obliged to function are clearly demonstrated by Czechoslovakia. The list of its independent international actions is long, yet in no instance do these conflict with any major Russian policy, just as the independent actions of Holland do not conflict with any major policy of Great Britain or the United States.

Another aspect of Prague-Moscow relations is the absence in the little Slav republic of historic forces which give rise to grievances and anxieties that Russia may in its own mind feel justified in harboring toward certain other border states.

Czechoslovakia is burdened with no feudal caste or a vigorous, age-old, anti-Russian tradition as are Poland and Hungary. Here is no German-blooded emperor and a pro-German court clique as in pre-war Bulgaria, which twice within a generation flung its overwhelmingly pro-Russian peasantry into war against Russia, once as an active ally of Germany and in World War II as an active collaborator against Russia. Here are no corrupt court circles and powerful landlord and official classes which, in pre-war Rumania, kept conspiring against Russia and joined Hitler in the war against her.

With the major portion of industry and all commercial banking and insurance nationalized, there is no longer the danger of native magnates conspiring with foreign cartels or governments against the Soviet Union. Now that the Russian armies have left the country, disaffected groups can no longer circulate horror stories about their misbehavior, in some instances so rampant and predatory that it frightened the population. In the cities of Žilina, Zlín, and Ružomberok I heard few and only minor complaints. The prophecies which were current in Prague, that in retaliation against Russian misbehavior the Czech population would smother the Communist party at the polls, have boomeranged with a vengeance on the prophets. One reason the Communist party polled the heaviest vote was the Czech desire, all the more earnest because of the feuds and clashes that encumber mankind, to demonstrate their faith in the military alliance with Russia.

Yet the alliance is as much a test for Moscow as it is for Prague. For the present there is no evidence that Moscow is subjecting Prague to pressure in the administration of its internal affairs. Moscow's loathing for collaborators with Nazi Germany is only too well known; it always metes out the sharpest penalties to those guilty of this crime. The Czechs have acted in their own way. Save in instances when a Czech was guilty of high treason, there have been no death sentences. There has been no blood purge such as Yugoslavia and Bulgaria have unrelentingly consummated. Not even Jaroslav Krejčí, the Premier of the Protektorat, has invoked on himself the death penalty. Yet while there have been caustic references in the Soviet press to "reactionaries" in Czechoslovakia, there has been no official or unofficial disparagement of Czech courts or Czech justice.

During the war Slovakia was an enemy country. It was flagrantly Fascist. It declared war on Russia, England, the United States. It mobilized a large army to fight on Russian land side by side with the *Reichswehr*. It is still riddled with Fascism and anti-Semitism. Russia might have occupied the country, exacted from it reparations, saddled it with military rule. She has done none of these things. True, the resistance forces in the country staged a brilliant revolt in Banská Bystrica in August 1944, but without American, British and particularly Russian aid the uprising never would have attained the scope and magnitude it did. Yet neither in the press nor in official pronouncements has Russia claimed credit for this aid.

To Slovaks the rebellion marks a turning point in their history. They celebrate it as a break with the Nazis and their own Fascism, as a day of glory and splendor, ushering a new epoch in their political evolution and their social emancipation. But to such spirited realists as the Russians a lone revolt in which only a section of the population participated cannot possibly shrive the nation of the sin it had committed against Moscow and the Allies. Yet the Russians have given no utterance to such sentiments. I have heard Russian writers and officers say that not only Slovakia but Bohemia and Moravia may yet pay a heavy penalty for the leniency which Bratislava and Prague have been manifesting toward the dissident and disruptive forces within the Slovakian borders. But these opinions were privately expressed. Not a word of such criticism has crept into the Russian press or into official Russian declarations.

In the pursuit of their bloodless, non-proletarian revolution, the Czechs have been disregarding the formula of class dictatorship. They want to do things their own traditional way. They aspire not only to the democratic ends which Russia keeps on emphasizing as her greatest goal, but they are striving to attain these through democratic methods. That the end justifies the means is not a traditional Czech way of thought. Against Russia's "democratic dictatorship" they pose their own "democratic Socialism."

They do not accept Russia's theory of class struggle as a weapon of advancement or a means of forging a new destiny. They are in no mood to countenance a monolithic political party such as Russia has achieved.

All this is contrary to the pattern of Soviet usage. Yet, to the best of my knowledge, there have been neither rebukes nor denunciations in the Soviet press. Russians who visit Czechoslovakia, soldiers and civilians, artists and engineers, carry away an exalted opinion. The order and discipline, the cleanliness and courtesy of the people, the beauty of landscape and the magnificent architecture, the advanced industrial system and the superb though mechanically unadvanced tillage of the land evoke ecstatic appreciation. A Russian young woman with close Communist affiliations in Moscow was asked after her visit to Czechoslovakia how she liked the country. She replied: "That's what we want all Russia to look like." Then there are Stalin's words to the Czech and Slovak trade-union delegation: "We shall learn from you and you will learn from us." There are also the Russian warnings to Beneš, which the Czech President has often made public, that he and his government must not repeat the errors which Russia committed.

Russia has been heedful of Czechoslovakia's change of policy toward minorities and has given it her unqualified support, not only in the expulsion of the German minority from her borders, in which England and America concurred, but in the exchange of populations with Hungary, which the Budapest Government has for a long time stubbornly been resisting. The quarrel with Poland over Těšín, which the Conference of Ambassadors had awarded to Prague in 1920, might have led to more than the war of words in which Poles and Czechs once indulged had it not been for Russia's unpublicized but firm support of the decision of the conference.

Though by her treaty with Czechoslovakia Russia was entitled to all the economic assets Germany had imported into or constructed in Czechoslovakia during the occupation, the Kremlin has made a gift of a substantial amount of these to the Prague Government. The gigantic plant for the manufacture of synthetic gasoline which the Germans had built in the town of Most and which, once it starts producing at full capacity, can supply all the country's needs for engine fuel, the Russians have turned over to Czechoslovakia without any indemnity. Other such assets inside Czechoslovakia, as well as Czech machinery which the Germans had moved to the Russian zone of Germany, they have likewise presented to Czechoslovakia without compensation. To a country that has been bankrupted by the German occupation these gifts are a welcome treasure.

In the early months after liberation, when European and world transport were shattered and Czechoslovakia lacked foreign exchange or loans with which to purchase raw materials for its industries, Russia came to her rescue. The steel plants were kept in operation largely with Russian ore, and the textile industry, disrupted and disorganized by the Germans, started putting itself together with the aid of Russian cotton, flax, and hemp. The immediate economic crisis was averted not by Russian charity but by a swift resumption of business relations, which have proved mutually advantageous but which, because of mammoth internal difficulties, required inordinate Russian effort and good will to execute.

Despite these manifestations of friendliness the question persists: Will Russia pursue its present policy of non-interference or will it at some future date engulf Czechoslovakia and merge it with the Soviet Union?

Russians fume at the mere suggestion of such an eventuality. To them, posing the question is equivalent to an impeachment of their good faith and to charging them with the very rapacity of which they incessantly accuse "monopoly capitalism." The leadership of the Czech Communist party and the non-Communists who share its sentiments on this subject—and their number is neither small nor unimpressive—fully endorse the Russian attitude. To them, too, any aspersion on Russia's good faith spells no honest doubt, no earnest quest for truth, but a deliberate effort to whip up bad blood—not only between Moscow and Prague but between Moscow and the non-Soviet world.

Yet the Kremlin does not act on mere impulse, in disregard of purpose and results. One therefore must ask what it can gain from a forcible inclusion of Czechoslovakia in the Soviet Union, whatever the mode of achieving the feat. The very first and inevitable consequence would be a fresh and bitter tension between Russia and the outside world. It would arm Russia's enemies everywhere, particularly in Europe and America, with explosive ammunition for an intensification of their war by the written and spoken word against the Kremlin and against Communists. It would unsettle as no other immediate incident or circumstance the entire structure of European peace, particularly in Germany, whose people would in their own way array themselves for the conflict with Russia, for which they have been hoping since the day of their capitulation to the Allied armies. The peace for which Russia longs as desperately as any nation would be subject to fresh and violent shocks. The charges of Russian imperialism might be considered serious enough to invite reprisals, political and economic, from quarters that have the means and the power to wreak them. Most manifestly it would enhance the already deep cleavage between the Soviet and non-Soviet world. If it provoked a civil war in Czechoslovakia—and who is there to guarantee that it would not?—it might conceivably result in the annihilation of a large part of the country, its people and resources. Whatever the final outcome might be, Czechoslovakia would cease to be the land of promise that the Czech and Slovak peoples hope to make of it.

A stern and turbulent internal crisis, even if by some miracle a civil war were averted, would shake the country and for quite obvious reasons. Once a part of the Soviet Union, its internal economy and politics would of necessity be integrated with those of Moscow. Bent as is Moscow on gigantic industrial-ization, which inevitably swallows tons of gold or its equivalent into capital investment, the material standard of living, because of the consequent paucity of consumers' goods, would drop to the level of Russia's, and its rise would depend not on its own productive energies and faculties but on the plans that Moscow would initiate and fulfill for the entire Union. In other words, Czechoslovakia would be called upon to make inordinate sacrifices for the upbuilding of the heavy and machine-producing industries of which it already has an abundance for its own national needs, all over the vast and far-flung Soviet domain. There no doubt are Czech Communists who might perhaps welcome the sacrifice. Their reasoning from their standpoint would be logical enough. Had Russia commanded a higher standard of living she would have shared it with Czechoslovakia; why, then, should not Czechoslovakia, with her small though superior industry, help the peoples of the Soviet Union in their struggle for a higher level of living? But such Communists would constitute only a small fraction of the Czech and Slovak populations. No amount of propaganda, however eloquent, no vigilance, however stern, could persuade or coerce so eminently middle class a people as the Czechs and so flamingly supernationalistic a people as the Slovaks, including the overwhelming mass of Communists, to embark on so strenuous a feat of self-denial.

Political integration with Moscow would be no more welcome than economic consolidation. It would subvert the historic heritage and denature the immediate aspiration. It would set at naught Stalin's oft-repeated admonition to Czechs and Slovaks, Communists and non-Communists, that they must work out their destiny in their own way in conformity with their own culture, their own needs, their own historic inheritance.

One must of course allow for the imponderables which the future may unleash and which are screened from the vision and the intelligence of mortal man. Historians and other students of the contemporary scene must be aware of the admonition of Professor Fisher, the noted British historian, that "in the development of human destinies the play of the contingent and the unforeseen" must ever be reckoned with. If the world were to divide into two federations, one under the sponsorship of Moscow, the other under the patronage of Washington, Czechoslovakia would embrace the Moscow federation, though insisting on the retention of its present independence in internal affairs. Nor is it beyond possibility that the Soviet Union and Czechoslovakia will, in the faraway future, attain a common level of culture and well-being, and confluence of these two streams of Socialism would then be natural though not necessarily inevitable. But in this book I am concerned with the two countries as they are and are destined to remain for some years to come. For Russia to seek the forcible absorption of Czechoslovakia would not only be a repudiation of all the utterances that have come from the Kremlin and from Czech Communist leaders on the relations of the two nations, but would spell disaster for both countries.

Left to itself, Czechoslovakia is an extraordinary asset to Russia. Russia needs manufactured goods, particularly the high-grade machinery for which Czechoslovakia is noted, and Czechoslovakia can absorb mammoth amounts of Russian raw materials. So cheered was Hubert Ripka, Prague's Minister of Foreign Trade, by the commercial agreement he had negotiated with Moscow on April 12, 1946, that he said: "Provided we are prepared to co-operate suitably with the scheme of Russia's general requirements, the Soviet system of five-year plans will guarantee us long-term orders which we greatly need for the planning of our production and which will guarantee continuity of employment."

So optimistic was *Pravda* of the results of the conference

between a Czech delegation and Russian leaders in July 1946 that it wrote: "Its results will aid the cause, fortifying European and general peace." So elated was *Práce* (*Labor*), Prague's trade-union daily, with the achievements of this conference that it commented: "Markets now seeking supplies will soon be saturated, and the capitalist system will glide into an economic crisis. The agreement with the Soviet Union, however, will enable Czechoslovakia to escape that crisis, for a considerable part of our exports will go to the Soviet Union which, thanks to its planned economy, does not know any crisis."

Time will tell whether these eloquent forecasts will come true. But they are indicative of the spirit of friendliness and co-operation that now prevails between the two nations.

The cultural bonds between them have always been strong by virtue of Russia's eminence in the arts, especially in dancing, music, literature. The Czechs have rendered into their own language more of the literary works of the old and new Russia than has any other nation in the world. These ties are destined to grow and multiply. In the development of certain engineering skills and in the building industry Czechoslovakia has much to teach Russia and is certain to become a popular school for Russian technicians and architects, even as Russia is certain to attract Czech students of physics and agronomy, of music and dancing, of folk art and stagecraft.

Intercourse between the two countries, not only economically but socially, is continually growing. Even as I write these words I read in the Czech press of the arrival of a large delegation of Russian students for a protracted stay in the country and of the departure of a large delegation of Czech students for a protracted journey in the Soviet Union. Athletic teams from both countries are continually holding contests with one another. Commissions of intellectuals and workers frequently travel back and forth. Russia has already favored Czechoslovakia with visits by some of her most noted musical and dancing ensembles, such as the Grigory Moiseyev Folk Ballet and the Red Army Choir, which American impresarios have sought in vain to bring to the United States.

Nor is this all. Whatever one may think of Russia's policy in the Balkans, the one supreme goal to which it is committed is the development and modernization of their economies. To the achievement of this purpose Czechoslovakia can make a stupendous contribution by exporting its superior technological skill and basic products, such as fabricated steel and machinery, so necessary in the upbuilding of an industrial society. Three thousand Yugoslav youths are already in Czechoslovakian schools and factories studying to become industrial experts. Others will follow, and not only from Yugoslavia.

Because of its geographic proximity to Russia, its racial affinity with the Slav peoples of the Soviet Union, its friendliness, its advanced industrial civilization, its highly cultivated skills and work habits, its ventures into Socialism, the absence of feudalism or native plutocracy, its faculty of reconciling ideological antagonism into workable policies, Czechoslovakia is an immeasurable asset to Russia, but only if left to its own way of attaining a new destiny. Common sense, therefore, would dictate a Russian policy of non-interference in the country's internal life. The only possible gain to Russia from a compulsorily Sovietized Czechoslovakia would be psychological or ideological, or rather egoistic: the pleasure of the proselytizer in a new convert, a reward which is irreconcilable with the robust materialist-mindedness of the Kremlin.

But the price of the pleasure, were it ever sought, would be beyond calculation. Even if the Czech Communist party could engineer a merger with the Soviet Union without a civil war, it would be obliged to subject the people to rigors and sacrifices that could never be enforced without Russian aid. The internal demoralization would be so disastrous, the international embroilments might prove so fateful, that the very thought of forcible Sovietization appears to this writer absurd and preposterous.

20. Great Britain

Great Britain was the first country to grant the new Czechoslovakia a loan. The sum was five million pounds and the transaction was consummated shortly before the proclamation of the nationalization decree. According to Zdeněk Fierlinger, who was Prime Minister at the time, this was the first loan of its kind to be extended to any nation in Europe.

That British bankers should disregard the implications of nationalization is in keeping with their historic policy of making a long-range appraisal of a purely business transaction. Had they cherished any misgivings of Czechoslovakia's capacity to repay the debt or had they been dominated by a desire to combat Socialism in the little Slav republic, they would have refrained from offering this sorely needed help. That they did not do so, particularly at a moment when Prague was uncertain and worried over its relations with the Western world, was a source of gratification and reassurance to the Czech Government and people.

Yet Great Britain has caused Czechoslovakia more irritation and perplexity and has wakened more dormant suspicions than any other Western nation. There was Winston Churchill's "iron curtain" speech of August 16, 1945, which rang around the world and whose loud echoes are still resounding everywhere. As late as September 1946 foreign businessmen who came to the Prague Fair asked this writer and others whom they met in hotel lobbies or at social gatherings where the "iron curtain" was of which Churchill had spoken. Without directly retracting the false accusation, the former Prime Minister, in his speech at Fulton, Missouri, in March 1946, in speaking of Czechoslovakia as a democracy, indirectly admitted his error. Yet because of his world prestige and the brilliance of his rhetoric the charge has sunk deep into the memory of hearers. Facing reporters on the *Queen Elizabeth* in late October 1946, while on his way to America, Jan Masaryk was again confronted with the query of an "iron curtain" over his country. On Czech minds the thrust has left a wound which will not readily heal.

There was the outburst of indignation in a large part of the British press and by noted Britishers against Czech treatment—or maltreatment—of Germans, which roused further resentment and evoked the ghost of Munich. In commenting on the outcry, *Narodný Osvoboženi,* the daily journal of the Legionnaires of World War I, wrote: "In Great Britain it is reported that Czechs are deporting Germans from their land, forcing them to leave their homes for the devastated Reich. Mr. Bertrand Russell is led by these reports to conclude that the Germans, with their gas chambers, acted more humanely than do Czechs now: death in gas chambers comes swiftly, while death from hunger and cold is a prolonged torment. Opinions on the subject may differ, but one thing Mr. Russell's words makes obvious—German gas chambers and Czech transports are of one and the same category. We do not know whether or not Britishers are aware that this systematic abrogation of basic moral distinctions brings automatically to Czech minds two names: Munich and Chamberlain. In the name of the noblest human ideals—peace among nations—Chamberlain perpetrated a base and immoral act. He justified it on moral grounds. His people accepted it with joy. If today a part of the British press comments on the Czech resolve to end once for all the German question as an act of Nazism, we cannot help thinking that such a press would be morally capable of another Munich and that it is deliberately preparing a pre-Munich condition in central Europe. The Germans who treated and killed people like vermin, according to them, should remain in the position from which they set out to conquer and destroy. It would be silly to deliver sermons on diplomacy to London. It might even be uninteresting to know what London thinks of us. It might, however, be interesting to inform certain factions of the British public what we think of such methods."

These words appeared not in a leftist but in one of the most moderate publications in Prague which has evinced particular admiration for Anglo-Saxon civilization and has been steadfastly championing close ties with Great Britain and the United States.

When a member of Parliament, in a burst of indignation against Czechs for their supposed maltreatment of Germans, proposed that a commission be sent to Czechoslovakia to investigate the alleged abuses, there was undisguised anger, though little of it was reflected in the press. At a reception tendered at the time by the Czech Foreign Ministry to the Student Congress, this writer heard Czech teachers and students express themselves with vigor and bitterness on the subject. One young woman, a student of philosophy at Charles University, declared, "If England imagines she can unload another Runciman on us, she had better remember that Russia might have something to say about it."

There were, of course, members of Parliament who treated with scorn the suggestion of a commission to Czechoslovakia, just as there were writers and editors who never joined in the clamor of condemnation and vehemently upheld the Czech resolve authorized by the Potsdam Agreement, which the British Prime Minister had signed to rid their little country of Germans. But Czechs cannot help remembering the events of Munich, when the opposition to Neville Chamberlain, which included Winston Churchill, was likewise loud, likewise vehement, but quite ineffective.

The note Sir Philip Nichols, the British Ambassador to Prague, addressed to Jan Masaryk, the Czechoslovakian Foreign Minister, on the subject of nationalization added to the prevailing irritation and misgivings. Mr. Masaryk never released the note to the press, native or foreign, but an editor of the London *Daily Express* happened to pass through the Czech capital at the time. He uncovered the note, cabled the story to his paper with the comment: "It has caused surprise and resentment. American concerns are also nationalized, but the Americans have been most friendly."

Since then there have been tilts between the British Embassy in Prague and the Czech Foreign Office over a number of issues which the Czechs regard as their own purely internal affairs. There was the protest in August 1946 by Evelyn Shuckburgh, British Chargé d'Affaires, against the exodus of Jews from Poland by way of Náchod, Czechoslovakia, to the Austrian and German zones of American occupation. After the pogrom in Kielce, Poland, July 4, 1946, panic-stricken Jews, threatened with further pogroms, began to flee from Poland. The Czechs permitted them to cross their frontier, provided transport and escort for them to the American zones. The British note demanded that no Jews be permitted entry unless they had entrance permits "to the country of ultimate destination." As no country anywhere would issue such visas to the fleeing Jews, the demand was tantamount to telling Czechs to close their borders to Jewish fugitives. The note ended with the words: "I am instructed to press strongly that, unless these immigrants possess genuine and valid entry visas for their country of ultimate destination, entry into or transit through Czechoslovakia should be firmly discouraged and if possible prevented."

The arrival of new crowds of Jews into DP camps in Germany, particularly Polish Jews who are fervently Zionist and would rather emigrate to Palestine than any other country in the world, seriously complicated the British crisis in the Holy Land. Yet Prague acted only out of magnanimity and by understanding with Warsaw, both fully appreciating the gravity of the Jews' position among the highly anti-Semitic Polish population. But British diplomacy in a strongly worded note protested the move, even though to Czechs it was solely an internal affair and an act of humanity made at substantial inconvenience and cost to themselves.

The attitude of the Czech Communist press toward British foreign policy brought another note of protest in August 1946 from Mr. Evelyn Shuckburgh. However flagrantly erroneous Czech Communist publications may have been in their interpretation and condemnation of British policy in Greece, or Palestine, or India, or Indonesia, it pursues no more hostile a line than does the British Communist press or the liberal and ultra-nationalistic American press, which never cease to fulminate against the Foreign Office for its actions in these countries. To expect Communist journals anywhere to approve or to remain silent on such actions is like expecting the Tory press to evince an attitude of benevolent tolerance toward Russian policy. Mr. Shuckburgh's note elicited an expression of regret from the Czech Foreign Office and the assurance that *Rudé Právo,* the leading Communist daily, was not reflecting the official view of the Prague Foreign Office. Non-Communist publications have again and again taken violent issue with

Rudé Právo over its attacks on British or American diplomacy. But the question which the British protest raises is this: Shall Czech Communists and other Czechs in Czechoslovakia have the same right as British Communists and non-Communists in Great Britain freely to criticize or denounce British policy in this or in that country? To Czech minds the fact that the Communist party happens to be at the moment the most powerful is no mitigating circumstance for the British protest, if only because Mr. Shuckburgh cited not a single instance of official endorsement of the attitude of the Communist press. In statements before Parliament and in interviews with foreign correspondents, including British, Klement Gottwald, the Communist Prime Minister, has emphasized the wish and the hope of establishing and expanding trade and other relations with Great Britain and America. He has not permitted the Communist press to sway his official attitude, as reflected in his acts and in his pronouncements. If, therefore, the Prague Government were to accede to the protest of the British Foreign Office and clamp a censorship on the Communist press, which it has not the power to do, it would thereby endorse the double standard of intellectual freedom which the London Foreign Office is to the Czech mind espousing, one for British Communists and non-Communists at home, and another for Czech Communists in Czechoslovakia or Czech non-Communists who might be severely critical of British foreign policy.

The issue was further complicated by Mr. Cecil Parrott, the British Press Attaché in Prague, who in reply to a request from the editor of the *Svobodné Noviny,* September 27, 1946, expressed his views on how relations between his country and Prague could be improved. In a lengthy statement Mr. Parrott complained that "day by day the Communist press is accusing us of all possible crimes in Indonesia, Palestine, and Austria." He cites the instance of *Práce,* the trade-union newspaper, in printing an article on Great Britain by a Britisher who is bitterly hostile to the Labor Government; and another of the weekly, *Kulturný Politika* (leftist but independent of party affiliation), which, though it has been receiving books and newspapers from London with the aid of the British Embassy, prints "unfriendly articles about us." That Great Britain has had a friendly press in Catholic and National Socialist and other journals, that the Social Democratic press has been neither bitter nor especially severe in its comments on British foreign policy were not mentioned by the British Press Attaché in his complaint. Czechs interpreted this censorious attitude as meaning only one thing: that whatever the policy of the British Foreign Office, Czechs may not question its wisdom or justice.

In terms of freedom of expression the issue again narrows itself down to the question: Shall Czechs, Communists and non-Communists, enjoy in their own country as full a measure of liberty to express themselves on British diplomacy as is accorded to Britishers in Great Britain? Whatever one's views on the subject, the fact is that Czechs have evinced no change of heart. But Mr. Parrott's statement, Mr. Shuckburgh's note and similar British representations, written and oral, stirred so much irritation among the Czech intelligentsia that an eminent member of the Prague Cabinet who is also an eminent leader of the Czech National Socialist party felt obliged to inform the British Ambassador that the attempt of the British Foreign Office to apply one standard of intellectual freedom to Czechs and to uphold quite another for the people in Great Britain was as ill-advised as it was dangerous.

But if there have been exacerbations there has been no lack of happy and tranquilizing association. There have been the visits of delegations of trade-union leaders and of Labor members of Parliament who have traveled widely, have met Czech leaders and people, and have given both hearty assurance of the good faith of the British people and of the support which

British Labor is ready to accord them in their Socialist program. There has been the visit of Sir Hartley Shawcross, Attorney General of the Labor Government and chief British prosecuting attorney at the Nuremberg trials, whose words of approval of the transfer of Germans were particularly welcome. There have been the visits of John Priestley, the author, and of Ellen Wilkinson, the British Minister of Education, who likewise spoke with hope and encouragement of the Czechoslovakian struggle toward a new way of life. There has been an exhibition of a library of two thousand books published in Great Britain during the war years, acquainting Czechs and Slovaks with the literary and intellectual developments in Great Britain during the years they were sealed off from the outside world. There have been further visits by noted Britishers, scientists and artists especially, whom the Czech public was eager to hear and to welcome. There have been exchanges of visits of young people. There is the Czech college in Hassobury, England, in which Czech students between the ages of sixteen and twenty spend ten months studying English language, literature, and British institutions. Above all, there have been the singularly well-organized ventures of the British Institute and of the British Council, which are housed in a former palace of Empress Maria Theresa in Prague, to bring to the Czech public a knowledge and appreciation of the best in British art and culture. The British Film Festival, the exhibition of British painting, the visit of the London Art Theatre, which gave performances in Shakespeare and Shaw, have brought enlightenment and edification. The clamorous enthusiasm with which Czech audiences greeted the Art Theatre must have been an experience the actors will ever remember and cherish. Whenever a Czech audience has the privilege of greeting a superior foreign theatrical or musical organization, whether British, Russian, or American, politics melt away like snow before fire, and art lifts people above the barriers of geography and nationality. There has been such a demonstration of British good will in the field of art and science and culture that the weekly, *Kulturný Politika,* ran a cartoon on its front page showing two Czechs facing an array of announcements of British offerings and one of them remarking to the other: "Look here, we have been discovered." The ironic implication, all the more meaningful to Czechs because of Neville Chamberlain's one-time reference to their land as "that little-known country," did not detract from the appraisal of the high quality of British cultural offerings.

The historic and intellectual ties between Czechoslovakia and Great Britain have been many-sided and at times powerful. Czechs know that the Hussite revolution, whose social heritage is acknowledged with equal enthusiasm by Communist and Catholic, derived much of its guidance and inspiration from John Wycliffe. "I am drawn to Wycliffe," wrote Hus, "by his reputation among good priests and with the University of Oxford and among people generally. I am drawn to him by his writings by which he seeks to bring all men back to the Law of Christ, and cause churchmen to spurn pomp and tyranny." Hus spoke affectionately of "the blessed land of England."

Lord Byron and, far more, Shakespeare and Shaw have played an eminent role in the development of Czech literature, the Czech theater, Czech intellectual life. Byron inspired the youthful Karel Hynek Macha to found the romantic movement in Czech poetry. Byron's *Childe Harold,* in translation, is required study in the secondary schools. As the defender of Greece, a small nation, Byron, losing his life in its fight for freedom, became a symbol of liberty all the more precious to Czechs because the Austria of those days had passionately striven to Germanize them and to put an end to their claims and hopes of an independent life.

Shakespeare and Shaw, like the great Russians, Tolstoy, Turgenev, Gogol, Dostoyevsky, had been intellectual and spiritual antidotes to the flood of Germanism amidst which they lived and which threatened to submerge them. Josef V. Sladek and Bohumil Stepanek gave the Czech people two complete and excellent translations of Shakespeare, and Erich Soudek is now making a third. Besides, there are many scattered translations of individual plays. Not a school of the theater that Prague has known—classical, realist, impressionist—but has given the tragedies and the comedies their own interpretations.

Because Czechs have had no upper class since the loss of their independence in 1620, an iconoclast like Shaw, who aimed his sharpest barbs at the upper class in his own land, has won a special place for himself in the Czech mind. London might have reviled the younger Shaw, but Prague always applauded him, and British visitors to Prague were unpleasantly impressed by Shaw's popularity there. Depicting the British upper class as neither giants nor heroes, neither sages nor even wise fools, Shaw flattered the little man, which the Czech essentially is. Shaw was the prophet of the new day when the little man could gather courage and strength of body and soul for the battle of his own emancipation and his own glorification. Shaw stirred national sentiment and helped galvanize the social-mindedness which the Czech had acquired from his Hussite heritage.

During the war years Czechs listened to the BBC with unfailing eagerness and regularity, despite German bans and the danger of forfeiting one's life by violating them. It had been a stupendous source of succor and faith. Winston Churchill's speeches were particularly welcome, and so highly appreciative were Czechs of the courage and the optimism he inspired that they named the handmade attachment to their radios for short-wave broadcasts "churchilka." *Máme to dobry* (all is well) became the customary greeting among Czechs after they had heard the nightly BBC broadcast.

British heroism during the war years was and still is lauded with enthusiasm. The *Rudé Právo,* which has been the cause of a diplomatic protest by the British Chargé d'Affaires, in writing of the Battle of Britain said: "Six years have elapsed since the German Luftwaffe, intoxicated with speedy victories in Poland, northern Europe, and France, sought to break the morale of the British people by murderous air attacks on open British cities and to force the British into capitulation. The whole world was watching the British Air Force with pride mingled with anxiety, and we in Czechoslovakia also remember our own Eagles—who fought on the first line of defenses of Britain, which at the moment were the defenses of the world.

"We remember those civilian and military heroes of Great Britain with the wish that the bloodshed in the fight against aggressors and murderers should not be forgotten but should accelerate the joint progress of the Allies in the building of the just and secure peace that is greatly needed by all tortured nations."

It is too early yet to make an appraisal of the lessons Czech exiles in London learned during their stay there, which are certain to exert no small influence on the future development of Czechoslovakia.

One particularly salutary lesson is already manifest: the increasing politeness of the Czech city police. Vaclav Nosek, the Communist Minister of Interior, who spent his years of exile in London, was so profoundly impressed by the politeness of the British bobby that he is seeking to inculcate it in the Czech police force.

On the eve of the arrival of the London Arts Theatre in Prague, *Svobodné Noviny,* organ of the Czech National Socialist party, in surveying the relations between Great Britain and Czechoslovakia during the past eight years wrote: "Because our affection . . . for the Soviet Union is not blind, we must cherish Western culture. To break with it would be dishonorable, might even bring evil consequences. . . . We hope that the country of Masaryk may become a . . . unifying force between the land of Dostoyevsky and the land of Shakespeare."

If these sentiments are to gain validity and power there must be an active appreciation by Great Britain of two aspects of Czech national life which are uppermost in Czech minds: respect for their internal policy, and the inviolability of the Prague-Moscow military alliance. "There are publications in Great Britain which are continually abusing us," commented a Czech editor, "but we do not rush with diplomatic notes of protest to the London Foreign Office. Reciprocity on this score we must have, even if we are a small nation and Great Britain is a great power."

Yet no Czech is taking a pessimistic view of future relations with Great Britain. Quite the contrary, the hope is growing that self-interest, if no other force, will in time awaken the Foreign Office to an appreciation of the fruitlessness of its efforts to make Czechoslovakia conform to policies and standards which the British people would never accept were anyone seeking to urge or foist it on them. There is universal and hallowed admiration for the British people and all they have achieved throughout their long and triumphant history. Britishers in ever-increasing numbers are coming to Czechoslovakia and have an opportunity to observe closely and openly its achievements, which in many ways parallel their own efforts to reshape their own economy and better their own lives. For international as well as for purely economic reasons Great Britain needs Czechoslovakia's friendship even as much as Czechoslovakia needs hers. There are no real conflicts between the two peoples. There are only social, cultural, and material bonds.

21. America

In 1929 a group of Mormons from Utah came to Czechoslovakia to open a mission. They were young men, some with a college education, all athletically inclined. They knew nothing of Czechoslovakia, not a word of the Czech language, and the Czechs knew nothing of Mormonism or Mormons. The youthful missionaries soon learned that Czechs were sports-minded and proceeded to teach them basketball, with which Czechs had already dallied at the Prague Y.M.C.A. In time the Mormons learned to speak Czech and the Czechs became such experts at basketball that in an international tournament in which Poland, Latvia, and Estonia participated the Mormon-coached Czech team won first honors. Basketball is now one of the most popular games in the country.

Softball was unknown in Czechoslovakia, and the Mormons again got busy. They had located some balls but were without bats. Searching around the basement of the Y.M.C.A., they found a supply of bats which the Y.M.C.A. secretaries who had been with the Czech Army in Siberia during World War I had brought with them but which the janitors of the building, ignorant of softball, had been busily chopping up for kindling wood. The Mormons rescued the remaining bats and presently registered another triumph in their athletic accomplishments.

Having learned the language and made themselves popular with the people, they proceeded to translate the book of Mormonism, Mormon songs, the Mormon "Word of Wisdom," and held meetings at which they both preached and gave concerts. In 1930, at the fair in the city of Pardubice, they held a Mormon exhibit in which they featured not only the "fruits of Mormonism," but the glories of Utah, "America's Wonderland." Three of the Mormon missionaries married Czech girls.

Mormonism was a little too much for Czech rationalism, and the religious following the missionaries attracted was limited to 210 members. But the brand of Americanism they embodied and symbolized—love of outdoors, of athletics, of singing, the ease with which they identified themselves with the native population, their superb physical appearance—made friends not only for them but for the country they represented.

The Y.M.C.A. came from America and grew up with the first republic. Its contribution to sports, physical culture, and good-fellowship, regardless of religious or political persuasion, made it a popular institution. Like all alien influences, intellectual or institutional, which have come to Czechoslovakia, it yielded to native influence, particularly to Czech humanism. Unlike other Y.M.C.A.s in Europe, it chose to emphasize not the purely national but the distinctively international character of its services. It called itself not the Czechoslovakian Y.M.C.A. but the Y.M.C.A. of Czechoslovakia. In the days when Communists were treated with obloquy, it welcomed them into its ranks. It has insured immortality for itself by the community Christmas tree it introduced. Brilliantly illumined with electric lights, the tree first made its appearance in the city of Olomouc in 1926. In a country where Christmas is invested with romance and beauty, it evoked an instantaneous and hearty response. It was in tune with folk tradition and the spirit of cheer of the Christmas festival. Since then every community in the country has had its public Christmas tree, as impressive a feature of Christmas celebration as midnight Mass on Christmas Eve or the endless round of social events that enlivens every home in the land.

Links between Czechoslovakia and America, now as in the prewar years, have been many and fraternal. There is hardly a family but has blood ties with America, for one and a half million Czechs and Slovaks have made America their home. Known as Bohemians, the Czechs have been among our sturdiest and most prosperous pioneers. In honor of the quality of their citizenship and in recognition of the merits of the culture which they brought with them, the University of Texas maintains a department of Czech language, history, and literature. The states of Kansas, Iowa, and especially Nebraska are dotted with thriving Bohemian communities.

The wife of Thomas Masaryk, founder of the first republic, and the mother of Jan Masaryk, the present Minister of Foreign Affairs, was a girl named Charlotte Carrigue, from Brooklyn, New York. Woodrow Wilson was one of the architects of the first republic, and until the Germans removed it and melted it into scrap, the bronze statue to the professor-President in front of the railroad station, named for him, was one of the more impressive monuments of Prague. Schools, streets, squares bear the name of Woodrow Wilson.

Like Russia, America had no part in Munich. That catastrophe was the consummation of French, British, and Polish diplomacy. Though helpless to avert it, Washington never accepted it or any of its consequences. As Laurence Steinhardt, the American Ambassador at Prague, pointed out in a lecture at Charles University, the Czechoslovakian flag was kept flying in America throughout the years of German occupation. Immedi-

307

ately after Munich, when on Göring's demand Beneš resigned from the presidency, and even before he departed from Prague, the University of Chicago offered him a chair. Beneš lectured there for a year.

Franklin Roosevelt's devotion to small nations, especially those who fell victim to Nazi military might, has made him a heroic figure in the Allied nations, but nowhere more beloved than in Czechoslovakia. His war speeches, with their accent on humanist ideas, found fervent response among the embattled Czechs. Like Woodrow Wilson, Roosevelt has attained the stature of a national hero.

For a small country, Czechoslovakia was one of the best trading partners America had in pre-Munich days. In 1937, the last year of its independence, one tenth of its exports were found on the shelves of American shops. They were chiefly commodities that offered little or no competition with native products. Thrifty and prosperous, pre-war Czechoslovakia proved an excellent customer and an unexcelled business risk.

In pre-Munich years thousands of American tourists traveled to Czechoslovakia and were impressed by the beauty of its architecture, the grandeur of its scenery, the friendliness of its people, and the choice gifts they could purchase in glassware, china, textiles, ceramics, other typical Czech crafts.

Since the end of the war America's contribution to the rehabilitation of the country has been stupendous. On leaving Czechoslovakia the American Army that liberated the northern provinces donated to the Prague Government equipment and raw materials worth several million dollars. The American Red Cross contributed supplies to the amount of $3,000,000; the National Catholic Brotherhood, $1,000,000; Czechoslovak American Relief, $3,500,000; and there was another $1,000,000 of gift packages. The Export-Import Bank granted a credit of $20,000,-

ooo for cotton, $2,000,000 for tobacco. Another $10,000,000 credit
was used up for the purchase of surplus army supplies in
Europe. America's contribution to UNRRA aid in Czechoslovakia was $206,000,000, almost three fourths of the amount ap-
propriated. UNRRA aid was no loan but an outright dona-
tion which the Czechoslovakian Government has used for purposes of relief and rehabilitation. American products were so
skillfully advertised by American labels, tiny American flags,
American stickers, that—contrary to reports which certain members of the American Embassy in Prague lavishly submitted to
Washington complaining that Czechs associated UNRRA with
Russia because the chief of the mission was a Russian and because some of the supplies were transported through the Russian zone—the very word UNRRA became identified with
America. This was, of course, an error and an injustice to the
other nations, particularly to Canada and Great Britain, which
had contributed substantially to UNRRA funds. UNRRA foods,
raw materials, agricultural and other machinery are some of the
reasons for the remarkable recovery the country achieved within
the first year and a half after liberation.

No outside contribution has been so timely and precious as
the service rendered the country by the American Medical Mission which the Unitarian Service Committee sent in the summer of 1946. Made up of fourteen distinguished professors from
the universities of Harvard, Columbia, Chicago, Iowa, New
York, Cincinnati, Tufts College, and the American Academy of
Orthopedic Surgeons in Lincoln, Nebraska, the mission constituted what was actually a "faculty on wheels" which journeyed
from one end of the country to the other. Never before had a
similar mission made so complete and so brilliant a medical
survey of a nation. The professors visited hospitals and medical
schools, treated patients, performed operations, conducted clinical conferences, delivered hundreds of lectures, and distributed

a large number of medical journals, books, and clinical films, some of which were furnished by the State Department.

Dr. Alexander Brunschwick of Chicago University created a sensation which made newspaper headlines with his pneumonectomy, the first of its kind performed in Czechoslovakia. The incident was not without a touch of drama. While examining patients at Olomouc the famous surgeon came upon a case of cancer of the lung. "If only we had anesthetic equipment we could operate on the man," he said. There was no such equipment in the hospital, so the Czech medical staff announced. But one Czech physician volunteered the information that they had received equipment from UNRRA which was new to them. Thereupon Dr. Emory Rovenstein, the anesthetist of the mission, asked to examine the mysterious equipment, which proved to be a most up-to-date anesthetic outfit. Not only the operation but the American division of functions between surgeon and anesthetist was a revelation to Czech physicians. They were surprised when they heard the surgeon inquire of the anesthetist, "Shall I give him a blood transfusion?" It was new to them that while the surgeon wielded the scalpel the anesthetist worried about the patient and kept him alive.

This is only one example of the new methods in medicine the mission introduced. Patterned after the German system, Czech medical schools had been teaching such subjects as physiology, biochemistry, microbiology, and pharmacology through lectures, whereas in American schools the emphasis is on laboratory work. The American method has the double advantage of making the study concrete and bringing teacher and student into close personal relationship.

The body of recommendations which the mission has made is something new in the international brotherhood of culture and science. If fully and faithfully realized, it will not only rehabilitate Czech medicine, which held a high place in pre-war Europe, but will lift it to new levels of accomplishment in teaching, in research, and in practice.

Since Prague has always been the seat of science and learning in central Europe, attracting to its university students from the Balkans and particularly from the Slav countries, the American contribution to Czech medical knowledge is certain to be disseminated through these other lands. If the bonds with American medical science are diligently maintained and the interchange of research and discovery continues unhampered, Prague may yet become one of the great medical centers of Europe.

Interest in America, as in Great Britain and Russia, is deep and universal. The daily newspapers feature advertisements of foreign-language courses in English and Russian. No other languages are so eagerly and comprehensively studied.

Though the Medical Mission, in this writer's judgment, has made by far the most distinguished contribution to post-war Czechoslovakia, other American agencies are continuously rendering the country special services. The United States Information Service is publishing a daily news bulletin, non-partisan in character and packed with the important news of the world, which is distributed to newspapers and magazines. The Information Service maintains a reading room in which one hundred American magazines, popular, literary, scientific, religious, are daily open to the public. It is building up a large and highly comprehensive reference library. It is supplying the Prague Ministry of Education with documentary and other films, informative and educational, for use in schools. American Institutes are springing up all over the country and so are the Friends of America.

In anticipation of tourists especially from America, the Ministry of Foreign Trade is preparing special literature on travel and recreation in Czechoslovakia and is busy rebuilding the spas and resorts which were popular in pre-war years. Like Paris, Prague suffered little destruction during the war and may yet vie with the French capital as a tourist center. The country has a special appeal for the lover of outdoor life: game for the hunter —chamois deer, wild boar, lynx; wild birds such as ducks, geese, partridge, pheasant, and snipe; fish for the angler—salmon, trout, carp; and the lure of forest and mountain, stream and lake, for the devotee of nature.

Popular good will for America is everywhere strikingly manifest, and so keen and widespread is interest in America that the College of Philosophy at Charles University, Prague, has established a chair in American literature and the history of American civilization. Zdeněk Vančura, a youthful scholar who spent two years as a post-graduate student in Columbia and other American universities, has been appointed head of this chair. The Sorbonne of Paris and Upsala, Sweden, are the only other universities on the European continent that maintain similar chairs.

Yet something new has come into the life of the country which poses a question concerning the future relations between America and Czechoslovakia: the revolution with its sweep into a Socialist economy, and the military alliance with Russia. The classic land of private enterprise in the world today, its immense riches and fabulous industrial progress and scientific attainment the outgrowth of private enterprise and under its control, America has not yet acquired the economic and diplomatic experience fully to appreciate or appraise an economic system at such radical variance with its own as the economic order of the new Czechoslovakia. It is therefore understandable that diplomatic and other observers should survey the Czechoslovakian scene with distrust, often enough with contempt—understandable, though hardly conducive to understanding.

Let the following incident speak for itself.

One morning an executive of the nationalized Baťa industries in Zlín called on this writer with the request that he help locate the families of two American fliers whom a Gestapo officer had shot in a little wood outside of Zlín on October 14, 1944. The Americans had been participating in a raid on a synthetic-gasoline plant. Their plane was damaged, and on reaching central Moravia they landed by mistake at the Zlín airdrome, which at the time was a German flying school. Quickly realizing they were within an enemy camp, they managed by some miracle to take off again but were forced down only five miles away.

A Czech gamekeeper saw them get out of the plane. He went over and talked to them. They turned over to him some of their personal belongings—clothes, shoes, souvenirs—which he hastily buried in heaps of leaves. While he was gone for his dogs and firearms, the Germans came. The gamekeeper heard five shots from a sub-machine gun. It was the Gestapo man firing at the Americans. The Germans buried the murdered fliers in a remote corner of the cemetery in the near-by village of Napajedle, and as soon as the Czechs learned of it they secretly placed floral wreaths on the grave of the Americans.

A few days before the Baťa executive called me, the people of Zlín and vicinity had accorded the fliers the highest honor within their power. They exhumed the bodies and reburied them in the public square of Napajedle, immediately in front of the village church. A crowd of five thousand, including the highest government officials in the province, a company of infantry, Boy and Girl Scouts, factory workers, and peasants, attended the funeral. The coffins were draped in American flags and were carried to the public square in the body of a plane from the Baťa aviation factory, to the accompaniment of a funeral march played by a military band.

Now the local authorities wished to communicate with the

families of the fliers. They knew their names but not their home towns. Would I help locate the families?

The Czech executive left with me the police record of the story and a sheaf of photographs of the funeral, the grave, the modest monument, topped by an American flag, erected to the memory of the American youths, all of which I turned over to the American Military Attaché in Prague.

Two days later the Baťa executive came back to see me. Glum and dispirited, he said:

"You must excuse me for troubling you again. I have just had a painful experience at the American Embassy, and I don't know what to make of it." He said he had inquired of an official in the economic section as to the possibility of obtaining credits and raw materials in America for the Zlín shoe factories, and the American had replied: "You work for Joe [Stalin]; go and get your credits and raw materials from him."

The American official did not speak for the Embassy, nor for the State Department, least of all for the American people. His attitude is significant only because it demonstrates the readiness with which diplomatic representatives associate Prague's nationalization with Russian domination and with the ruin of everything they deem civilized and sacred. So frequent and so voluble were American allusions to "this Bolshevik nonsense," or "Russian-bossed Bolshevism," that to reassure Czech public opinion Ambassador Laurence Steinhardt, in an interview with a reporter from the Prague *Foreign Trade Journal,* spoke with appreciation of Czechoslovakia's efforts to reorder its economic life in its own way. Officially the State Department has manifested no open antagonism to nationalization.

But the note the State Department addressed to the Czechoslovakian Chargé d'Affaires in Washington on September 28, 1946, suspending negotiations for a loan and canceling further sales of surplus army property, has brought to the surface an undercurrent of tension between America and Czechoslovakia. The episode dramatizes the delicacy of Prague's international position.

Incidents and situations which have ruffled American sensitiveness and which served as the immediate cause of the action of the State Department are a matter of record. Prague has been tardy in settling the claims of American citizens for properties which have been nationalized or seized by squatters. The number of these claims is not small: 1,085, ranging from up-to-date factories built by Americans with their own capital, to cottages that are the properties of American citizens. Squatters have been a source of perpetual harassment to the Prague Government, which is deluged with complaints not only from foreigners but from its own citizens, from Jews who have returned from concentration camps or from service in the Czech Army in Russia or the West, from Czech citizens and anti-Fascist Germans who had eluded the Nazis during the occupation. Still, the tardiness or inability of the government to expel illegal occupants from American possessions a year and a half after liberation, and to come to an amicable settlement for properties that had been nationalized, has irked American representatives in Prague, especially in the light of all the generous help that has come from America since liberation.

The gist of the American grievance against Prague was expressed in the official American summary received by the American Embassy in Prague of the reasons which actuated the State Department in terminating negotiations for an American loan. Among other things, the summary spoke of an "indication of misinterpretation by Czechoslovakia of motives in extending economic assistance to European countries. This was explained as owing to support by Czech officials of statements of Soviet officials that the United States was using its credits and ability to make loans in order to further economic imperialism of the

United States, which statements, it is understood, were made in Paris and appeared in the press."

Accusations of American imperialism, often couched in violent language, have appeared, but solely in the Communist press. Occasionally factual situations in America have been distorted or falsified and again solely in certain ultra-leftist journals.

But the sinning has not been one-sided. A section of the American press has treated the new Czechoslovakia with abundant good will and understanding; and another section, which associates the word nationalization with havoc and terror, rarely refers to the little country save in terms of denunciation and obloquy. Once while calling on the editor of a Czech publication I was shown a copy of a highly circularized American magazine with a sensational story of the reign of Russian terror in the Czech capital. The editor shrugged and dismissed the story and the charge it embodied with a laugh. "We are a small nation," he said. "We have learned to laugh at a lot of things that are said against us."

Yet there have been occasions when the Czech press, Communist and non-Communist, has demonstrated singular forbearance toward America. The Slovakian Fascist Government, including Josef Tiso, the president, who had invited a German Army to shoot down the Slovakian uprising in Banská Bystrica, fled for safety into the American zone. On learning of the escape, Prague authorities demanded the extradition of the war criminals so that in accordance with the Moscow agreement of October 1943 they could answer for their evil deeds before a Slovakian court. The immediate incarceration of these men in a Slovakian jail would have dealt a severe blow to their underground followers and would have discredited the false claim which they were energetically circulating through their highly ramified grapevine, that America and Great Britain were protecting their leaders. It took Prague five months to achieve the extradition of Slovakia's one-time Fascist leaders. Whether or not it was Great Britain which obstructed prompt action on Prague's demand, as was explained by Americans in Prague, does not detract from the forbearance demonstrated by the Czech and Slovak press. Not once did any newspaper or journal allude to the incident one way or another.

More striking was the attitude of the press toward the so-called Štěchovice incident. On February 11, 1946, American officers and soldiers from the American zone in Germany, after spending the night in Prague, proceeded to a wood near the Štěchovice dam and, under their own military guards, began the excavation of cases of documents which the German Ministry of State had buried there. "When challenged by the commander of the local garrison who came to inquire into the proceedings," reads an official Czech report on the subject, "the American officer in charge refused to give a satisfactory explanation, stating that he was under secret orders and working with the consent of the Czechoslovakian authorities. The group continued their work on Tuesday [following day], and when a Czechoslovakian soldier approached the place he was fired upon by an American guard." The excavation was undertaken with neither the authority nor the knowledge of the Czechoslovakian Government. Had not the Czechs been a coolheaded people, the firing on the soldier might have resulted in bloody retaliation and the incident might have provoked a serious diplomatic crisis. The American Embassy apologized for the infraction of the nation's sovereignty, and the documents that were unearthed were delivered to Prague. Some of the American soldiers were detained for interrogation. None was imprisoned, and only two weeks after the event did the Prague Telegraph Agency issue a calmly worded report on the subject. The Catholic press made no comment on the unfriendly act, and only on March 5 did the Communist *Rudé Právo* print a brief paragraph of indignant criticism. The incident was passed over by the public and the press with neither pronounced acrimony nor bitter rhetoric.

The sharp attacks in the Communist press and nowhere else on American foreign policy synchronized with the growing tension between Russia and America at the Paris Conference. However unjustified the attacks may have been, the question is whether America, like Great Britain, is applying a double standard of intellectual freedom, one for itself, another for a nation that is not a big power and which by its very place on the map must always find itself in the thick of the diplomatic battle between America and Russia. Diplomatic pressure may for a time silence an explosive editor or an unreasonable commentator, but only for a time, particularly as America is in no position to silence its own ultra-nationalist press which periodically launches hostile campaigns against the Prague Government. If the American interpretation of "friendliness" carries with it the implication that a foreign nation must acquiesce in United States foreign policy or that the press of *all* parties must refrain from disparaging this country or from ascribing to it motives that exasperate America's sense of morality—then, despite all the bonds of friendship and all the fraternal relations between the two peoples, tension, instead of abating, must increase. It is inconceivable that the Communist press in any country, including Czechoslovakia, should favor America in any tilt it may engage with Russia, any more than that the ultra-nationalist press in America would uphold Russia in any conflict with America.

Yet however provoking to American diplomacy may have been the tardiness of the Prague Government in acting upon the economic claims of American citizens, however exasperating the denunciations in the Communist press, or the support the Czech delegation at international conferences accords Russian proposals, the real reason which prompted the action of the State

Department on September 28, 1946, was the decision, frankly communicated to Czech representatives in Paris, that it is not in American interests to help Czechoslovakia reconstruct its industries. The news of this decision reached Prague long before the suspension of the negotiations for the loan. Whether or not the decision is permanent only time will tell. On the date this book appears negotiations for the loan may or may not have been resumed, the loan may or may not have been granted. But the basic issue it involves, namely, Czechoslovakia's relationship with Russia, transcends in importance press campaigns in either country and any other grievances America may harbor against the Prague Government.

The non-Communist press was neither tardy nor evasive in its solemn evaluation of this issue. Immediately after the announcement of the suspension of the loan and under the significant title, "West and East," *Svobodné Noviny,* spokesman of the Czech intelligentsia, which has been particularly friendly to America and Great Britain, wrote as follows:

"That we should act as a 'bridge' between West and East has evidently caught our fancy. . . . But we must be conscious of the fact that we cannot safeguard the security of our state merely by relying on the decency of others. . . . We must understand that each and all of us are the guarantors of our state, and our diplomacy must create the conditions favorable to our becoming an important factor in central Europe. Nowadays central Europe is the continuation of eastern Europe, the core of which is represented by the Slavonic states. *Here and nowhere else must we stand.* Our urgent and vital tasks are set in this political sphere, and we must work toward its political unification, not to be drowned in it, but to cast into it the anchor of our security. . . . We shall gain the sympathy of the Western states. But because we wish to gain the sympathy of the West we have no other way forward but the one mentioned. This road may not look pleasant to many of us; it would be much easier 'to burn candles before all saints.' However, the security of our state is at stake, and this is manifestly the major concern of every one of us."[1]

Obzory, the intellectual and literary organ of the Catholic party, was no less solemn and explicit in the warnings it sounded.

"It is futile to shut our eyes," wrote the editor, "to the unpleasant reality that for some months American diplomacy has manifested no understanding of the needs and the demands of the Czechoslovakian people. This showed itself at the Paris Conference, where American representatives opposed the eviction of the Hungarian minority from Slovakia and finally counseled that the problem of the Hungarian minority be solved by ceding to Hungary certain Slovakian districts which are thickly inhabited by Hungarians. . . . Now the unfavorable attitude has become even more pronounced by the breaking of negotiations for the loan. . . . Back of these steps against Czechoslovakia is the growth of the great and powerful conflicts between Russia and America. Many actions which have resulted in unfavorable consequences for Prague are directed against Moscow."[2]

At the time of the incident this writer attended a small gathering of intellectuals in Prague. In the course of the evening's discussion someone posed the question: What would happen were Moscow to inform Prague that, since its alliance with the Soviet Union was stirring up trouble for it in America or Great Britain or both, Moscow was ready to dissolve it?

"Our people," was one comment, "would be so panic-stricken they would think the world was coming to an end."

"It would be a diplomatic atomic bomb on us," was another comment.

"We might even get down on our knees and beg Moscow to reconsider its decision," was a still further observation.

[1] *Svobodné Noviny,* October 18, 1946.
[2] *Obzory,* October 19, 1946.

The alliance is of infinitely greater import to Czechoslovakia than to Moscow. In time of war Russia can withdraw into its own immense spaces, tamed and untamed, nurse its wounds, and gather fresh strength for a counterattack. But if Czechoslovakia found itself involved in a war between America and Russia it would be at the mercy of every weapon, including the atomic bomb, which America might hurl at her. Small as it is, exposed to air attacks, its industry, whether reconstructed with or without American credits, would, even in the absence of an atomic bomb, be blown to dust and cinders. The country would be a scorched earth, so bleak and desolate that it could not hope soon or ever to recover. No nation anywhere has more to lose from a possible war between Russia and America or has more to gain from a continued peace between the two. That was why an eminent Czech scholar well known in the West, on learning of the action of the State Department, was constrained to remark: "America has made a test in a place where it is least justified. It is quite incredible."

Whatever the real motive behind the policy, whether it is American reluctance to aid a nation whose economy is antagonistic to capitalism, or because of its close relations with Russia to add to Czechoslovakia's peace or war potential, neither Czech leaders nor the Czech press interpret it as a reflection on Czechoslovakia's business integrity, the fear that it might default on its indebtedness. They appraise it chiefly as an American weapon in the diplomatic conflict between Moscow and Washington.

Whether or not America reverses its stand as conveyed to Czech envoys during the Paris Conference, and if so, whether at some future time she again reverts to the view that an industrially reconstructed Czechoslovakia is "not to her interests," the small nation is proceeding on the assumption that no real war clouds are darkening the horizons of Europe. On the day that the Czech press informed the public of the American action it also carried news of a credit of twenty million dollars advanced to Czechoslovakia by Brazil. The nation is embarked on a stupendous program of reconstruction. With or without American loans it will proceed to modernize and expand its industry. It will do so even if it has to tighten its belt and endure severe privations during the Two-Year Plan which is to lift production and the standard of living to ten per cent above the pre-war level. It is continuing to cultivate friends wherever it can find them, and to solicit credits wherever there is hope of obtaining them. India and Egypt have been particularly friendly; both need Czechoslovakia's machinery and both have surplus funds. So have Switzerland and Sweden and the South American republics. Besides, Czechoslovakia is a member of the International Bank, and its search for credit is in some measure certain to be gratified by this institution. The sums sought are governed by Czech calculations as to their own ability to pay. This fact Hubert Ripka, its Minister of Foreign Trade, has consistently emphasized. It will make no blind plunge into borrowing, even if there were lenders eager to pour gold into the coffers which the Germans have looted. Therefore, the action of America is of more moment because of the policy and attitude which inspired it than because of the funds it withheld.

The nation's only fear, a very great fear, is a revived Germany with her seven-to-one superiority in man power. Because of this fear it will neither sacrifice nor weaken its alliance with Russia, whatever the cost. If America or Britain were to drive it into a position where it had to choose between West and East, it would unhesitatingly choose Russia as the only pillar to which it can fasten the hope of national survival. This is the meaning and the only meaning of the comments I have quoted and others which might be quoted from the non-Communist press, and this is the prevailing sentiment of the people. "Here and nowhere else must we stand," would become the policy and the slogan of the nation. Memories of Munich and the betrayal by the West are too fresh and too poignant for them to turn their back on the East.

In the American scheme of things Czechoslovakia, because of its size and remoteness from the American scene, may appear of small consequence. Yet because of its geography and the orderly and rational manner in which it is seeking to adjust itself to the new times, it holds an eminently strategic position in the Europe of today, far more so than at any time in its history.

Meanwhile, all leaders and all parties, including the Communist, are on record as espousing a policy, however difficult of fulfillment, which shall bind the little nation in real friendship with the West and East.

22. The Slovakian Triumph

I journeyed to Banská Bystrica, the Slovakian mountain town, to attend the celebration of the first anniversary of the Slovak uprising against Nazi Germany and their own Fascist regime. I had no more than reached the overcrowded, banner-draped town than I was buoyantly aware of the contrast between the people there and in Prague. Slavs like the Czechs, Catholics like most Czechs, with an affinity in language almost as close as that between Americans and Britishers, Slovaks are yet a people apart in their outward demeanor and in their inner make-up. More volatile and more boisterous than Czechs, they are also more sensitive and gayer. Their eyes are more flashing, their faces more expressive. They gesture more profusely, talk more expansively. They laugh more readily, hate more fiercely, forgive less easily. Neither as rational, cultivated, nor reasonable as Czechs, they are quicker to feel offense and to resent aspersion, however indirect, or if only uttered in jest. Their intonation is softer, their voices more melodious. More gullible than Czechs and more vain, they are also more approachable, easier to know.

324

Covetous as Czechs seldom are, they are yet more generous. More spontaneous than Czechs, they are less reliable and rarely self-critical. The Czech may be niggardly in promises but is punctilious in fulfillment. The Slovak is flush with promises, wayward in fulfillment. Breaking an engagement or being recklessly late rouses neither compunction nor regret. To the Czech discipline is a habit, almost a rite; to the Slovak it is a burden, often a nuisance. He does not mind jostling or being jostled, as the milling crowds in Banská Bystrica so tumultuously demonstrated. He has something of the *shirokaya natura*—the big heart of the Russian—the exaggerated self-glorification of the Pole, plus a hidebound provincialism of his own, attributes of which no one would accuse the Czechs. "The Czech thinks, but the Slovak feels," is a common saying among both peoples.

With the Hussite heritage in his blood, the Czech grew up with the nineteenth century, was tempered by its machine age, matured by its politics, hardened by its rationalism, elevated by its humanism. Not the Slovak. With the exception of a very small group of rebellious priests and brooding intellectuals, the Slovak missed the nineteenth century as completely as though it had never been. Through no fault of his, he slept through this age of stormy awakeners and brilliant awakening. Nor had the preceding eight centuries jolted him out of his intellectual torpor. His Hungarian masters had lulled and stunned him into a somnolence out of which he was powerless to rouse himself. That was why he trailed in the very rear of the procession of the modern world, far behind the Czechs, far behind all Western peoples, far behind his own Hungarian masters. What saved him from complete submergence and obliteration was his extraordinary virility and his unconquerable racial consciousness. Despite the allurements that Magyarization flaunted before him, especially after the 'thirties of the last century, he clung to his language and folkways as to a hallowed command

325

or a physiological compulsion. There were exceptions, of course: Slovaks who forswore their racial heritage for the worldly advantages the disinheritance dangled before them. But their number was small. Peasant that he was, living in a sequestered world, the Slovak dug himself deep into his racial and communal roots, even as a hibernating animal digs itself deep into the earth, and for the same reason—to shelter himself against predatory intruders.

He had never lifted himself out of his frustration and sequestration high enough to have merited the honor and the responsibility of a high office in the church in which he devoutly worshiped. There had been only one Slovak bishop, Stefan Moysas, before the rise of the Czechoslovak Republic in 1918. Only Hungarians held high church offices, and they rarely evinced any sympathy or understanding of Slovak self-assertiveness. Slovak priests were educated in schools and seminaries permeated with a Hungarian tradition which stemmed from one of the oldest and most unrelenting feudalisms in Europe. No other professional schools for students of any subject were accessible to a Slovak, unless he renounced his nationality. This fact must ever be remembered in the study of turbulent Slovakia and in the appraisal of the befuddled Slovak mentality.

"The trouble with us Slovaks," said a Slovakian superintendent of schools to this writer, "is that we have no history." Not quite true. Mere survival is history, but in the case of the Slovak it was a history of retardation and resignation. When the emancipation finally came in 1918, with the establishment of the first republic, there were Slovak masses who were more dazed than overjoyed by the event. They were afraid of the new liberties lest the Hungarian masters again pounce on them and drive them back into meek subservience. About half of them were illiterate. They had not their own educated class to guide and govern them. Only about twenty Slovaks were competent to teach in high schools, seven hundred more to perform similar services in elementary schools, or to act as clerks in post offices and other administrative posts. Nor could this be otherwise in the light of the subversions and suppressions they had suffered under Hungarian mastery, which had permitted only 140 Slovak elementary schools, not one high school, not one business school, not one industrial school, not one technical school, and of course no university. The Hungarians tolerated only one daily newspaper in the Slovak language, only one library, in Turčanský Svatý Martin, home of the Slovak *Matica*—mecca of Slovak culture.

If Slovakia was to be lifted to the level of enlightenment of the Czech country, it had to be succored on a gigantic scale, and only the Czechs were in a position to proffer the much-needed aid. By the thousands they migrated to Slovakian towns and villages and instantly set about reorganizing and rebuilding the country. For twenty years Slovakia boomed with effort for a new land, such as it had never been in all its history, with schools, libraries, highways, railroads, factories, though nowhere nearly enough of them, and with an expanding national consciousness. More than one and a half million acres of arable land, which had been the possession of Hungarian and Austrian nobles and Jewish landlords, were divided among 198,786 peasant families. Instead of only 140, there were 3,277 elementary schools, 246 high schools, all in the Slovak language. Fourteen teachers' colleges, twenty commercial schools, thirty-two technical schools and industrial institutes, and a university, the first in the history of the Slovak people, also flourished. Twenty million books and brochures had rolled off the Slovakian presses. The progress Slovakia had made within twenty years, principally through the help of the more cultivated and competent Czechs, was unrivaled anywhere in central Europe.

Yet as population grew, as natural wealth accumulated, as

culture throve, dissidence mounted. More and more Slovaks who graduated from high schools and colleges coveted the government positions Czech pioneers were holding. They became increasingly resentful of Czechs, regarded them as aliens and intruders. More lax and more impatient of discipline than Czechs, they were irked by Czech insistence on punctuality and rectitude. Nor were Czechs who rudely flaunted their superiority before the excessively sensitive Slovak, wanted even as university professors. There were Czech educators who derided the Slovak language, spoke of it as a corrupt derivative of Czech. The petty intelligentsia and the shopkeepers were particularly acrimonious in their resentment of Czech domination.

The sole exception was the Slovaks of the Evangelical faith. Better educated in the mass than the Catholic Slovaks, they had not quite slept through the nineteenth century. Evangelical pastors and laymen kept contact with their co-religionists in Germany, England, and America, often went on trips to these countries, studied there, absorbed new ideas of government, economics, sociology, literature, and other arts. Relations between them and Czechs might now and then be strained, but never to a point of snapping the fraternal and racial bonds that held them together. They had a brotherly feeling toward Czechs, and to them Jan Hus was likewise a hero and an apostle of a new world and a new life. To this day the Evangelical Slovaks make use of the Czech translation of the Bible and of Czech hymnbooks. But the Evangelicals constitute only about one sixth of the population in Slovakia.

The spearhead of the dissident movement was Andrej Hlinka, a Catholic priest of peasant parentage from the village of Černová, outside the town of Ružomberok. Though officially the village is termed a "street" of Ružomberok, it is a community of its own, with its own history, its own way of life, its own loyalties, its own historic traditions. I went to this village in the summer of 1946. As I walked its streets, accompanied by a young priest, I could not help being impressed by the sturdiness, the piety, the backwardness, and the liveliness of its people. Young and old greeted the priest with the expression, "Praised be Jesus Christ," and wherever we went we were accorded simple but gracious and hearty hospitality.

The hillside cemetery opposite the beautiful white church which was built in the early part of the century by the initiative and assiduous efforts of Andrej Hlinka told a dramatic tale, not only of the village, but of the spectacular career of the priest and of the tyrannies old Hungary had with a nonchalant ease perpetrated on the beaten and impoverished Slovakian peasantry. Save for the two marble tombstones over the graves of Hlinka's parents and his uncle and aunt, there were only wooden crosses to mark the burial places of the villagers— that is, of those recently put to rest. The old graves were shapeless mounds of earth overgrown with rank grass and weeds, with not a sprig of a flower to adorn them, with not a sign of a cross or anything else to identify or commemorate the dead. Here was none of the outward reverence for departed kin that is so universal a feature of Czech village cemeteries, where a monument, however humble, marks each grave, with flowers over and around the neatly kept tombs, with the little basins of water with which to wash the tombstone or to freshen grass and flowers, with the little paraffin lamps inside a glass enclosure to light on solemn occasions, with all the other little reminders of tenderness and love for those who are no longer among the living. The harsh life the Slovak peasantry knew did not cultivate in them the special refinements and the deep filial sentiments that are so glowingly in evidence in the Czech countryside.

The most impressive feature of the cemetery in Černová is the huge weather-beaten marble memorial to the fifteen villagers, among them two young girls, whom Hungarian gendarmes shot on October 27, 1907. The monument is a symbol not only of the martyrdom of the village, but of Andrej Hlinka, its most celebrated son. Because Alexander Parvy, the Hungarian bishop of Spiš, Slovakia, had branded Hlinka as a Pan-Slav and a traitor to Hungary, he imposed on him the severest discipline within his power. On May 4, 1906, he suspended him *ab officio,* and on June 18 of the same year suspended him *ab officio et ordine,* which banned him from celebrating mass, from administering the rites of confession, from burying the dead, and from performing the other functions of his calling. Josef Fischer, a priest of German descent, was appointed to his place in the church in Ružomberok. But when the village church was finished the villagers appealed to the bishop to permit their own Andrej Hlinka to celebrate its opening. Again and again the villagers appealed. Again and again their appeal was rejected. Hungarian nationalism, and nothing else, was the cause of this rejection, and it only served to stir to fever heat the Slovak consciousness of the villagers of Černová. They were determined to prevent Josef Fischer from dedicating the church. When the priest who had replaced Hlinka, accompanied by a representative of the bishop and an organist, drove in a coach into the village, the peasantry cried out, "Why have you come? We haven't invited you." When the uninvited guests made an effort to proceed, the villagers stopped them. Thereupon Hungarian gendarmes opened fire and fifteen men and women fell dead.

This incident was a turning point not only in the relationship between Hungarians and Slovaks but in the career of Andrej Hlinka, who was an irrepressible champion of Slovakian emancipation. Persecuted and martyred, he had become a national hero, and not only to the Slovaks. Czechs befriended him, collected funds for him, conspired with him, and sheltered him from the Hungarian police and from Hungarian persecution. He had aroused the interest and sympathy of Seton-Watson, a Scotch professor of history, who dedicated thirty years of his life to aiding him and other Slovaks in their battle for independence.

Eloquent, ambitious, strong-willed, audaciously outspoken, Hlinka was yet, in the words of Seton-Watson, who knew him more intimately than any other foreigner, indeed than most Czechs and most Slovaks, "a twelfth-century priest." The disparity between him and Masaryk in learning, in humanistic thought, in progressive outlook on the world, particularly on the new Czechoslovakia, was immeasurable. Masaryk looked ahead; Hlinka looked backward. He had never assimilated and never really understood, as had Masaryk, the meaning of democracy as it developed in the Western world. He hated Hus and the Hussite movement and all the other struggles for enlightenment in Czech history and in the modern world. An impassioned nationalist, he was yet an implacable paternalist, stalwart in the conviction that a people must be ruled rather than led, must be commanded rather than educated into social responsibility. Not democracy but theocracy was his political creed. Therefore, conflict between him and Masaryk, between Prague and Bratislava, was inevitable, and Hlinka was quick to exploit the resentment of Slovaks against the presence of Czechs in positions of authority in Slovakia, and against all the errors that Czechs committed in their relations with Slovaks. This conflict was all the more keen because the growing Slovak merchant and industrial class resented the presence of the more affluent, more experienced, more businesslike Czech capitalists.

Hlinka rallied an ever-increasing following. The more powerful he grew, the more vocal he became in his dissidence, the more violently he denounced Prague, the more assiduously he nurtured the spirit of separatism, the more clamorous was his demand for complete and immediate autonomy for Slovakia.

The mass of the clergy supported him, but a significant minority was passionately arrayed against him. Vividly I remember the afternoon in 1938 which I spent in a café on the banks of the silent and swift-flowing Danube in Bratislava with the late Monsignor Okánik, who had only words of scorn and excoriation for Andrej Hlinka. Monsignor Jüriga, another eminent Catholic clergyman, never missed an opportunity to inveigh violently against Hlinka's obscurantism. "Is there any country in the world," he once said, "in which our Church and our clergymen are treated with greater respect and greater solicitude? Think of it, if a parish is too poor to pay a priest a living salary, the government makes up the difference. Have you got anything like that in America? Of course not. The Church in Slovakia has kept all its lands, has many schools, and in all our schools, all over the republic, religious instruction is given to those who register a desire for it; and again the priest is honored. I don't understand this man Hlinka." There were other priests who felt as did Okánik and Jüriga, but they were in a hopeless minority.

When the Nazi menace had made the Czechoslovakian skies black with storm, Hlinka's obduracy remained unshaken. For him there was no retreat; there was only advance, regardless of consequence. His twelfth-century mind could not rise above personal frustration and national recrimination. When the republic needed unity as desperately as a choking man needs air, he kept hewing away at disunity. Though officially he proclaimed he did not seek a dissolution of the republic, everything he said and did was thinning and cleaving the bond between Czechs and Slovaks. Not even a visit from his old friend, the afore-mentioned Professor Seton-Watson, Slovakia's stanchest and most indefatigable champion, moved him to a change of heart. All of this was happy news to the Hungarian irredentists and feudal lords, inside and outside the Slovakian frontier, and even more to the Nazi conspirators in the Sudeten-land and to Hitler himself.

Hlinka died in August 1938, on the eve of the Munich crisis. I attended his funeral in Ružomberok, where he had been living for some years. Among the stacks of floral wreaths that decked his bier, none were more resplendent than those presented by K. H. Frank and Konrad Henlein, Hitler's shrewdest and most ruthless agents and disciples in Czechoslovakia.

Immediately after Munich, Slovakia erupted into a fierce crusade against Czechs and Jews and only in a smaller measure against its own more progressive groups. Bratislava was plastered with billboards reading, "Czechs and Jews, get out," and re-sounded with the crash of broken windows and often enough with the thud of broken heads. Vindictive racialism was ramp-ant, and Fascism was fattening on the ruins of the shattered republic.

The new leader was Josef Tiso, a Hungarian-educated Slovak priest. Nowhere nearly as impressive a personality as Hlinka, his manner was more suave, his method more secretive, his aim more far-reaching. Draping himself in Hlinka's mantle, he led his little nation straight into Hitler's camp. On the fourteenth of March 1939, after a conference with Hitler in Berlin, and on Hitler's demand, he announced Slovakia's independence. The very next day Hitler marched into Prague. Slovakia became an "independent" state, with Tiso as its president. Persecution of Czechs and Jews gained in momentum and brutality. But while Czechs, abandoning home and hope, could flee into Moravia and Bohemia, the Jews had no road of escape. There were priests, like Monsignor Augustine Pozděch, who after liberation became vice-chairman of the Slovakian National Council, who pleaded for tolerance. But they were voices in the wilderness. Slovaks, who had themselves been one of the most persecuted peoples in Europe, were, now that power had come to them, now that Tiso and his colleagues were galvanizing their minds with a medieval obscurantism and steeling their ordinarily generous impulses against the grace of compassion, the most jubilant and most cruel persecutors of Jews, next to the Germans. They did not kill like the Germans, but they terrorized and tormented no less unfeelingly, and looted no less zealously.

Andrej Hlinka may not have been a Judophile, but he respected Jews and frowned on anti-Semitic outbreaks. Had he been alive, he would have thundered against pogroms. No Slovak Jew I know but is agreed on this point. Tiso evinced not a shred of Hlinka's tolerance. He and his government actually paid Hitler the sum of five hundred German marks or twenty-five hundred Slovak crowns, the equivalent of eighty dollars per person, for ridding the Slovak lands of Jews. From such traffic in human lives dictator Horthy of Hungary and dictator Antonescu of Rumania recoiled with dismay, if not with dread. But Tiso stuck to his bargain.

Since Hitler was rounding up Jews in all countries he had mastered, without tribute to anybody, the "sale" in Slovakia was a shrewdly calculated business artifice, which yielded immense profit to the Germans, immense loss to Slovakia. The sums Slovakia owed Germany for "ridding the country of Jews" was charged against raw materials, particularly lumber, which Germany was feverishly lugging out of the country. Within the brief span of six years Slovakia was despoiled of thirty years' growth of timber, or "green gold," as Slovaks speak of their forest treasures.

Monsignor Pozděch and his small following among the clergy fumed at Tiso's murderous transaction in Jewish lives. Some of them had the temerity to voice their protests openly and vigorously to the callous, headstrong, and all-powerful Tiso. But he was beyond persuasion. When news first reached him that Jews were being killed in gas chambers he dismissed it as "Jewish

materials were pumped ouc of the country in an ever-swelling flood. The national economy was subverted; the national debt skyrocketed. The country enjoyed the false prosperity of a regime that held together only by virtue of foreign bayonets.

Greater than the economic was the social cost. A young generation was growing up with only contempt for the former republic and all it had meant and symbolized in Slovakia's rise during the years of its existence. Democracy it flouted and denounced as the plague and obsession of degenerate civilizations. Not a book with an inkling of progressive ideas but was seized and destroyed. Hitler and Tiso were the heroes of youth. With a population of only two and a half millions, Slovakia became the mecca of a dark civilization, pillared by four malevolent *isms*—anti-Czechism, anti-Semitism, Fascism, supernationalism.

All was well so long as Germany was winning battles. But a day of reckoning was approaching. As the Red armies were crashing closer and closer to Slovakia, Slovaks, including Hlinka Guards and other Fascists, began to ponder the consequences of a Russian victory. In the West, too, the Germans were suffering disaster. If the Red Army overran Slovakia it would be treated as an enemy country that had sent a large army to fight side by side with Germans on Russian territory. Retribution would be grim, and Slovakia would have no friends and no defenders in the Allied world. It would bear the stigma of a Fascist land, and it would suffer the burden of a military occupation. It would lose its immediate good living. It would be saddled with reparations. It would be obliged to expiate its sins throughout years of subordination and subjection to the very Russia it had been taught to hate and had been made to fight.

The more Slovaks pondered the inescapable consequences of imminent German defeat, the blacker loomed the impending collapse of Tiso's regime, and the more alarmed they became of their own fate and their own future. How could they absolve themselves of the guilt in which they were so hopelessly enmeshed?

The time was ripe for Communists, Socialists, anti-Fascist intellectuals, Evangelical pastors, and Catholic priests who had gone underground and were fighting a hopeless though valiant battle against Tiso. They had been waiting for the opportune moment when they could muster a large enough army to wage open war on the Bratislava Government. They mobilized Slovakian disaffection into an ever-growing army of rebels, many of whom, I must emphasize, were recruited from yesterday's Fascists. The Czechoslovak exile government in London, aided by the British and the Americans, lent its untiring help. Russia sent experienced partisan leaders to help the movement. Finally the revolt broke out and Tiso's defenders were routed out of Banská Bystrica and other places. Alarmed, Tiso called on the Germans for help. He would fight his own people with foreign bayonets if only he could retain power over the country. Nazi legions hastened to their ally's aid and soon checked the resistance movement. But not for long. The Red Army was pushing onward. The country was breaking up. The Tiso regime was crashing apart like ice floes in spring. Demoralized, leaderless, frightened, his followers, now that his end had come, abandoned Tiso as readily as they had once rallied to his Fascist banner. He and his government fled for safety into the American zone. Banská Bystrica had triumphed, and the very name of the town has since become identified with Slovakia's rise against Fascism.

Now I was there to attend the celebration of the first anniversary of the historic event. The town and the surrounding countryside were swarming with holiday makers and echoed and re-echoed with gay shouts and lilting tunes. Banners, bunting, costumes, flowers dazzled the eye. Here were color and drama and a loud negation of the erstwhile leadership and the erstwhile dispensation. The heroes of yesterday, the dead and the living, whom Hlinka and Tiso had anathematized as enemies of Slovakia, were heroes again. Masaryk, Beneš, Štefánik, the Slovak who had been one of the founders of the first republic, were acclaimed once more. No one mentioned Hlinka except in scorn. No one alluded to Tiso except in wrath.

It was all in boisterous contrast to the other national Slovak gathering I had attended in the same month of August seven years earlier in the town of Ružomberok. The occasion then was Hlinka's funeral. Compounded with the grief of the moment over the passing of the leader was an emotion of acrimony against Czechs and against all Slovaks who had been bitter against Hlinka. Here were all Hlinka's leaders and disciples, dressed in black and bursting with sullenness, some openly crying for revenge on Prague. True, Czechs were Slavs like Slovaks, but they were not Slovaks. The two nations would have to go their separate ways. Slovakia, too, had a glory and a destiny all its own, and no one would be permitted to tarnish the one or frustrate the other. Supernationalism was loud and defiant.

I could not help contrasting the Slovak leaders of those days with the ones I was now meeting. The new men were much younger, more mellow, better educated, many of them speaking English, French, German, which they had learned in exile as soldiers in Allied armies, as associates in foreign embassies or at home. They were the flower of Slovakia's new and progressive —that is, anti-Fascist—intelligentsia. Charming and courteous, they made supreme hosts. If the meat rations were scanty, the wines inferior, it was the best the ruined country could afford. For the first time since their arrival in Czechoslovakia foreign correspondents had their fill of fresh grapes, of which there were none in Prague, and of apples, too, which, even if unripe, were better than none.

These young Slovaks were as lavish with answers to questions as they were with their hospitality. They took criticism with a grace which could not help soften the language of the critic. Not a harsh word did any of them utter against Czechs. Unlike Hlinka's followers, they saw no future and no hope for their little and dismally backward country except in a union with Czechs. Nor were they unmindful of the task confronting them and of the shortcomings of their people, who had overwhelmingly rallied to the banner of Tiso's Fascism. They knew the thorny path ahead and the struggle before them for the re-education and rehabilitation of the minds and the sentiments of the people to the new ideas of government and the new conditions of living. Glib and eloquent conversationalists, they brimmed over with optimism.

The festivities rose to a climax with the parade in honor of President Beneš and the other dignitaries, including Prague's diplomatic corps, who had made a special journey to Banská Bystrica. Louder and livelier were the shouts "Long live Beneš!" Brighter and gayer were the triumphal arches with the flaming legends of loyalty and devotion to the new and resurrected republic. Beneš was visibly moved and pleased, for never before had he been accorded so tumultuous and so joyful a welcome in Slovakia.

The day was as if made for festivities, with warm sun and bright skies. Though uniformed partisans and legionnaires of World War I and units of Slovak infantry and artillery, accompanied by brass bands, lent a military coloration to the event, it was the village folk from the near-by mountains who invested it with an unmistakably national flavor. Few Slavs anywhere can match the Slovakian peasantry in love of color, in skill in needlework, in the gift of decorating a pine sapling or an ordinary hayrick so that it glows like a variegated flower bed. With boisterous pride and merry abandon, village after village passed the reviewing stand, now in horse and wagon, now in ox-drawn hayrick, afloat with the splendors of ribbons, flowers, bunting, and spectrum-like costumes. The girls and the women inside danced and leaped, sang and shouted, and made the very heavens gay with their revelry.

There was nothing solemn about any of the events or festivities. The emphasis of song and speech, official and unofficial, was not on past quarrels, past acrimony, past sacrifices, past sorrows, but on immediate triumph, immediate jubilation.

"With harmonious and courageous co-operation," said Beneš, "we can in due time build in Czechoslovakia a corner of real paradise."

These were brave and eloquent words, and the tumultuous applause which greeted them testified to a hearty acceptance of their meaning and their promise. Yet as one swallow does not make spring, so a lone uprising, even if celebrated a year later by an assemblage of festively clad and gay-hearted men and women, does not cleanse a nation of the malignities engendered by nine centuries of serfdom under a foreign power, interrupted only by a brief sojourn in the modern world, and reinforced by six years of triumphant Fascism.

23. The Slovakian Shadow

Accompanied by the Rev. Fedor Ruppeldt, the Evangelical pastor at Žilina, I drove to Ružomberok, the birthplace of Slovakian dissidence and Fascism. I wanted to see it again and observe the changes, if any, it had undergone since the collapse of Tiso's Fascist state and in what measure it shared or reflected the spirit of liberation from its own former self, which was so tumultuously celebrated in Banská Bystrica.

As we were slowly ascending a hilly road my companion, sweeping the surrounding scene with his eyes, said, "Our Slovakia is so beautiful; someday it will be another Switzerland."

Twilight was falling over valley and mountain, over wood and stream, and the glints and hues in the sky, the dusky shimmer of the broad Váh River that skirted intermittently along the highway lent more than verbal substance to the ecstatic outburst.

Slightly smaller in territory than Switzerland, with a population of only two and a half instead of Switzerland's four and a half millions, Slovakia is one of the most scenic countries in Europe. It boasts no Alpine grandeur, not even in the high Tatra

Mountains, nor does it sparkle with lakes like Switzerland. But its forests and mountains, its bracing climate and its wealth of mineral springs, its torrential mountain streams and the still, swift-flowing Danube give it a natural splendor unrivaled by any of its immediate neighbors. Here nature is rugged and beautiful, delighting the eye, elating the mind. Here is a sportsman's paradise—hunting and fishing, skiing and skating, mountain climbing and flower gathering. Here in summer are birds of rare plumage and rare song, with grove and orchard resounding with melody, with the high-soaring skylarks in the valley showering the very grainfields with ceaseless and cheery tunes. Here are some of Czechoslovakia's most celebrated spas and pleasure resorts, and here one can lose himself in ease and expansiveness, in fun and fancy, in high adventure and blithe revelry.

Here, above all, is an ancient peasant civilization aglow with legend, afloat with tradition, with scarcely a village but boasts its own wisdom and its own lore, in song and story, in custom and costume, and in a piety that never palsied the urge for gaiety and never suffered the premise that to please the flesh is to lose the soul. Up in the Tatras, on the high plateaus, driven there centuries ago by Turkish and Hungarian invaders, and as if seeking to reach out for protection to the very God they had enshrined in their hearts, are peasant communities—mere hamlets—that are epics of human fortitude. Neither wind nor blizzard, neither the rigors of nature nor the remoteness from fellow men have daunted the quest for peaceful retreat. Over these plateaus broods a poetic primitiveness, unchanged through the centuries, as if rooted in the rock and grass out of which it has sprung; swathed in a melancholy murk, it is yet abrim with a hardy hopefulness. Tunes and legends keep the past alive, not a past of sanguinary encounters between man and man, but of man's ceaseless tussle with nature and exulting in man's mastery of the inanimate world about him. In these lofty mountain plateaus is a world that is above and aloof in fact and in spirit from the turbulence of our times, from the inner torments that beset man in the flourishing valleys below. Spring is sudden and brief, summer is brilliant and gay, autumn is as flitting as spring, winter is long and arduous. But man, humble and sturdy, remains master of his own little world.

We were in the valley, now, climbing a mountain road. We passed village after village, here and there scarred by war, with the freshly planed timbers looming on doors and walls like white patches on the deepening night, with the lights in the low, commodious cottages twinkling like stars in a darkening sky. Save for electric lights, there was nowhere a sight or sound of the modern age, nowhere a glimpse or a clank of a mechanized implement such as invests a Russian village with a steely maturity that is in sharp contrast to muddy streets and thatch roofs. In this part of the world there is scarcely a break in the "design for living." There is no perceptible or audible rift in the ancient harmony of life, no improvisation and no invention, not yet anyway. The old world is the new world, the old age is the new age, lambent with memory, suffused with sentiment, with the patriarchal family still swaying the motives and actions of man. Hence the not unnatural incongruity of Fascists in the days of Tiso shielding Communist sons and brothers from the reach of the law, and now, with Fascism in collapse, Communists reciprocating the sentiment and shielding Fascist sons and brothers from the clutch of the new law that is upon the land. This is a part of the history and reality of Slovakia, which accounts not a little for the rough political climate of the country.

Yet in these villages lies Slovakia's richest treasure—its peasant humanity, as dormant with unrealized gifts, as dowered with untapped bounty as the very nature of which my companion spoke with such fervor, and no less ready for exploration and cultivation. If only all the new leaders and teachers and, even more, the petty intelligentsia, which was the backbone of the Fascist regime, can shake themselves loose from the thousand-year-old servitude to Hungary with its once feudal glamor and feudal false face, and from the allurements of the brief and deceptively flashy Fascist years, which, with the collapse of Germany's might, came to an abrupt and disastrous end, crashing the country's inflated prosperity into an abyss of misery and chaos. No people anywhere carry the burden of the remote past borrowed from the traditions of an enemy and of its own immediate yesterday with less grace and with so much danger to themselves.

At last we arrived in Ružomberok and drove around and around. With its glistening pavements, its extraordinary neatness, its blocks of superb buildings—homes, shops, schools, offices, cafés—and with the walls of mountain in the background, it rose as sturdy and majestic as when, seven years earlier, I had first glimpsed it in wonder and veneration. Prague's ungrudging generosity and Hlinká's ambitious foresight had transformed the bedraggled little trading center of Hungarian days into a lively community with no sight of or smell of slum.

One avenue we passed bore the name Masarykova Ulica—Masaryk Street. The Masaryk against whom Hlinka and his disciples had thundered denunciation and imprecation was restored to the good graces of the town. Another street was named after Beneš, still another after Stalin. This was revolution in a country like Slovakia.

Cafés were bright with lights. Despite the drizzle, sidewalks teemed with promenaders, laughing and chattering boys and girls, the boys mostly in military uniform. Life had come into its own again, breezy and spirited, though inside the full-lighted cafés the soft-spoken waiters, sporting dignified black ties, fetched every guest who found a seat at a table a plate brimful with thick potato soup and a cup of ersatz coffee as execrable as I had yet tasted. That was all the evening menu allowed in the early months of liberation.

We drove up to the street stairway that ascended to the Town Hall Square, subsequently rechristened Hlinka Square. Here Hlinka had had his new home, new offices, new schools, his old and beautiful church. Here germinated the disaffection which on Hlinka's death sprouted into full-grown Fascism, with Nuremberg laws, with forcible expulsion of Czechs, with the sale of Jews, with uniformed storm troopers named Hlinka Guards, with much of the paraphernalia gleefully borrowed from Nazi Germany. We climbed the high and winding staircase, and the first thing that caught my eyes in the glare of the street light was the new name of the place—Square of the Revolution. "Town Hall Square," "Hlinka Square," "Square of the Revolution"—three phrases designating more clash and upheaval, more disaster and triumph, more confusion and hope, than the Slovaks had known in the preceding one thousand years.

I searched the corner of Hlinka's home where at the time I attended his funeral, rising on a lofty pedestal, stood the marble bust of Professor Seton-Watson with a dedication in English reading: "In recognition of his thirty years' work for the Slovaks, erected with gratitude by the young Slovak generation." After Munich and at the professor's request, as if anticipating the inevitable act, the bust was removed and the dedication was plastered. Now it was back again on the lofty pedestal and the dedication was once more uncovered.

"Where was it kept?" I asked the Slovak policeman who came over to greet us.

"In the museum," he said. "After it was removed Hlinka's bust was put in its place. Now Hlinka's bust is in the museum and the professor's is back here."

No small defeat this was for the once thriving and tumultuous Hlinka party. This, too, spelled revolution.

Rising out of the stairway in marble and granite was a new edifice I had not seen in 1938. "What is this?" I asked the policeman.

"The Hlinka mausoleum," he answered. But now the body was there no more.

"Did partisans take it out?" I asked.

"Oh no, they had no chance," the policeman explained. "Late one night Hlinka's followers drove up with a covered truck, stole the body, and raced out of town."

"Where is the body now?" I asked.

"Nobody knows. Some say it was driven across the border to a monastery in Austria, and others say it is somewhere in Bratislava."

Still another defeat, indeed a defamation of the once mighty leader of the Slovak People's party. The Hlinka person, the Hlinka tradition, the Hlinka symbol had disappeared from the scene which he had once cloaked with the power and magnetism of his person.

The church was open and I walked inside. It had not changed since the time I had joined the procession of mourners who filed by the open coffin in which lay the body of the priest, gleaming cross in the waxen hands, purple robe and purple cap accentuating the pallor and the dignity of the sunken face. In the brilliant light of the glistening chandeliers, Slovak men and women, boys and girls were on their knees intoning a hymn. The singing was hearty and melodious—congregational or choral singing has ever been the special gift of Slavs, of Slovaks as much as of other members of the race. The scene around was peaceful and radiant, with flowers and embroideries enhancing the brilliance of fresco and statuary. Here was no awareness of social storm or social rift. Here were only sanctified solemnity and deep-souled faith. Thus political storms erupt and subside, armies arrive and depart, leaders rise and fall, ideas sweep in and out of the mind of man, but devotion to the old faith remains unshaken and untarnished.

A long block away from the square, rising out of a pall of darkness, was the old Jesuit monastery. We went up there to interview the rector. A man in his position, I thought, would have an illuminating comment to make on the events of the times. A young and handsome novitiate with short-cropped hair and in a long black robe took our names, ushered us into a high-ceilinged, modestly furnished room, and, excusing himself, left. Soon he returned and announced that Rector Grieger would be glad to talk to us. We were not long in waiting. The rector presently appeared, a man of about fifty, of medium height, with not even the ample black robe concealing the slenderness of his figure. He walked with a swift and sprightly step, and his pale face was livened by large and glowing eyes. He had a fluent command of French and German and understood some English. He was the acme of courtesy and talked in a slow, resonant voice, interspersing his speech with graceful gestures of his small white hands. Yes, he said, he was in the town when the revolution occurred. No, there had been no serious disturbances, hardly any bloodshed. The Red Army had stayed only three days, and he had heard of no misbehavior of Russian soldiers. Yes, they visited the monastery. Two officers came one evening, called him out, and said they would have to search it for possible German fugitives or spies. He interposed no objections, though he assured the Russians there were no Germans within the monastery's walls. They insisted they would have to make a search and they did. They were quite pleased when it was over that no enemies had found refuge there. They were friendly and cheerful, and the rector treated them to wine and sausage sandwiches. They drank and ate, and when they left they shook hands with the rector and wished him good health and good luck. That was the only experience he personally had had with Russians during their stay in Ružomberok.

"How do you look on the economic revolution in your country?" I asked.

"Well," he said, smiling, "I have no riches, I have no property. None of us in the monastery has. I am the real Communist. The robe I wear is not mine, the shoes I have on are not mine. Both belong to the monastery. I am its ward and servant. The food I eat, the books I study, the bed I sleep in—nothing is mine. I live no better than my associates or my students or the people who are otherwise associated with the institution. We share everything alike. I have no bank accounts. When I go somewhere on a trip the treasurer gives me my expenses. On my return, if I have any money left, I give it back to him. I live poor. I shall die poor. What can a Communist have against me? The accumulation of personal wealth means nothing to me." Not once did he raise his voice; not once did he inject emotion into his words. Composed and serene, he seemed as unworried by the revolution as though it had never happened. "Only one thing," he said, "is disconcerting—they have taken the schools away from us."

He was referring to the law passed in April 1945 by the Slovak National Council, disestablishing the church schools and creating a new unified secular school system for all children, regardless of religion. I told him that I had seen priests coming out of the public schools in Žilina accompanied by crowds of children.

"These priests were teachers in the church schools, and now they teach in the new schools because there are not enough other teachers to staff them," explained the rector.

"Has there been any interference in the teaching of religion in the new schools?"

"No. The law makes religious instruction compulsory two

hours a week except for children whose parents request the principal in writing for an exemption from such instruction. Of course our Slovak parents never make such requests."

"Is the state still paying the clergy its salaries?"

"Yes, no change in this respect."

"Has there been any official closing of churches?"

"No, I don't know of any."

"Has there been any interference with religious worship or with anything in the observance of your faith?"

"None at all. In this institution we are carrying on as we always have. We are quite crowded because we have had to move the theological seminary from Banská Bystrica."

I put these questions to the rector because only a few days earlier I had received in my American mail a printed copy of a complaint addressed to the State Department by certain Slovakian groups in America, charging the Slovakian National Council and the Red Army with the closing of churches and with attacks on the Catholic faith. Whatever the source of the information on which it was based, this eminent and scholarly churchman did not confirm it. His words were a disavowal of the charge.

Strikingly enough, the Bratislava *Pravda,* official Communist daily, in its issue of April 6, 1946, printed a story that bears significantly on the subject of the Catholic faith in Slovakia. "The District Committee of the Communist party in Senica," reads the story, "has offered its aid in the rebuilding of the celebrated Calvary shrine in the town of Šaštín. The shrine suffered serious war damage and is in a lamentable condition. Everybody will of course contribute to the beautiful cause of restoring the precious monument. It is especially desirable that the rehabilitation be completed before May, when masses of religious folk come there on pilgrimages. Contributions for the rebuilding of Calvary are to be sent to the Citizens' Credit Institute."

The Communist party actually soliciting contributions for the rehabilitation of a religious shrine, not as a historical museum but as a place of worship and pilgrimage for the devout Slovak masses! After reading this announcement it was easy to understand the anachronism I had observed in the classroom of a village school, on the front wall of which hung the portraits of Pope Pius XII, President Beneš, and Josef Stalin—symbols of the forces that are grappling for reconciliation in Slovakia: Czech humanism, Roman Catholicism, and Russian anti-capitalism. I use the word anti-capitalism advisedly, because Slovakian Communism as propounded by the Communist party is stripped of the philosophical and sociological features that would make it offensive to the devout Catholic population. "We tell our people," said the party secretary of Ružomberok, "that the aims of our party are the fulfillment of Christian teaching." Two thirds of the members of the Communist party are practicing Catholics. About seventy members are priests. Even in as devout a village as Černová, Hlinka's birthplace, the Communist party polled 120 votes in the elections of May 1946. The conflicts and the compromises between Catholics and Communists in Slovakia gain meaning and drama from the fact that, unlike the Czechs, the Slovaks, except the Evangelicals, never had been shaken by a reformation or any intellectual and political rebellion.

In the summer of 1946, when I went back to Slovakia, I searched out Monsignor Posděch, eminent churchman and political figure. Throughout the years of Tiso's Fascism he had been an uncompromising opponent of the president-priest and all he represented. He defended Czechs, he succored Jews. He remonstrated with Tiso for his anti-Semitism, his anti-Czechism, his intellectual obscurantism. Twice he had been under arrest, once by the Slovak and once by the German police. But he never wavered in his convictions, never compromised his ideals. That is why his moral authority is so high among his people and among all others, including Jews. He has been a father and a brother to the bereaved and the persecuted.

No one, I felt, was in a better position than he to make a judicious and balanced appraisal of the political struggles in his country, particularly of the position of the Church.

The monsignor was in the city hospital recovering from an operation on his leg. Though confined to bed, he appeared alert and vigorous, with a healthy color in his full and rounded face and a glow of energy and good humor in his finely rounded blue eyes. His speech was as frank as his manner, and he radiated a sturdy and cheering optimism. I asked to what extent the Catholic clergy had actively participated in the Fascistization of the country.

"We have eighteen hundred priests in Slovakia," he said, "and no more than ten or fifteen per cent rallied full-heartedly to Tiso's regime. The overwhelming mass of our priests live in villages, and for the most part they were minding their own business, doing their own work, and were not conniving in conspiracies to loot Czechs or Jews or to betray their country to Hitler."

"How many priests have been arrested since the liberation?"

"No more than fifty; too few, I must say, for some of them behaved quite badly. Now no more than ten are still in jail awaiting trial. The others have been released, and remember, these arrests were made not by the Russians but by our own Slovak Government."

"How many churches have been closed?"

"Not one. Some were badly damaged by the war. But not a single church or shrine has been closed by the Slovak National Council."

"Has there been a falling off in church attendance or any diminution in the devotion to the faith?"

"Quite the contrary. Our monasteries, for example, have never been so crowded with youths who want to consecrate their lives to Christ."

"Have church lands been nationalized or confiscated by the new land reform?"

"No, our church lands have remained untouched. Don't believe the stories which Tiso's followers are sending to America. Tiso is a traitor. He could have averted the Jewish tragedy. He had the power."

The churches and monasteries hold about 160,000 acres, of which close to one third is the property of the Hungarian archbishop at Esztergom.

"Are you optimistic of the future of your country?"

"Oh yes. Our people are sturdy and hard-working. Under competent leadership they will find their way to a new and democratic way of life."

Not only he but other leaders, Communists and non-Communists, brim over with confidence as to the future of Slovakia.

The outward social scene does inspire a feeling of peace, tranquillity, and reassurance. The old symbols of the Tiso regime have vanished. Neither in picture, poster, banner, nor slogan do they survive any more. Slovakia is attired in a new political cloak, every fold and line of which speaks death to the old and life to the new dispensation. The change is as complete as it is startling, but only outwardly. The malignant isms—anti-Czechism, anti-Semitism, Fascism, supernationalism, which attained a fearsome florescence during six years of Fascism—have not been uprooted. They had become too lusty a part of the life of the people for the fires of the Banská Bystrica, in which only a part of the population had participated, or for the flaming rhetoric of some of the new leaders to scorch them to extinction.

Had the new government been in a position to match the good

living which, by the grace of Hitler's favors and its own false economy, Slovakia enjoyed under the Tiso regime, its words and its promises might have found deeper and more universal response. But the war made even the pledge of such a fulfillment in the immediate future impossible. Fifty-nine hundred highway and seven hundred railway bridges were blown away; twenty-nine mountain tunnels were blasted; two thirds of the railroad tracks were gone. More than one third of the livestock had perished, and the harvest of grains—especially important because bread and porridge, as with Slav peasants everywhere, are the staff of life in the countryside—was less than one third normal in the summer of 1945. In the eastern part of the country, where the fighting was fiercest, more than one hundred thousand people remained homeless. The sudden reversal in the condition of living was a shock and an agony. That it was the price Slovakia was paying for its own Fascism and its political and military alliance with Nazi Germany only a small part of the population recognized, or is in a mood to this day to accept. In 1946, when economic recovery was so manifest that in the market place of Bratislava a nine-pound goose, all dressed and ready for the cook, sold for the equivalent of one and a half dollars in American money, the country was still simmering with underground restlessness and disaffection.

If only because there are scarcely any Czechs left in Slovakia, anti-Czechism, while still a weapon of Tiso's undercover followers, is no longer of serious consequence. The bitter memories of persecution and expulsion inspired by Hlinka and eventuated by the Tiso leadership are too fresh in Czech minds to tempt them ever again to seek domicile or opportunity in Slovakia. "One road to Calvary is enough in one lifetime," said a Czech teacher whom Hlinka Guards had chased out of the country without permitting him to take along his personal belongings. Slovaks are in control of their country. They hold the highest and the lowest offices. The agreement which they have worked out with Prague and which is neither autonomy nor federalism but a unification of the main policies of both lands makes it unnecessary for Czechs to take over any of the governmental functions in any phase of Slovak life.

Yet the idea of Fascism is not dead. It quivers with an energy that would be frightening if, as in the post-Munich days, there was a near-by powerful state like Nazi Germany to galvanize it into action. Supernationalism is still loud, though the old-time brashness has oozed out of it. This exaggerated self-glorification of a people who have given the world not a single personage of consequence, who have never initiated or been a part of any significant progressive movement in history, unless one excepts the union with Czechs during the first republic, may seem ludicrous, unless one remembers that it is an offshoot of the age-old servitude to Hungary and of a desperate yearning to compensate the ego for the barrenness of historical achievement and for the comparative lowliness of the prevailing civilization. It is refuge and hope, but untempered, save in certain small circles, by self-scrutiny and self-effacement. The lack of self-criticism among the Slovak intelligentsia is not the least of the contrasts between them and the Czech intelligentsia, who are sternly, often harshly, self-critical.

The fact is that Slovakia, because of its tragic history, is, like all backward countries that find themselves confronted with the challenge of the machine age and the surge of new and powerful ideas, a sick country, sick politically, sick intellectually, above all sick economically. The twenty years of the first republic had pushed it up high on the ladder of modern thought and modern industrial civilization, but not high enough for the Tiso regime, with the aid of Nazi Germany, to fail in pulling it down again. The landholdings of the peasantry are for the most part still puny and inadequate. Two fifths of the villagers possess only five or less acres per family, and one half of one per cent control one fourth of the arable land of the country. The new land reform contemplates a drastic readjustment, which, if faithfully achieved, will do more than any other circumstance, far more than all the oratory of all the political parties, to woo the peasantry into an increasingly loyal support of the new government.

Except in the rich Danubian valley and particularly in the mountain districts, where nature is especially niggard, the methods of tillage are as crude as they are primitive. The labor is all done by hand and largely with implements that in America are found only in museums. The cow, far more than the horse or the ox, does all the draft work. Add to this the ancient and barbarous distribution of the land into narrow spans, one sometimes miles away from the other, and one can appreciate the doleful plight of the peasant. Poor living, as much as lack of adequate education, has made him the victim of the underground whisperings and often the open incitements of Tiso's followers, who have kept alive in him his anti-Semitism, his distrust of progressive ideas, his readiness to follow the false prophet who brands everything "non-Slovakian" as sacrilege and treachery.

Despite their innate charm and vivacity, blocks and blocks of the Slovakian peasantry must still be spoken of as a "dark people," and the farther east and south one journeys, the more indigent the population, the darker their minds. When UNRRA food first arrived in eastern Slovakia, in one of the villages a rumor was spread that the tinned meats were human flesh. Alarmed, the villagers hastened to sell their coupons cheaply to Slovak speculators who originated the rumor so they could enrich themselves at the expense of the people they had duped.

Nothing is so illustrative of the similarity of certain groups of the Slovakian peasantry to the muzhik of czarist days as the anti-Jewish outbreak in Topolčany. By a decree of the Slovak Government of April 1945, all parochial schools were secularized, including, of course, the school in this village. Thereupon someone launched a whispering campaign that Jews were conspiring to seize it and make of it a Jewish school. How a handful of broken and impoverished Jews could achieve so audacious a feat no one paused to reflect, any more than muzhiks in the old days bothered to puzzle out for themselves how Jews could overthrow the Czar or seize for their own purposes the established Orthodox Church. In Topolčany, as in old Russia, the whisper stirred up sentiment against Jews, and local officials, again as in czarist Russia, made no effort to stop it or explain away its absurd intimations. The atmosphere was so tense that there was danger of an untoward incident causing an explosion. A Jewish physician in the employ of the government was vaccinating the children of the village, and when one child fainted a woman rushed to the window and cried out, *"Zamrelo,"* which is the Slovakian for "fainted," but the crowd in the street had mistaken it for *zomrelo*—died. The error resulted in a campaign gathering flamelike violence that the Jewish physician was deliberately murdering Christian children. Passion erupted and a pogrom followed.

On May 18, 1946, in the village of Namestovona Oravě, Grossman-Golan, public prosecutor of the People's Court, was murdered. Before his death he was made to sign the following statement: "I have been baptized and I have polluted the Roman Catholic creed."

There is a group of Jews, who were educated in Slovakian schools and who survived deportation and concentration camps and the partisan wars, who feel that Slovakia is their motherland and that it is their duty to remain there and devote themselves to the re-education of the people and the rehabilitation of the country. They are the only Jews who feel confident of their future. The others are seized with despair, especially the orthodox Jews, and are yearning for a chance to go anywhere in the world—Palestine, Africa, any of the Americas, where they can feel secure and rid themselves forever of the fears and vexations that beset their daily lives. "Two hundred of us," complained a young man, "organized ourselves in the concentration camp of Novaky into a partisan army. We fought in Batyovice, and fifty of our men lost their lives, while others became invalids. We should have gotten some consideration from the government, shouldn't we? When we came home and looked for work we were told that of course workers were needed, but when Slovak administrators learned from our names that we were Jews they found all the excuses in the world to deny us work. I am not saying that the men on the top level are guilty of injustice to us. But the men in the administrative positions are again and again making us feel that we are strangers, unwanted and unneeded. We're not even treated like stepchildren, but like intruders and interlopers, and the moral torture we suffer is as great as our physical want."

It is significant that the *Katolické Noviny* (*Catholic News*), the most widely read weekly journal in Slovakia, printed an article on September 15, 1946, under the title "How Shall We Behave toward Israelite Catholics?" The author exhorts the readers not to draw any distinction between Jewish converts and born Catholics. The fact that the leading Catholic publication deemed it necessary to print such an appeal a year and a half after liberation is testimony to the prevalence of anti-Jewish sentiments among the population.

Yet it would be as easy to exaggerate as to underestimate the gravity of Slovakia's disaffection or the dark-mindedness of a large section of its peasantry. For one thing, the govern-

ment, while not as vigorous as it might be in combating sub-
versiveness, fully appreciates its dangers. It is sensitive to the
obloquy the anti-Jewish outbreaks evoked on Slovakia, not only
in Prague but in foreign lands and particularly in America. In
the selection of officials it shows no anti-Semitism. Jews may
be seen in all government offices and in positions of high
responsibility.

Besides, the road to Tisoism is blocked, and there is no
near-by Hitler and a mighty *Reichswehr* to break it open again.
The reincarnation of the Fascist idea into a living force or a
ruling state is a lost hope and a lost cause. With its own powers
Slovakia is as helpless now as she was in the pre-Munich days to
perpetrate a radical and spectacular coup. While the old hates
and acrimonies are unextinguished, there is no powerful neighbor now to blow them into a devouring flame.

Now Slovakia is surrounded by nations in which the Fascist
idea may still be simmering, but without hope of coming to
a boil, if only because of Soviet Russia's vigilant proximity. If,
as is most unlikely, internal conspiracy and intrigue plunge the
country into complete economic breakdown, the resulting chaos
may bring forth a strong hand to whip the nation into order,
and it is certain, if only because of the geography of the country,
that the strong hand will emerge not from the right but from
the left. Only within the framework of the newly re-created
Czechoslovak state can Slovakia fulfill itself.

The new government, with its sweeping nationalization
program, is more keenly aware of Slovakia's economic backwardness than was the first republic. Then private businessmen,
especially Czechs, were more concerned with making their
enterprise profitable than in reshaping and rebuilding Slovakia's
economy. It is all different now under the system of nationalization. The large sum of $400,000,000, or one third of the
entire amount to be poured into the Two-Year Plan, will be

spent in Slovakia. The picturesque little country is to experience the greatest industrial boom it has ever known. The countryside is to be electrified; a huge chemical plant is to be erected in Novaky; the timber and mining industries are to be expanded and modernized; the metalworking factories are to be enlarged and mechanized; a new food industry is to be developed on an ample scale. For the first time in its history the nation's energies, with the aid of Czech finance and Czech experts, are to be directed to the full and planned exploitation of its own resources. Such development will draw away the surplus population from the rural community. There will be more land for the individual peasant family. There will be more goods in the country and more purchasing power to absorb them locally. Above all, the modern machine will help clear away the dark-mindedness of the more backward rural population. It will break down superstitions and prejudices that are a by-product of primitiveness. It has done so in other lands that have known an industrial renaissance, and in time it is certain to exercise no less salutary a transformation on the Slovak.

24. The Big Horizon

A Czech officer narrated to this writer an incident during the battle of Vyškov, Moravia, one of the more violent the Red Army fought in Czechoslovakia. It dramatizes what Czechs themselves often lament as a salient failing in their character.

A Russian general had made his headquarters in the home of a schoolmaster. For several nights he had not slept. His face was drawn and haggard, and as he sat at the table poring over maps he smoked one cigarette after another and refreshed himself with frequent swallows of cognac. There was a piano in the room and he asked the schoolmaster if he could play it.

"Yes," said the schoolmaster.

"I wish," requested the general, "you'd play a Strauss waltz."

Astonished by so unusual a request at so desperate a moment, the schoolmaster sat down at the piano and proceeded to play.

Suddenly the door flew open and a Czech woman, harassed and angry, burst into the room and, facing the general, cried: "General, your soldiers have taken away all my hens. Now I have no hens any more—all my hens are gone."

Tense with overwork and nervous strain, the general lost his temper, leaped to his feet, and clasping his temples with clenched fists, shouted: "What's the matter with you Czechs? Don't you see what's happening? A battle is raging, men are fighting, men are dying, we're spilling our blood to liberate your country, and you come to me and wail about your hens!"

After the woman was gone the general swallowed more cognac, lighted a cigarette, and as he sat down to his work he turned to the schoolmaster and said: "Play another Strauss waltz."

"Yes," commented the Czech officer who told the story, "we Czechs are always preoccupied with little things. We think of our hens even in the midst of a decisive battle for our liberation. We're such a 'small-minded' people."

Sternly self-critical, Czechs are disposed to overemphasize and exaggerate their failings. Yet, friendly and cultivated as they are, they evince an extraordinary, almost devout, regard for little things. They are sticklers for petty proprieties. They are squeamish about little irregularities. They loathe disorder and slovenliness.

Once, as I was walking out of my hotel, the porter stopped me and drew my attention to the end of the torn loop sticking out of my coat collar.

"It does not look nice," he said. "You'd better have it fixed."

Czechs abominate waste in land, in substance, in anything. They shrink from extravagance in language, in sentiment, in ways of living. A noted Russian war correspondent, while visiting Prague, invited several American journalists to his hotel room. As he was ordering drinks by telephone he said to the waiter jokingly, "Now remember, none of your puny Czech portions; fill the glasses to the top." Turning to his guests, he remarked, "Czechs are so funny; they measure *slivovice* like medicine, by the drop."

With his unbridled expansiveness, the Russian is amused by Czech frugality and often irritated by Czech punctiliousness in the observance of small amenities. Unromantic and rational, only in his appreciation of sports, and art—music, theater, dancing, poetry—does the Czech spill over with emotion. In Prague I attended performances of a Russian ballet and of the London Arts Theatre. The performers were literally swamped and stormed with curtain calls. When the famous Red Army Choir came to Zlín for an outdoor concert it was greeted by an audience of more than thirty thousand, and so insistent and tumultuous was the demand for encores that it sang itself into exhaustion.

If the Czech is scrupulously mindful of little things, he is, after all, a man of peasant lineage and peasant heritage. He is the peasant supreme, the man with a small landholding who knows that nature may be a little mother but is also a cruel stepmother. He must husband every mite of substance at his command, every spear of grass, every stalk of grain, every beet root he pulls up, as though it were all a treasure, the sole treasure in his life. Living away from the sea with its faraway horizons, its endless surge of energy, not even the master for three centuries of his landlocked little country, the Czech has schooled himself as a matter of physical and spiritual self-preservation to bring into play unobtrusively, sometimes secretly and subtly, all the powers of creativeness he could muster, not only of muscle, but of mind and heart. He could trust neither to vision nor miracle. His own foresight, his own toil, his own faith, his very smallness have been the sole source of his salvation.

He could not openly parade his defiance of the enemy within and without. He had to outsmart and outwit him even as, being a small landholder, he had to outsmart and outwit nature. Since the enemy—the Austrian court, the Austrian nobility, the German financiers and industrialists—was in command of the big

363

things in life—money, land, political power, social prestige—he had to preoccupy himself with the little things within his grasp —the *halar* or crown he earned, the strips of land he cultivated, the hen and the pig he raised, the book he read, the song he sang. He toiled today so he could feel secure tomorrow—secure against the whims of nature, against the intrigues of man, against the failings and imperfections of his own self.

Yet the leaders who have sought to mold the mind and fashion the spirit of the people have by contrast peered beyond the little world in which the individual Czech dwells. They were men of big horizon. They swept their eyes to near-by and far-away places for a vision of the new truth and the still newer truth by which man could better his life. Preoccupied with the destiny of their people, they probed with the dispassionate inquisitiveness of a scientist the dreams and deeds of others, with a view to understanding and perfecting themselves and applying what they deemed wise and good and, above all, feasible to the needs and perplexities of their own little nation. Parochialism and dogmatism were sins of which, in the light of Czech history, their fiercest enemies could not accuse them. This was so with the youthful St. Wenceslaus, democrat-prince, patron saint of the country, who knew Greek and Latin and strove, even as do the leaders of today, to fuse the values of the East and the West into a social harmony of its own, and who to this day is glorified for his gentle nature, his democratic demeanor, his readiness to compromise, with honor and dignity, quarrels with the external enemy.

This was so with King George of Poděbrady, who proclaimed that it was better to surround oneself with friends than with walls, and who made an energetic though unsuccessful effort to unite the nations of Europe for the mutual defense of European civilization against the rising and powerful Turk.

This has been especially so with the succession of remarkable men beginning with Jan Hus and ending with Eduard Beneš, Monsignor Šrámek, and the rising, if not yet fully tested, Klement Gottwald, who have sprung from the land, sons of peasants.

The moral interpretation of politics which Hus enunciated and with which he had sought to invest Czech individual and communal life, has been the most powerful tool in the regeneration and rebirth of the Czech nation. Not a leader of stature in the past, Catholic or Hussite, realist or positivist, but wielded it in his own fashion and on behalf of his own people.

The moral and intellectual legacy Hus bequeathed to his people has kept the mind of the intelligentsia open to the fresh currents of thought that swept Europe and America, however advanced and radical, and has lifted their eyes to the horizon beyond their frontiers. Hence the first republic, with what was for its time a singularly progressive system of social legislation, the high level of popular education, the prodigious industrial expansion, and the accent by Masaryk and his followers on the ethical Hussite approach to law, politics, economics, social reform. The business group and the wealthy land proprietors, who on the fall of the first republic and with the aid of Nazi Germany rose to power and proceeded of their own accord as much as because of Nazi prodding to scrap the old institutions and uproot the old heritage, so completely discredited themselves with the clergy, the people, and above all with the intelligentsia, that on the collapse of Germany they were engulfed in the flood of popular indignation and wrath.

"How do you explain," I asked a university professor, "that in your country the Communist and the Catholic manage to get along so much better than in other countries?"

"Because," came the reply, "there is a Hus in the Czech Communist and a Hus in the Czech Catholic."

The Bright Passage

It is one of the great paradoxes of our time that a nation which, including its factory workers, is so middle class in its cast of mind and way of life, with a hallowed regard for the little world which the individual has built round his own self, should be the first in Europe to enact so far-reaching a change in the ownership of industry and finance. Yet in Czech eyes the new dispensation signalizes no break but an expansion of the pattern of their history, intended to meet the challenge of the new day without recourse to battle and blood. Social Democrats and Communists have no doubt been responsible for the magnitude of the nationalization program, but the principle of nationalization was never disputed by the other parties, all of which accepted it as the sole road to national salvation.

Because of its mastery of the machine age, the magnitude of the nationalization program, the century-old association with Western culture, the geographic proximity and age-old racial and cultural bonds with Russia, above all the military alliance with the Soviet Union, Czechoslovakia, more than any nation in Europe, is the acid test of the Socialist idea and of the diplomacy of the big powers.

It would be easy to emphasize and dramatize immediate setbacks and failings—the abuses, especially during the first year of liberation, by National Councils and Factory Committees; the incompetence of newly appointed directors and managers of factories; the overcluttered bureaucracy in the administrative offices, the excesses of overzealous and unscrupulous police functionaries. There are foreign diplomats and other foreign observers who, on the basis of reverses suffered and perversities committed, predict imminent collapse of nationalization and of all the other innovations that have been proclaimed. Czechs who loathe the new social order, who hanker after the return of the pre-Munich scheme of things, and who are essentially of what is known as the Prague middle class with its *zlata mladež* —golden youth—echo and re-echo similar sentiments. Their language drips with melancholy foreboding. They never cease to speak of troubles and catastrophe ahead.

The Prague correspondent of the Associated Press and this writer were once invited for a drive by a group of highly educated and widely traveled Prague residents. "Have you heard," said one of them, "what the Russians are going to do the coming winter? They are going to send to Prague 150,000 soldiers and 750,000 more to the outskirts of the vicinity." But only a few weeks later the Russian and American troops withdrew from Czechoslovakia.

A European-trained newspaperman once created a sensation with a story that seven thousand Jews in Czechoslovakia had committed suicide during the first half year after liberation. The story had been floating around Prague for some days, and no British or American journalist would bother with it, for the truth was that only fourteen Jews had taken their lives during that period. The explanation of the guilty newspaperman was that he had obtained the story from a Czech whose word he had no reason to question. There are plenty of Czechs, almost all of them in Prague, who are so fiercely determined to discredit the government of the National Front and its leaders that they deliberately search out foreign residents, especially journalists and diplomats, to whom they can narrate stories of gigantic corruption and catastrophe, in the hope that these will find their way into the foreign press or will be transmitted to Foreign Offices.

Every capital on the Continent, including Prague, seethes and reeks with rumors so sensational that, as one American correspondent expressed himself, "If I started cabling them I would make the front page every day, but within a week I'd be fired."

The Bright Passage

Failings and excesses are openly and often acridly aired in the Czech press, and people all over the country are so candid and voluble in the expression of opinions and criticism that no party, even if it wished, could conceal misdeeds from the public. On the occasions when the revolutionary impulse of the Communist party or certain groups within its ranks sought to override constitutional or legal barriers, the joint action of the other parties and the outcries in the press brought a halt to the attempted dereliction.

"Democracy," said the late Thomas Masaryk, "means discussion." When there is more than one party in a country and when, as in Czechoslovakia, all enjoy equal liberty of speech and assembly, and when elections are unencumbered with pressures and subterfuges that favor one party to the exclusion of others, not only is discussion as irrepressible as the urge to power and triumph, but also party rivalry.

Considering the brevity of the time which has elapsed since liberation, only one and a half years on the date these words are written, the astonishing features on the Czechoslovakian scene are not the irregularities and subversions committed, but the orderliness and tranquillity that prevail. The recovery the country has already achieved is stupendous. Increase in factory output is constantly mounting. Foreign trade is continually expanding and is beginning to girdle the globe. Thanks in no small measure to contributions from UNRRA and to the remarkable diligence of Czech and Slovak farmers, the standard of living has risen perceptibly. The principle and practice of freedom in every field of human endeavor, save in economic practices that infringe on the nationalization decree, have been accorded ever-increasing clarification and validation. Association with the West and the East has been gaining in magnitude.

Open as it is to the flow of new ideas from the outside world, Czechoslovakia, despite the mishaps of yesterday, the irregu-

368

larities and perplexities of today, can look forward to a flourishing tomorrow and to an unfolding of native creativeness such as it has perhaps never known in its history. Now that the German minority has been largely evacuated, the one internal force that had always harassed and frustrated native effort is cleared away.

But if the country is to triumph in the experiment of revolution by evolution, two conditions are indispensable: internal tranquillity and freedom from drastic external interference. If a hopeless internal cleavage should occur, anything might happen. Were the Communist party to manipulate itself into dictatorship, the cleavage would be inescapable. Yet considering the culture of the country, the character of the people, such manipulation, were it seriously attempted, could only fail. If the Communist party should abrogate its present platform of national rejuvenation, its membership would shrink and it would be hopelessly routed in a forthcoming election.

The greatest of all dangers is powerful external pressure. If one or more of the big powers, whether because of immediate irritation or long-range policy, whether because of fear of the success or the failure of the Socialist idea, sought to impose its will on the little nation, Czechoslovakia's powers of resistance might be taxed to exhaustion. Like a plant that draws nutriment from its own soil and its own supply of moisture and sunlight, the new Czechoslovakia must draw sustenance for survival and growth upon its own resources, natural and human. Nutriments of foreign origin it must distill and apply in its own way by its own hand and for its own good, as it has always done. The whispered counsel of elder statesmen from the West, with the refrain, "Come back to us," like the notion of shifting the little nation into the Russian fold, is equally futile and dangerous.

"We are a people," reads a declaration signed by Dr. Jan Belehradek, the only Czech scholar who since the day of Hus has had the honor of being twice elected to the rectorship of

The Bright Passage

Charles University, and by František Halas, the most widely acclaimed Czech poet, "which has always demonstrated the faculty to create its own ideas of civilization in close harmony with world civilization. We never blindly accepted ideas but richly re-created them and furthered them in our own manner. Christianity came to us from the East and the West. In the course of a long process we re-created it and brought it to a climax in our [Hussite] Reformation. We adopted and refined it and fitted it into universal values. We have already accepted several forms of Socialism and have achieved certain Socialist experiments of our own; what we are living through today and what we are destined to experience tomorrow, if only we are permitted peace, is for the present our greatest experiment in a Czech type of Socialism which could aid in the realization and the stabilization of the basic concepts of world Socialism."[1]

These words embody the essence of the spirit of the Czech revolution. If left to itself, Czechoslovakia is in a position to make a significant contribution to the peaceful resolution of the economic and ideological battles of today. If it fails in its purpose it will be because of the rivalries and jealousies of the big powers rather than its own shortcomings. Yet save for those who long for the return of the vanished era of the pre-Munich days, none in the country is counting on failure. The overwhelming mass of the people believe in themselves and the future.

[1] *Právo Lidu,* November 7, 1946.